# Hidden Heroes

## America's Military Caregivers

Rajeev Ramchand, Terri Tanielian,
Michael P. Fisher, Christine Anne Vaughan, Thomas E. Trail,
Caroline Epley, Phoenix Voorhies, Michael William Robbins,
Eric Robinson, Bonnie Ghosh-Dastidar

Sponsored by Caring for Military Families: The Elizabeth Dole Foundation

For more information on this publication, visit www.rand.org/military-caregivers.

Library of Congress Cataloging-in-Publication Data is available for this publication
ISBN: 978-0-08330-8558-0

Published by the RAND Corporation, Santa Monica, Calif.
© Copyright 2014 RAND Corporation
RAND® is a registered trademark

Cover design by Dori Gordon Walker

Support RAND
Make a tax-deductible charitable contribution at
www.rand.org/giving/contribute

www.rand.org

# Preface

After a decade of war, supporting returning service members, veterans, and their families remains a national priority. Addressing the treatment and recovery needs of those who have been wounded, ill, or injured has been a special area of focus. This most recent cohort of wounded, ill, and injured veterans—those who served after September 2011—benefited from improved battlefield medicine and rehabilitative services that allowed them to return to their homes and communities much more rapidly than cohorts before them. In their recovery and reintegration, many of these veterans are aided by the support and assistance of nonprofessional or informal caregivers: individuals who provide a broad range of care and assistance with activities of daily living, such as bathing, dressing, and eating, and who help them relearn basic skills, arrange and take them to medical appointments, manage their finances, and care for their children.

While much has been written about the role of caregiving for the elderly and chronically ill and for children with special needs, little is known about the population of those who care for military personnel and veterans, referred to as "military caregivers" in this report. An earlier RAND report, *Military Caregivers: Cornerstones of Support for Our Nation's Wounded, Ill, and Injured Veterans* (Tanielian et al., 2013), summarized the scant literature on this group and outlined the need for continued research to understand the characteristics and needs of this population. This report summarizes the results of a two-part study designed to describe the magnitude of military caregiving in the United States today, as well as to identify gaps in the array of programs, policies, and initiatives designed to support military caregivers. The findings from this study will be of interest to policy and program officials within the agencies and organizations that sponsor and implement caregiver support programs.

This report was prepared as part of a research study funded by Caring for Military Families: The Elizabeth Dole Foundation. The research was conducted within RAND Health in coordination with the National Security Research Division, divisions of the RAND Corporation. A profile of RAND, abstracts of its publications, and ordering information can be found at www.rand.org. This research study was co-led by Rajeev Ramchand and Terri Tanielian. Questions about the study and the report may be directed to Rajeev_Ramchand@rand.org or Terri_Tanielian@rand.org.

# Contents

# Figures

# Tables

# Summary

Many wounded, injured, or disabled veterans rely for their day to day care on informal caregivers: family members, friends, or acquaintances who devote substantial amounts of time and effort to caring for them. These informal caregivers, who we term *military caregivers*, play a vital role in facilitating the recovery, rehabilitation, and reintegration of wounded, ill, and injured veterans. The assistance provided by caregivers saves the United States millions of dollars each year in health care costs and allows millions of veterans to live at home rather than in institutions.

Yet the toll of providing this care can be high. A preliminary phase of our research commissioned by Caring for Military Families: The Elizabeth Dole Foundation (*Military Caregivers: Cornerstones of Support for Our Nation's Wounded, Ill, and Injured Veterans*, Tanielian et al., 2013) found that time spent caregiving can lead to the loss of income, jobs, or health care and exact a substantial physical and emotional toll. To the extent that caregivers' well-being is compromised, they may become unable to fulfill their caregiving role, leaving the responsibilities to be borne by other parts of society. Most of this prior research focused on caregivers in general, with little evidence about the impact of caregiving on military caregivers specifically. In recognition of their growing number, particularly in the wake of the conflicts in Iraq and Afghanistan, it has become paramount to understand the support needs of military caregivers and the extent to which available resources align with those needs.

This report presents results from the second phase of our analysis, which represents the most comprehensive examination to date of military caregivers. It examines the characteristics of caregivers, the burden of care that they shoulder, the array of services available to support them, and the gaps in those services.

## Study Purpose and Approach

To inform an understanding of military caregivers and efforts to better support them, the goals of our analysis are threefold:

1. **Describe the magnitude of military caregiving in the United States,** including how caregiving affects individuals, their families, and society. We describe the number and characteristics of military caregivers and their role in ensuring the well-being of their care recipient. We employed a social-ecological framework to assess the effects of caregiving on military caregivers, their families, and society more broadly. We also examine how these effects differ across cohorts of veterans.

2. **Describe current policies, programs, and other initiatives designed to support military caregivers**, and identify how these efforts align with the needs of military caregivers. We review the existing policies and programs and assess how these initiatives address specific caregiver needs.

3. **Identify specific recommendations for filling gaps** and ensuring the well-being of military caregivers.

To address these goals, the study team performed two tasks: a nationally representative survey of military caregivers and an environmental scan of programs and other support resources relevant to the needs of military caregivers.

### Caregiver Survey

We conducted the largest and most comprehensive probability-based survey to date of military caregivers. One respondent from each of the 41,163 households that participate in the KnowledgePanel (an online panel of households designed to represent the U.S. general population of non-institutionalized adults) was invited to complete a screener to determine eligibility for the survey across one of four groups: military care recipients, military caregivers, civilian caregivers, and non-caregivers. Of these 41,163 households, 28,164 (68 percent) completed the screener. We also drew upon a supplementary sample of post-9/11 family caregivers from the Wounded Warrior Project (WWP) to ensure an adequate number of these military caregivers in the final sample, which was blended into the KnowledgePanel sample using a statistical algorithm to create weights to account for systematic and observed differences between the groups. From these samples, we interviewed 1,129 military caregivers (including 414 post-9/11 caregivers).

In addition, we interviewed samples from two other groups for comparison: 1,828 civilian caregivers and 1,163 non-caregivers. These comparison samples provided information about the extent to which outcomes among military caregivers are unique and shed light on whether the policies and programs that exist for caregivers more broadly can be similarly marketed and offered to military caregivers, or if they need to be adapted to cater to this group.

### Environmental Scan

Prior environmental scans have offered some insight into caregiver services in specific areas, sectors, or populations—for example, respite services available at a state level—but no studies have examined the full spectrum of services available for military caregivers within the United States on a national level. We used a multipronged search strategy that included web searches, sorting through the National Resource Directory, consultations with nonprofit staff and subject matter experts, attendance at relevant meetings and events, and snowball sampling among service organizations (i.e., asking organizations about other organizations they knew of that offer programs and services to military caregivers). We also conducted interviews with the organizations that offered services involving direct or intensive interaction with caregivers (see the "Common Caregiving Services" box for a listing of these types of services). A total of 120 distinct organizational entities were identified. Using a structured abstraction tool, we gathered information to document the publicly available information about programs that support caregivers. We added to this information using a semistructured interview tool to gain additional insights and information from 81 of the organizations. We asked questions to understand the history, origin, funding source, and objective of the programs. We also asked detailed questions about eligibility criteria, types of services offered, mode/mechanism of delivery, and whether any data had been gathered to assess the impact of the program on caregivers.

## Results

### Post-9/11 Military Caregivers Differ from Other Caregivers

We estimate that there are 5.5 million military caregivers in the United States. Of these, 19.6 percent (1.1 million) are caring for someone who served in the military after the terrorist attacks of September 11, 2001. In comparing military caregivers with their civilian counterparts, we found that military caregivers helping veterans from earlier eras tend to resemble civilian caregivers in many ways; by contrast, post-9/11 military caregivers differ systematically from the other two groups.

Table S.1 details some of the key differences among these populations. In sum, post-9/11 caregivers are more likely to be

- younger (more than 40 percent are between ages 18 and 30)
- caring for a younger individual with a mental health or substance use condition
- nonwhite
- a veteran of military service
- employed
- not connected to a support network.

### Post-9/11 Caregivers Use a Different Mix of Services

We found that 53 percent of post-9/11 military caregivers have no caregiving network—an individual or group that regularly provides help with caregiving—to support them. Perhaps because they lack such a network, post-9/11 caregivers are more

## Common Caregiving Services

These are some of the most common services offered by programs that assist military caregivers:

- **Respite care:** Care provided to the service member or veteran by someone other than the caregiver in order to give the caregiver a short-term, temporary break
- **Patient advocate or case manager:** An individual who acts as a liaison between the service member or veteran and his or her care providers, or who coordinates care for the service member or veteran
- **A helping hand:** Direct support, such as loans, donations, legal guidance, housing support, or transportation assistance
- **Financial stipend:** Compensation for a caregiver's time devoted to caregiving activities and/or for loss of wages due to one's caregiving commitment
- **Structured social support:** Online or in-person support groups for caregivers or military family members (which may incidentally include caregivers) that are likely to assist with caregiving-specific stresses or challenges
- **Religious support:** Religious- or spiritual-based guidance or counseling
- **Structured wellness activities:** Organized activities, such as fitness classes or stress relief lessons, that focus on improving mental or physical well-being
- **Structured education or training:** In-person or online classes, modules, webinars, manuals, or workbooks that involve a formalized curriculum (rather than ad hoc information) related to caregiving activities.

**Nonstandard clinical care:**

- **Health care:** Mental health care that is (1) offered outside of routine or traditional channels such as common government or private sector payment and delivery systems, or (2) offered specially to caregivers.
- **Mental health care:** Health care that is (1) offered outside of routine or traditional channel such as common government or private sector payment and delivery systems, or (2) offered specially to caregivers.

**Table S.1**
**Key Differences in Caregiver Populations**

| Characteristics | Post-9/11 Military | Pre-9/11 Military | Civilian |
|---|---|---|---|
| Caregiver relationship to person being cared for | • Spouse (most common): 33%<br>• Parent: 25%<br>• Unrelated friend or neighbor: 23% | • Child (most common): 37%<br>• Spouse: 22%<br>• Parent: 2%<br>• Unrelated friend or neighbor: 16% | • Child (most common): 36%<br>• Spouse: 16%<br>• Parent: 10%<br>• Unrelated friend or neighbor: 13% |
| Percentage of caregivers age 30 or younger | 37 | 11 | 16 |
| Percentage of caregivers between ages 31–55 | 49 | 43 | 44 |
| Percentage of caregivers with nonwhite racial/ethnic background | 43 | 25 | 36 |
| Percentage of caregivers employed | 76 | 55 | 60 |
| Percentage of caregivers who have support network | 47 | 71 | 69 |
| Percentage of caregivers who have health insurance | 68 | 82 | 77 |
| Percentage caregivers who have regular source of health care | 72 | 88 | 86 |
| Care Recipients | | | |
| Percentage of care recipients with VA disability rating | 58 | 30 | N/A |
| Percentage of care recipients with mental health or substance use disorder | 64 | 36 | 33 |

likely than other caregivers to use mental health resources and to use such resources more frequently. Similarly, they use other types of support services more frequently, such as helping hand services, structured social support, and structured education and training on caregiving (see the "Common Caregiving Services" box for a description of common support services).

## Military Caregivers Perform a Variety of Caregiving Tasks

Post-9/11 military caregivers also differ from other caregivers in that they typically assist with fewer basic functional tasks, but more often assist care recipients in coping with stressful situations or other emotional and behavioral challenges. Tasks that all caregivers perform are sometimes grouped into two categories: activities of daily living (ADLs) and instrumental activities of daily living (IADLs). ADLs describe basic functions, including bathing and dressing. IADLs are tasks required for noninstitutional community living, such as housework, meal preparation, transportation to medical appointments and community services, and health management and maintenance.

Post-9/11 military caregivers perform fewer ADLs and IADLs than pre-9/11 and civilian caregivers, largely because their care recipients require less assistance with these types of tasks. When such help is required, most post-9/11 military caregivers help with these tasks. Nonetheless, civilian and post-9/11 military caregivers report spending roughly the same amount of time per week on caregiving, regardless of their era of service; however, those who serve as caregivers to a spouse spend the most time caregiving per week. Post-9/11 caregivers were more likely to report that they had to help care recipients cope with stressful situations or avoid triggers of anxiety or antisocial behavior.

How much time does caregiving demand? For all caregivers, this demand is substantial. In general, civilian caregivers tended to spend more time each week performing these duties than pre-9/11 military caregivers, though the time was comparable for post-9/11 military caregivers. Seventeen percent of civilian caregivers reported spending more than 40 hours per week providing care (8 percent reported spending more than 80 hours per week); for post-9/11 military caregivers and pre-9/11 military caregivers, 12 and 10 percent, respectively, spent more than 40 hours per week.

### Caregiving Imposes a Heavy Burden

Caring for a loved one is a demanding and difficult task, often doubly so for caregivers who are juggling care duties with family life and work. The result is often that caregivers pay a price for their devotion. Military caregivers consistently experience worse health outcomes, greater strains in family relationships, and more workplace problems than non-caregivers, and post-9/11 military caregivers fare worst in these areas.

Military caregivers consistently experience poorer levels of physical health than non-caregivers. In addition, military caregivers face elevated risk for depression. We found that key aspects of caregiving contribute to depression, including time spent giving care and helping the care recipient cope with behavioral problems. Perhaps of even greater concern, between 12 percent (of pre-9/11 military caregivers) and 33 percent (of post-9/11 military caregivers) lack health care coverage, suggesting that they face added barriers to getting help in mitigating the potentially negative effects of caregiving.

The impacts of caregiving on families are more pronounced among post-9/11 military caregivers, largely because of their age. Of all caregivers caring for a spouse, post-9/11 military caregivers report the lowest levels of relationship quality with the care recipient. This difference is largely accounted for by the younger age of post-9/11 military caregivers, but it still places these newer romantic partnerships at greater risk of separation or divorce.

As noted earlier, the majority of military caregivers are in the labor force. Caregiving also has an effect on absenteeism. Civilian caregivers reported missing 9 hours of work on average, or approximately 1 day of work per month. By comparison, post-

9/11 military caregivers report missing 3.5 days of work per month on average. The lost wages from work, in addition to costs incurred associated with providing medical care, result in financial strain for these caregivers.

## Most Relevant Programs and Policies Serve Caregivers Only Incidentally

Our environmental scan identified more than 100 programs that offer services to military caregivers (see the "Common Caregiving Services" box). However, most serve caregivers incidentally (i.e., caregivers are not a stated or substantial part of the organization's reason for existence, as evidenced by its mission, goals, and activities).

Figure S.1 categorizes these programs according to the types of services (as described earlier in the "Common Caregiving Services" box) that each offers to caregivers. We found that 80 percent of these programs are offered by private, nonprofit organizations; 8 percent by private, for-profit organizations; and 12 percent by government entities.

These programs tend to be targeted toward the care recipient, with his or her family invited to participate, or toward military and/or veteran families, of whom caregivers are a subset. These programs either make services available for family caregivers, or they serve military families and within that group offer services for the caregiver subset. There are two primary reasons for this: First, most programs limit eligibility to primary family members. This limitation excludes caregivers who are either in the

**Figure S.1**
**Services Offered to Military Caregivers by Organizations Identified in the RAND Environmental Scan**

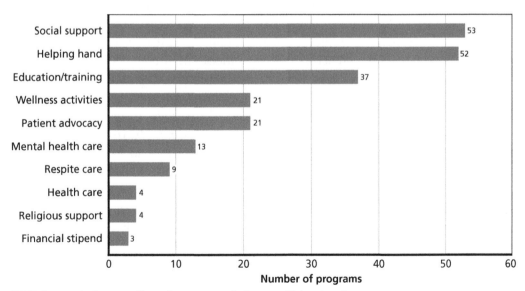

NOTE: An organization may offer various programs that span multiple categories.

RAND RR499-S.1

care recipient's extended family or are not related to the care recipient. Second, many of these programs are geared toward caregivers for older populations, and thus typically limit eligibility to those caring for someone age 60 or older. Post-9/11 caregivers—more than 80 percent of whom are under age 60—are hit particularly hard by this focus on older caregivers.

Of services targeted to caregivers, we examined the goals of the services provided, grouped them into four categories, and assessed their alignment with caregiver service use and needs, noting programmatic gaps in some areas.

*Services helping caregivers to provide better care (patient advocacy or case management and structured education or training).* More than 34 percent of post-9/11 caregivers reported difficulties because of medical uncertainty about the care recipient's condition; half that share of pre-9/11 and civilian caregivers reported such difficulties. We also found that post-9/11 caregivers reported greater challenges obtaining necessary medical and other services for their care recipients as compared with other caregivers. While many programs offered patient advocacy and case management support, only 20 to 30 percent of all caregivers were using this type of program. Among those who did, post-9/11 military caregivers rated them as significantly more helpful than did other caregivers.

*Services addressing caregiver health and well-being (respite care, health and mental health care, structured social support, and structured wellness activities).* We found that caregivers have consistently worse health outcomes than non-caregivers, and post-9/11 military caregivers' outcomes are consistently the worst among caregivers. Close to half of all post-9/11 military caregivers do not have such coverage, and only four programs specifically target caregivers in this area (12 offer some form of mental health care). Respite care is offered by only nine organizations, though notably fewer post-9/11 military caregivers (20 percent) have used respite care than civilian caregivers (29 percent). In contrast, more programs promote caregiver wellness via structured wellness activities (e.g., fitness classes, stress relief lessons, or outdoor physical activities) for caregivers and their families.

*Services addressing caregiver and family well-being (structured wellness activities, religious support networks, and a "helping hand" [direct support, such as loans, donations, legal guidance, housing support, or transportation assistance]).* To address the issue of lower-quality family relationships, religious programming and structured wellness activities are often geared toward families.

*Services addressing income loss (financial stipend).* Finally, only three stipend programs (primarily for post-9/11 caregivers or those who care for the elderly) exist to help offset income loss that results from caregiving. This seemingly important service helps address the financial challenges that caregivers report having and that may result from, among post-9/11 military caregivers, a largely employed group of caregivers who miss, on average, 3.5 days of work per month. However, among those who received a monthly stipend or caregiver payment from the VA, pre-9/11 caregivers rated it as significantly more helpful than did post-9/11 caregivers.

## Caregivers Need Help with Future Planning

As younger caregivers age, the demographic composition of caregivers and the dynamic relationship between caregivers and care recipients will change, signaling the need for long-term planning. This need is likely more pronounced for post-9/11 military care recipients, who are younger and may be more vulnerable than pre-9/11 and civilian care recipients, particularly those relying on parents and aging spouses.

Critical aspects of planning include financial, legal, residential, and vocational/educational planning. Lack of knowledge about services available for aging care recipients, or being ill-informed about how to access such services, may hinder some caregivers from making future plans for their loved one, while the emotional toll that such planning takes may also affect caregivers' ability to make concrete future plans.

Few of the military caregiver–specific programs we identified offered specific long-term planning assistance to military caregivers. Beyond the usual advice for planning legal issues for the care recipient (powers of attorney, living wills, estates and trusts), there is little guidance to help military caregivers address long-term needs for themselves. Planning for the caregiver's own future can provide security for the care recipient's future as well, particularly if the caregiver becomes incapacitated by poor health or dies.

## The Burden of Caregiving Affects Society

While the value of caregiving may be high for the care recipient and helpful for defraying medical care and institutionalization costs, the burden of caregiving exacts a more significant toll on the economy. As a consequence of the impact in the employment setting, as well as excess health care costs to tend to their own increased health needs, caregivers confer costs to society. Using literature from the civilian caregiving setting, as well as from studies on the effects of mental health problems on society, we estimate that the costs of lost productivity are $5.9 billion (in 2011 dollars) among post-9/11 caregivers.

To mitigate these costs over time, efforts to address and mitigate the negative consequences and increased costs of caregiving can potentially increase the value that military caregiving confers on society. Future studies that gather more detailed information and data about the effectiveness of various caregiver support interventions and their impact on the costs of lost productivity (at both the individual and societal levels) might inform the business case for increasing support for this vulnerable population.

## Recommendations

Ensuring the long-term well-being of military caregivers will require concerted and coordinated efforts to address the needs of military caregivers and to fill the gaps we have identified. To address these concerns, we make recommendations in four strategic areas. We highlight our key recommendations here.

### Empower Caregivers

Efforts are needed to help empower military caregivers. These should include ways to build their skills and confidences in caregiving, mitigate the potential stress and strain of caregiving, and raise public awareness of the caregivers' value.

- **Provide high-quality education and training to help military caregivers understand their roles and teach them necessary skills.** Training caregivers can help them play their roles more effectively and enhance the well-being of the wounded, ill, or injured veterans they are caring for.
- **Help caregivers get health care coverage and use existing structured social support.** Ensuring that caregivers have health care coverage is critical to their continued health and well-being. Likewise, peer-based social support programs to address feelings of isolation are vital to improve caregiver connectedness and build supportive networks.
- **Increase public awareness of the role, value, and consequences of military caregiving.** Public awareness or education will raise the profile of military caregivers and help ensure that their needs are addressed and their value recognized. This step may also help additional members of this group self-identify and seek support.

### Create Caregiver-Friendly Environments

Creating contexts that acknowledge caregivers' special needs and status will help them play their roles more effectively and balance the potentially competing demands of caregiving and their own work lives.

- **Promote work environments that support caregivers. Provide protection from discrimination and promote workplace adaptations.** While federal law offers protection from discrimination against caregivers in the workplace, practices and policies for accommodating caregivers' needs and improving support for caregivers in the workplace can reduce absenteeism and improve productivity. One example includes employee assistance programs, which can provide counseling support and referrals for additional resources.
- **Health care environments catering to military and veteran recipients should make efforts to acknowledge caregivers as part of the health care team.** Military caregivers assume responsibilities to help maintain and manage the health

of their care recipients. Performing these tasks effectively requires that they interact regularly with health care providers: physicians, nurses, and case managers. Health care providers can facilitate caregiver interaction with the health care system by acknowledging caregivers' key role in helping veterans navigate the system and providing necessary supplemental care.

## Fill Gaps in Programs

As we noted, programs relevant to the needs of military caregivers are typically focused on the service member or veteran, and only incidentally related to the caregiver's role. In addition, we observed specific gaps in needed programs. Therefore, eligibility issues and specific programmatic needs should be addressed.

- **Ensure that caregivers are supported based on the tasks and duties they perform, rather than their relationship to the care recipient.** Programs should extend eligibility to all caregivers who might benefit from them, including extended family and friends. Organizations that serve wounded, ill, or injured service members and veterans and who serve caregivers who are family members, or those that serve military and veteran families and serve caregivers who have also served, will need to consider how to expand eligibility to include extended and nonfamily caregivers. In addition, the most notable gaps in programmatic support were resources that connected caregivers with health care coverage (nearly one-third of post-9/11 caregivers lacked coverage) and financial support to compensate caregivers for income loss and other expenses.
- **Respite care should be made more widely available to military caregivers, and alternative respite strategies should be considered.** To the extent that adverse outcomes associated with caregiving (e.g., depression) are influenced by time spent caregiving, finding temporary relief from caregiving appears critical. Respite for military caregivers should be considered carefully, and existing programs for patients with cancer, the frail/elderly, care recipients with dementia, or the physically disabled may need adaptation to better serve military care recipients.

## Plan for the Future

Ensuring the long-term well-being of caregivers and the agencies that aim to support them may each require efforts to plan strategically for the future, not only to serve the dynamic and evolving needs of current military caregivers, but also to anticipate the needs of future military caregivers in a changing political and fiscal environment.

- **Encourage caregivers to create financial and legal plans to ensure caregiving continuity for care recipients.** Organizations that serve military caregivers can fill a gap in services by creating and sharing guidance about long-term financial and legal planning. Programs that are available in these areas typically address the needs of those caring for the elderly or for persons with dementia and Alzheimer's, focusing expectedly on retirement and estate planning. Planning for post-9/11 care recipients needs to be different. These plans need to address financial stability for caregivers and their families and may include strategies to make up for lost wages and retirement and pension benefits. The plans also need to factor in the financial stability of the care recipient, who may need resources to buy caregiver support if the current caregiver is unable to continue in that role. Legal plans need to prepare powers of attorney and executors for estates or trusts, and may also require that new guardians and caregivers be appointed in the event that the current primary caregivers are no longer available.

- **Enable sustainability of programs by integrating and coordinating services across sectors and organizations through formal partnership arrangements.** The large number of current organizations raises two sustainability issues. First, if services are not coordinated, they can become a "maze" of organizations, services, and resources in which caregivers can become overwhelmed (Tanielian et al., 2013). Second, attention and commitment for supporting veterans and their families is currently high, but public interest may fade in future years, potentially translating into decreases in the level of private and philanthropic support for the many nongovernment programs (Carter, 2013; McDonough, 2013). One way to address both issues is to create formal partnerships across organizations. Effective partnerships will require exploring opportunities for true coordination, including the creation of coalitions.

- **Foster caregiver health and well-being through access to high-quality services.** High-quality support services are needed to boost caregiver effectiveness and reduce the negative effects of caregiving. The Institute of Medicine (National Research Council, 2001) has defined high-quality medical care as care that is effective, safe, caregiver-centered, timely, efficient, and equitable. This definition applies to support programs as well. At present, however, little is known about the quality or effectiveness of available military caregiver programs. High-quality programs are important because research has shown that quality care can improve outcomes. Understanding the quality of services requires measuring and assessing the structure, process, and outcomes associated with these services. Evaluating all of the identified programs in our scan was beyond our scope. But we also did not hear of caregiver support programs conducting rigorous evaluations or studies to document their effectiveness, or that they had implemented continuous quality improvement initiatives. Currently, the Family Caregiver Alliance and Rosalynn Carter Institute for Caregiving maintain databases on evidence-based programs, and the Family Caregiver Alliance resource includes information about model programs and emerging practices. In addition, the VA is funding research projects to assess the effectiveness of caregiver services and interventions. Organizations that implement military caregiver programs could benefit from using these resources to inform their own service delivery. Over the long term, demonstrating program value may require that organizations also evaluate the extent to which their services are improving outcomes for participants.

- **Invest in research to document the evolving need for caregiving assistance among veterans and the long-term impact of caregiving on the caregivers.** This study provides a snapshot of the needs and burdens of military caregiving. While we can provide a glimpse into the future of military caregiving by looking at the characteristics of post-9/11 caregivers and the factors that might affect their caregiving demands, we can only make projections. Similarly, while the needs of pre-9/11 veterans may be what post-9/11 veterans will eventually require, there are differences in the make-up and expectations of the pre-9/11 and post-9/11 generations. In the future, additional rigorous, cross-sectional research like ours can shed light on the needs of caregivers and how their needs compare to those presented here. In addition, longitudinal studies and evaluations are needed to document changing needs over time and the effectiveness of programs and services intended to meet those needs.

## The Bottom Line

Military caregivers play an essential role in caring for injured or wounded service members and veterans. This enables those for whom they are caring to live better quality lives and can result in faster and improved rehabilitation and recovery. Yet playing this role can impose a substantial physical, emotional, and financial toll on caregivers. Improving military caregivers' well-being and ensuring their continued ability to provide care will require multifaceted approaches to reduce the burdens caregiving may create and to bolster their ability to serve as caregivers more effectively. Given the systematic differences among military caregiver groups, it is also important that tailored approaches meet the unique needs and characteristics of post-9/11 caregivers.

# Acknowledgments

The successful completion of our study relied upon many individuals and organizations. We wish to thank the many stakeholders who contributed time and information, particularly representatives from organizations who participated in interviews and reviewed our program profiles.

We thank the individuals who took the time to participate in our survey, as well as the team at GfK Custom Research who facilitated the implementation of the survey, including Sergei Rodkin, Beth Jaworski, and Mansour Fahimi.

We are grateful for Senator Elizabeth Dole's inspiration, vision, and support in commissioning this study. We thank the team at the Elizabeth Dole Foundation, including Carol Lindamood Harlow, Steven Schwab, and Gia Colombraro, for continuous assistance and support. We also acknowledge the support and encouragement that Melinda Farris provided throughout the study.

We are indebted to our RAND research support team, including David Adamson, Stacy Fitzsimmons, Racine Harris, Jeremy Kurz, Maggie Snyder, Clare Stevens, and Lance Tan. We thank our colleagues, Margaret C. Harrell, Susan D. Hosek, and Carra Sims, for reviewing our protocols and advising us on specific issues throughout the course of the study.

We thank our quality assurance reviewers for their constructive reviews: Charles C. Engel, Carrie Farmer, John R. Campbell, and Susan Paddock. Collectively, their comments and feedback greatly enhanced the final report. We also thank our report production team of editors and designers, including Arwen Bicknell, Steve Kistler, and Dori Walker.

Finally, we are especially grateful to the men and women who have served and are currently serving as part- or full-time caregivers; we thank them for their time and service to our nation.

# Abbreviations

| | |
|---|---|
| ACL | Administration for Community Living |
| ACS | American Community Survey |
| ADA | Americans with Disabilities Act |
| ADL | activity of daily living |
| AoA | Administration on Aging |
| BIA | Brain Injury Alliance |
| CAN | Caregiver Action Network |
| Cause | Comfort for America's Uniformed Services |
| CI | confidence interval |
| CMS | Centers for Medicare and Medicaid Services |
| CVOHSA | Caregivers and Veterans Omnibus Health Benefits Act of 2010 |
| DCoE | Defense Centers of Excellence for Psychological Health and Traumatic Brain Injury |
| DoD | Department of Defense |
| DoL | Department of Labor |
| EEOC | U.S. Equal Employment Opportunities Commission |
| EOD | Explosive Ordnance Disposal |
| FCA | Family Caregiver Alliance |
| FMLA | Family and Medical Leave Act |
| FPL | federal poverty level |
| HCBS | Home and Community-Based Services |
| HHS | Department of Health and Human Services |
| IADL | instrumental activity of daily living |
| IOM | Institute of Medicine |
| IPF | iterative proportional fitting |

| | |
|---|---|
| KP | KnowledgePanel |
| M | mean |
| MDD | major depressive disorder |
| NAC | National Alliance for Caregiving |
| NAMI | National Alliance on Mental Illness |
| NDAA | National Defense Authorization Act |
| NGO | nongovernmental organization |
| OAA | Older Americans Act |
| OEF | Operation Enduring Freedom |
| OIF | Operation Iraqi Freedom |
| OND | Operation New Dawn |
| OR | odds ratio |
| PHQ-8 | eight-question Patient Health Questionnaire |
| PTSD | posttraumatic stress disorder |
| RAS | Relationship Assessment Scale |
| RCI | Rosalynn Carter Institute for Caregiving |
| SAFE | Support and Family Education |
| SCAADL | Special Compensation for Assistance with Activities of Daily Living |
| SE | standard error |
| SF-36 | Short Form 36 |
| TAPS | Tragedy Assistance Program for Survivors |
| TBI | traumatic brain injury |
| USO | United Service Organizations |
| VA | Department of Veterans Affairs |
| VBA | Veterans Benefits Administration |
| VHA | Veterans Health Administration |
| WHODAS-2 | World Health Organization Disability Assessment Schedule 2 |
| WWP | Wounded Warrior Project |

# CHAPTER ONE

# Introduction

Approximately 22 million veterans live in the United States today (Department of Veterans Affairs [VA], 2013a). These veterans span multiple generations and eras of service, from World War II to the most recent conflicts in Iraq and Afghanistan. Data from the VA indicate that roughly 3.8 million of these veterans receive compensation for a documented disability that resulted from a disease or injury incurred or aggravated during active military service (VA, 2013a).[1] The number and proportion of disabled veterans has increased significantly since 2001, largely as a result of the conflicts in Iraq and Afghanistan. While advanced technologies and battlefield medicine enabled low rates of overall deaths from these conflicts, a significant number of individuals have experienced disabling wounds, illnesses, and injuries as a consequence of their military service.

Alongside these wounded, ill, and injured service members and veterans exists a cadre of individuals who help care for them, whom we term *military caregivers.* While health care providers may diagnose conditions and prescribe the treatment, it is these other individuals who provide support with activities of daily living (ADLs) such as bathing or dressing, help manage medications, provide transportation to medical appointments, help the disabled up and down stairs, and aid in other ways. And while health care providers are essential facilitators in the acute and long-term recovery and reintegration of wounded, ill, and injured service members, they were trained and educated specifically for their selected vocations. Though essential to the survival and quality of life of those they support, most informal and military caregivers did not choose caregiving as a vocation and may have little training. Their spouse, child, parent, friend, coworker, or neighbor was taken ill, injured, or wounded, and they stepped forward to take care of them.

Military caregivers are heroes in their own right, but their efforts are often unrecognized. They serve in the shadow of war, as their caregiving responsibilities persist for months and years after conflicts end. The men and women who have made sacrifices for their country often receive honors, awards, and benefits in recognition of their

---

[1]   This is often referred to as a service-connected disability.

service—accolades and opportunities that they rightly deserve. Their caregivers help the disabled walk and eat, tend to wound care, or take them to their medical appointments, and rarely receive honors and awards. These caregivers are an incidental population, one that has received policy attention only as a consequence of the focus on the ones for whom they provide care. Yet their value is enormous. Military caregivers provide benefit to not only their loved one, but also to society. The care they render helps reduce health care costs to the government and society.

In this report, we focus on the caregiver as the primary population of interest. We want to understand the needs of the caregivers as a population and examine how their needs may vary according to their own characteristics, as well as the characteristics of the individuals for whom they are caring.

Military caregivers serve an essential role in facilitating the recovery, rehabilitation, and reintegration of the wounded, ill, and injured. Caregiving duties, though, often come with consequences. Caregivers themselves may feel overwhelmed or unprepared for the duties they are now expected to perform, and these feelings and burdens can translate into mental and physical illness. Their caregiving responsibilities may also alter—in both positive and negative ways—the dynamics within their families, including marital quality and the ability to care for their children. There are also impacts on society at large, as caregiving responsibilities may affect whether individuals can remain productive at work and whether they remain in or leave the workforce altogether.

Though research has looked at the health and well-being of wounded, ill, and injured military personnel and their families, and the effect of deployment on family well-being, there is little known about military caregivers. While some small-scale studies have focused on military caregivers, no large-scale studies have been conducted. This report aims to fill that gap. We conducted a national survey of military caregivers and an environmental scan of the policies and programs that currently exist to support them. Building on these data, this research report aims to:

- describe the magnitude of military caregiving in the United States, including how caregiving affects individuals, their families, and society. We describe the number and characteristics of military caregivers and their role in ensuring the well-being of their care recipient. We also assess the effects of caregiving on military caregivers, their families, and society and examine how these effects differ across cohorts of veterans.
- describe current policies, programs, and other initiatives designed to support military caregivers, and identify how these efforts are—and are not—meeting the needs of military caregivers. We review the existing policies and programs and assess how these initiatives address specific caregiver needs.
- identify specific recommendations for filling gaps and ensuring the short- and long-term well-being of military caregivers.

## A Social Ecological Framework of Military Caregiving

Prior studies in the civilian care setting have discussed the benefits, costs, and value of caregiving at multiple levels. Research has shown that the presence of an informal caregiver can improve care recipients' well-being and recovery, and reduce medical costs by enabling home-based or community living for the disabled (Feinberg et al., 2011). In addition to documenting these potential benefits to the care recipient, studies have described the benefits and costs of caregiving in terms of its impact on caregivers, their families, their workplaces, and society more broadly (Feinberg et al., 2011). For example, AARP projected the value of family caregiving in 2009 to be $450 billion as measured by unpaid contributions (Feinberg et al., 2011), while others have shown the costs to society in terms of the impact on lost productivity, lost income, and increased health care costs. This impact is felt within the business community, but also within the U.S. economy more broadly. MetLife estimated that the costs associated with caregiving for the elderly cost U.S. employers approximately $13.4 billion in excess health care costs per year (MetLife, 2010). In a separate study, using data from a Gallup survey, Witters (2011) estimated that the lost productivity due to absenteeism among full- and part-time caregivers cost the U.S. economy more than $28 billion.

Recognizing that military caregivers are situated within these larger contexts, and to understand how military caregiving affects both individuals and the other systems in which they interact, we approached the study of military caregivers using a social ecological framework that acknowledges a dynamic relationship between individual and environmental factors, as depicted in Figure 1.1. At the core of this framework is a current or former member of the U.S. military who is injured, ill, or wounded, along

**Figure 1.1**
**The Social Ecology of Military Caregiving in the United States**

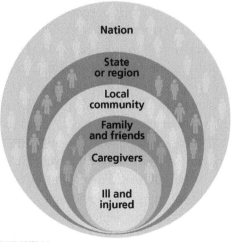

Nation

State or region

Local community

Family and friends

Caregivers

Ill and injured

RAND *RR499-1.1*

with his or her caregiver. At this level, our study explores the relationship between the care recipient and the caregiver, and how facets of caregiving may influence the caregiver's health and well-being. We also examine the programs and resources available both to enhance caregivers' technical skills to provide care and to ensure their own health and well-being. Caregivers also exist within larger social structures that both are affected by and influence the care that caregivers provide, and which can also impact the caregiver's health and well-being. Families and communities influence the network of individuals whom caregivers can rely upon and the resources available to help perform caregiving tasks; at the same time, caregiving may strain family relations or affect community engagement, including employment and performance at work. The resources that are available to help support care recipients, their caregivers, the caregivers' families, and the communities in which they reside are influenced in many ways by larger social structures, namely state and federal policies. Thus, the burdens of caregiving may ripple throughout these other populations of families and communities. These other populations may act as buffers or reinforcements, enabling the caregiver to perform more optimally with fewer consequences and the care recipient to thrive.

In the remainder of the report, we examine the characteristics of caregivers and their caregiving situations with an appreciation for these multidirectional influences. We also discuss how the impacts of caregiving may change over time and discuss potential future implications and downstream costs and benefits of military caregiving.

## Terms and Definitions

In this report, we have adopted specific terms to refer to the caregiver population. To make comparisons with other research studies, and to help align programs and policies that may use different definitions, we define these terms.

We use the term *caregiver* to refer to the individual, who may be a family member, friend, or neighbor, who provides a broad range of care and assistance for, or manages the care of, an individual with a disabling wound, injury, or illness (physical or mental). We use this term generically throughout the report to include anyone who serves in this capacity, regardless of whether they are related to the individual, live with the individual, or are caring for a person with injuries or physical or mental illness. They may provide this service part or full time. A caregiver differs from a *care provider*, who is trained and hired to deliver or provide services to a care recipient. Care providers may include health care professionals or allied health professionals that render treatment, therapy, rehabilitative, or care management services. These individuals often have specific professional licenses or certifications and are reimbursed for their contributions.

We apply the term *military caregiver* to a caregiver who is providing care to a current or former member of the U.S. Armed Forces. *Post-9/11 military caregiver* (or *post-9/11 caregiver*) refers to a military caregiver providing care to a service member or veteran who served in the armed forces after September 11, 2001, regardless of whether he or she also served prior to 2001. *Pre-9/11 military caregiver* (or *pre-9/11 caregiver*) refers to a military caregiver providing care to a service member or veteran who served in the armed forces before September 11, 2001, and not after that date. This date is important in that it distinguishes among cohorts of veterans entitled to newer benefits and among programs intended to address the needs of current and former military personnel who supported the recent conflicts in Iraq and Afghanistan. Thus, we compare the experiences of caregivers by the era of service of their veteran throughout our analyses.

In describing the population of caregivers who provide assistance to individuals who never served in the Armed Forces, we use the term *civilian caregiver.*

We use the term *care recipient* to refer to the person for whom caregivers are providing care. We also use this term generically throughout the report to include anyone who receives caregiving support. A *military care recipient* is a care recipient who is a current or former member of the U.S. Armed Forces.[2]

Finally, we use the term *caregiver incidental* and its inverse, *caregiver specific*, to describe programs included in our environmental scan. The latter describes programs for which caregivers are a stated or substantial part of the organization's reason for existence, as demonstrated by its mission, goals, and activities. We use a similar rubric for describing organizations that are either *military incidental* or *military specific.*

## Organization of This Report

This report is divided into five chapters. In the remainder of this chapter, we provide the relevant background and context for this study. We do so by reviewing the earlier work RAND and other researchers have conducted on military caregivers, and then provide an overview of the primary methods used for the current study: a nationally representative survey of military caregivers and an environmental scan of the programs that serve them. This is followed by a short overview of federal and state policies relevant to military caregiving.

Chapter Two focuses on the characteristics of caregivers and care recipients. In this chapter, we quantify and describe the number of military caregivers and also describe the types of relevant medical conditions borne by military care recipients, the ways in which these wounded, ill, or injured service members and veterans rely on military caregivers, the tasks that military caregivers perform, the network of other people caregivers rely on for support, and the nature and types of support programs available to military caregivers. This chapter also presents the specific demands that caregivers face in providing care to service members or veterans.

Chapter Three describes the consequences faced by military caregivers as a result of their caregiving role. It begins by describing the health and well-being of caregivers

---

[2]  Wounded, injured, and ill service members remain in the military for a period of time during their treatment and recovery before separating to veteran status. Some may elect to stay within the military through policies for allowing them to continue on active duty.

and, when possible, how caregiving itself may contribute to these outcomes. We then describe how caregivers' families are affected by caregiving, and the consequences that caregiving has on caregivers' work or careers. In these sections, we also present specific challenges that military caregivers have in caring for themselves, their families, and in managing their finances and careers. We describe the programs and resources available to caregivers and how programs and resources may, or may not, meet these needs. We also discuss where caregivers are currently accessing support services and the reasons why some are not accessing services at various organizations.

In Chapter Four, we present a series of analyses and a framework for considering the future of military caregivers, the service members or veterans they are caring for, and society. We also discuss the long-term issues facing caregivers in light of the dynamic and evolving nature of their roles and their capabilities for fulfilling these roles, highlight the long-term planning issues that may soon become relevant (if they are not already) to caregivers and care recipients, and the changing landscape of resources that exist to support them.

Chapter Five summarizes our main findings as they relate to the overall impact of caregiving at the individual, family, and societal level, and present recommendations that, if enacted, will fill gaps and ensure long-term sustainable support for military caregivers.

Throughout the report, we have included a series of discussion boxes. These provide more in-depth discussion about select issues identified in our analysis that warrant future research. We also highlight key findings in boxes that accompany many sections of the report.

A series of appendixes provide greater detail about the methods employed for the national survey (Appendixes A and B), our enumeration procedures (Appendix C), and the environmental scan (Appendixes D and E). Appendix F provides additional details on federal and state policies and programs relevant to military caregivers. Descriptions of organizations and programs excluded from our environmental scan are included in Appendix G. Detailed descriptions of programs identified in the scan are included in a separate, online Appendix H.

## Study Overview

*Hidden Heroes* represents the second of a two-phase study that RAND conducted on military caregivers in the United States. It is based on primary research from two key sources: a nationally representative survey of military caregivers and military care recipients, and an environmental scan of the policies, resources, and programs available to military caregivers.

Before describing the current phase, we review the results from Phase I of our work, *Military Caregivers: Cornerstones of Support for Our Nation's Wounded, Ill, and*

*Injured Veterans* (Tanielian et al., 2013). We also present an overview of recent research on military caregivers that helped inform the current research project. We then describe our methods for both the survey and environmental scan.

### *Cornerstones of Support:* A Review

In *Cornerstones of Support*, the first phase of our study, we reviewed the existing literature to document what was known about the characteristics and roles of military caregivers. Many studies had examined the characteristics of caregivers and value of caregiving in the United States, but those studies had primarily focused on caregivers in the civilian sector. While studies acknowledge variability of caregiving across individuals, they generally converge on the important role that caregivers play in providing critical acute and long-term care and support—often enabling their care recipients to remain out of institutions, to experience speedier recoveries, and live fuller, more independent lives in spite of their disabilities. However, these studies also revealed the burdens that the tasks and time associated with caregiving place on many who assume these roles. Civilian caregivers are at increased risk for health problems and deterioration, mental and emotional distress, isolation, and loss of income. As a result, caregivers absorb many social, legal, and economic costs, which may have greater consequences for society.

Though the research base on military caregiving is limited, *Cornerstones of Support* provided some information about this population, including how it might resemble and differ from its civilian counterpart. Past research reported that the overwhelming majority of military caregivers were women caring for their husbands, and most lived with their veteran care recipient. The existing literature and our own discussions with groups of military caregivers themselves revealed that military caregivers performed similar tasks to civilian caregivers: providing support and assistance with ADLs as well as with instrumental activities of daily living (IADLs, defined in more detail in Chapter Two). But these data also highlighted challenges unique to military caregivers, who often struggled with assisting their care recipients with multiple and severe injuries or illnesses, navigating complex systems of care, and tending to the often invisible disabilities associated with posttraumatic stress disorder (PTSD) or traumatic brain injury (TBI).

*Cornerstones of Support* also highlighted the need for better data on the unique experiences of military caregivers. As we describe in detail in the next section, existing research drew largely upon small-scale studies or studies that used a convenience-based approach to gather the perspectives of caregivers. Specifically, there was a need for:

- a survey of military caregivers large enough to enable researchers to examine the unique experiences of those individuals caring for service members and veterans from post-9/11 conflicts; e.g., Operation Enduring Freedom (OEF), Operation Iraqi Freedom (OIF), and Operation New Dawn (OND)

- a study that used a probabilistic sampling strategy that would recruit caregivers regardless of whether they were part of an existing caregiving network
- a comprehensive scan and analysis of the programs and resources available to military caregivers today.

*Hidden Heroes* represents Phase 2 of the RAND study and attempts to fill each of these three gaps.

## Past Surveys of Military Caregivers

Recent surveys of military caregivers provide an important foundation for this study and are described in Table 1.1. Several of the previous studies focused on caregivers of veterans or service members with specific health conditions; namely TBI (Griffin et al., 2012; Phelan et al., 2011), spinal cord injuries (Robinson-Whelen and Rintala, 2003), and PTSD (Calhoun, Beckham, and Bosworth, 2002). Two studies were broader surveys of military caregivers (National Alliance for Caregiving [NAC], 2010) or military caregivers and care recipients (Van Houtven, Oddone, and Weinberger, 2010). Prior to our report, the largest and most comprehensive survey of military caregivers was carried out by NAC and published in 2010, using a "snowball" method in which the organization contacted a set of veterans through veteran service agencies and asked those veterans to pass the survey invitation to their primary caregiver, ultimately recruiting 462 military caregivers. We will review the specific findings of these studies in later chapters; in general, the NAC survey and others revealed that military caregivers are predominantly women who provide many different types of care for their care recipients, and who struggle with the strain of caregiving and its emotional and financial effects.

While informative, existing studies of military caregivers are limited, primarily by the strategies that authors use to recruit, or "sample," caregivers in the study. Sampling military caregivers is difficult because there is no accurate way to identify all military caregivers in the United States, obtain their contact information, and ask them to participate in a survey. Military caregivers are spread out all over the country, in urban and rural areas, and there is no official registry of military caregivers that could be used to contact them. Given the difficulty in identifying and contacting these individuals, researchers have relied on organizations that support or provide care for veterans and/or military caregivers as a means to recruit caregivers for surveys (or ask veterans about their caregivers). This is a very targeted and efficient way of identifying military caregivers, because these organizations either have rosters of members who are military caregivers, or they serve ill or wounded veterans who could then relay the survey to their primary caregiver (e.g., veterans served by a VA hospital). As shown in Table 1.1, previous surveys have used this method exclusively to recruit military caregivers to participate in surveys.

Though efficient, such convenience-based methods of obtaining survey respondents have certain limitations that could lead to biased results. First and foremost,

**Table 1.1**
**Previous Epidemiologic Studies of Military Caregivers**

| Author | Sample | Number of Post-9/11 Caregivers | Description of Sample | Main Findings |
|---|---|---|---|---|
| Bass et al., 2012 | 486 military caregivers | Not reported | Caregivers of veterans in five cities who were diagnosed with dementia and who were contacted either through their physician or through VA medical records | Higher veteran behavioral problems was associated with greater caregiver need and poorer psychological adjustment; greater ADL dependency was associated with more caregiver stress |
| Griffin et al., 2012 | 564 military caregivers | 564 | Caregivers of veterans who were released from four VA rehabilitation centers with a diagnosis of TBI | Most caregivers were women; a quarter provided care over 40 hours a week; 60 percent were the sole caregiver |
| Phelan et al., 2011 | 70 military caregivers | 0 | Caregivers of veterans who were released from four VA rehabilitation centers with a diagnosis of TBI | Perceived caregiver discrimination and stigma was associated with poorer psychological adjustment |
| NAC, 2010 | 462 military caregivers | Approx. 175 | Caregivers of veterans using veteran service agencies and survey solicitations through organizations that serve military caregivers | Compared with national statistics on nonmilitary caregivers, military caregivers were found to be younger, serve as caregivers longer, and have greater caregiver burden, stress, and financial strain |
| Van Houtven, Oddone, and Weinberger, 2010 | 42 veterans and 17 military caregivers | Not reported | Veterans and their caregivers who accessed home and community-based services at the Durham Veterans Affairs Medical Center | More than half of caregivers were interested in training, but perceived barriers (e.g., transportation); almost a quarter screened positive for probable depression |
| Robinson-Whelen and Rintala, 2003 | 348 veterans with caregivers | Not reported | Veterans with spinal cord injuries who received treatment at the Houston VA and had at least one caregiver | One-third of caregivers were in poor/fair health; over half reported no one else was available to provide care if the main caregiver becomes unable |
| Calhoun, Beckham, and Bosworth, 2002 | 71 military spouses who were caregivers | 0 | Spouses or partners of Vietnam veterans recruited from a VA PTSD clinic | Caregivers of veterans with PTSD experienced more burden and worse psychological outcomes than those caring for veterans without PTSD |

there is a possibility that respondents from convenience-based samples are systematically different from the population of interest they are intended to represent. For example, military caregivers recruited through caregiver organizations may be better connected to services and more knowledgeable about programs than caregivers who do not belong to these organizations. The possibility that military caregivers recruited through convenience samples are different from other military caregivers raises a concern about the generalizability of the findings; that is, the results from convenience surveys may not be representative of all military caregivers in the United States. For example, if researchers surveyed military caregivers through the VA, the respondents would not include people who provide care for those ill or wounded veterans who are not eligible for VA benefits, or who do not access them for other reasons. Thus, the results from surveys based on either of these approaches will not account for the total number of caregivers in groups that did not get surveyed or how they would have responded to the survey.

Finally, with any survey, there is a certain amount of variability in the confidence with which results can be generalized to the population of interest. This variance is often called "sampling error," and it represents the fact that the survey did not sample the entire population, just a portion of the people in it. Estimating sampling error in convenience-based samples is problematic. It relies upon knowing the underlying characteristics of the population that the survey respondents are meant to represent. If basic characteristics of the population are unknown, as with military caregivers, then it is not feasible to estimate the sampling error. Even if population characteristics are known, estimating sampling error with convenience-based samples is not always very precise.

To account for the limitations of convenience-based samples, "probability-based" random samples are usually preferred. Probability sampling relies on ensuring that every member of the population has a chance of being surveyed, and that those designing the study know every member of the population's probability of being selected to be a part of the sample. A small group of the population is then randomly selected to participate in the study. This approach enables researchers to estimate the characteristics of an entire population or enumerate a population subgroup with statistical confidence. Importantly, sampling error can be estimated and accounted for in the survey results, enabling researchers to empirically quantify the confidence of our estimates. Thus, probability-based survey samples are best for drawing conclusions about the characteristics of the population of military caregivers, while convenience-based samples provide targeted access to a group of caregivers of interest.

As we will describe, RAND's Survey of Military Caregivers used an approach that blended both a probability-based sample and a convenience-based approach. We relied on a probability-based sample for estimating the prevalence of military caregivers and their needs, but we also gathered a convenience-based sample of military caregivers from the Wounded Warrior Project® (WWP). Our process for blending the samples is described in more detail in the next section. Our main reason for gathering the convenience-based sample from WWP is that there were likely to be a relatively small number of caregivers for post-9/11 service members and veterans in the probability-based sample. Just as the veterans of the conflicts in Iraq and Afghanistan represent a smaller proportion of the overall living number of veterans in the United States, we suspected there would be a similarly lower proportion of the living military caregivers serving post-9/11 veterans compared with caregivers for veterans of prior eras. However, we were interested in learning specifically how post-9/11 military caregivers differed from other military caregivers. Augmenting the probability-based sample with a convenience-based sample and implementing statistical procedures allowed us to increase the number of post-9/11 military caregivers in our study and thus reach reliable conclusions about this group while removing any potential bias brought about by using exclusively a convenience-based approach.

### RAND Survey of Military Caregivers

Between August and October 2013, RAND conducted an online survey of military caregivers with an existing, probability-based sample of households in the United States supplemented with a convenience-based sample of post-9/11 military caregivers. We present a brief overview of the survey here; readers interested in more detail should refer to Appendixes A and B.

The probability-based sample came from KnowledgePanel (KP), an online panel of households that is designed to represent the U.S. general population of non-institutionalized adults. One respondent from each of the 41,163 households that are part of the KP panel was invited to complete a screener to determine their eligibility for the survey across one of four groups: military care recipients, military caregivers, civilian caregivers, and non-caregivers. Of these 41,163 households, 28,164 (68 percent) completed the screener.

A complementary sample of military caregivers was drawn from the WWP database of military caregivers. WWP is a nonprofit organization founded in 2003 to honor and empower wounded warriors who incurred a physical or mental injury, illness, or wound coincident to their military service on or after September 11, 2001. WWP maintains a database of names and contact information of individuals who have registered with the organization and self-identified as caregivers of wounded, ill, or injured OEF/OIF/OND veterans. Each registrant in this database must supply information about the veteran they care for, which WWP uses in turn to verify affiliation with a wounded, ill, or injured OEF/OIF/OND veteran.

In addition to military care recipients from KP and military caregivers from KP and WWP, we chose to sample two control groups for comparative purposes. Our sample of civilian caregivers from KP provides information about whether the characteristics and outcomes observed among military caregivers were unique to military caregivers or were common among all caregivers. This information may be helpful to inform whether the policies and programs that exist for caregivers more broadly can be similarly marketed and offered to military caregivers, or may need to be adapted to cater to that group. For example, we show in Chapter Two that one-third of post-9/11 military caregivers are spouses of the person they are caring for, though only a quarter of pre-9/11 military and 16 percent of civilian caregivers are spouses of the care recipient. Programs that are geared to adult children caring for their elderly parent (for example, by providing images in marketing materials) may be relevant to post-9/11 military caregivers, but may need to be adapted to better target this group. Similarly, we chose to interview a sample of non-caregivers because we were interested in comparing certain outcomes experienced among military caregivers with non-caregivers. Figure 1.2 provides a schematic of our survey approach, the groups sampled, and the total number of respondents from each.

**Eligibility criteria.** Eligibility criteria for each of the four groups of respondents are described here.

- *Military care recipients* came exclusively from KP and identified as having reported (a) having ever served on active duty in the U.S. Armed Forces or in the reserves or National Guard; (b) requiring assistance as a result of an illness, injury, or other condition or impairment (including mental health condition); and (c) having at least one person who is a family member, friend, or neighbor who helps the veteran/service member due to their illness, injury, or other condition but does not get paid for it.

- *Military caregivers* were identified from KP and WWP as not meeting criteria of a military care recipient and reporting that (a) they provide unpaid care and assistance for, or manage the care of, someone who is at least 18 years old and has an illness, injury, or condition for which they require outside support; (b) the person for whom they provide care is a current or former member of the U.S. military, National Guard, or reserves; and (c) their relationship to the person is not as someone hired to provide care in exchange for financial compensation, or to provide volunteer caregiving services through a program or agency.

- *Civilian caregivers* came exclusively from the KP sample and were identified as reporting that they did not meet criteria as a military care recipient or military caregiver but that (a) they provide unpaid care and assistance for, or manage the care of, someone who is at least 18 years old and has an illness, injury, or condition for which they require outside support, and (b) their relationship to the person is not as someone hired to provide care in exchange for financial compensation, or to provide volunteer caregiving services through a program or agency.

- *Non-caregiving controls* did not meet any of the aforementioned criteria; in addition, they were required to report that they do *not* provide unpaid care and assistance for, or manage the care of someone who is *younger than* 18 years old and has an illness, injury, or condition for which they require outside support.

**Figure 1.2**
**Schematic Representation of RAND Survey of Military Caregivers**

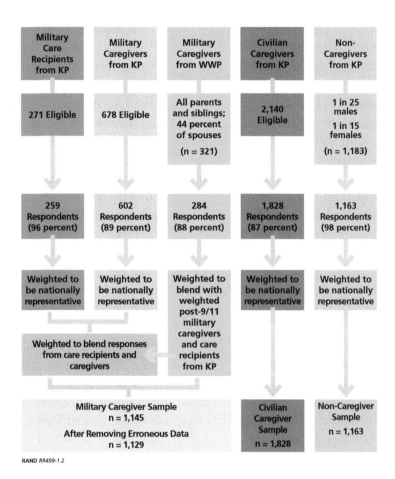

RAND RR499-1.2

**Weighting.** Analyses of data from the KP panel are weighted so that results are representative of the noninstitutionalized U.S. population. As described here (and in more detail in Appendix B), these weights were modified to improve the representativeness of the sample specifically for the U.S. population of military caregivers, military care recipients, civilian caregivers, and non-caregiving controls.

**Combining data from three groups of military caregivers.** We asked military care recipients a series of questions about their caregiver that aligned with questions asked of caregivers themselves. Similarly, we asked military caregivers a series of questions about their care recipient that aligned with questions asked of care recipients themselves. We used a statistical raking algorithm known as iterative proportional fitting (IPF) to create weights to account for our sampling strategy, which may overrepresent military care recipients who are healthier, and, by design, excludes those who are institutionalized. Variables used in this procedure included whether the care recipient lived with the caregiver, had a TBI or another neurological condition, had a VA disability rating of 70 percent or above, and his or her level of functioning. Also included among the variables was whether the caregiver had any support providing unpaid care (i.e., a caregiving network), and the amount of time s/he spent caregiving.

We combined data from WWP with the KP panels of military caregivers to increase our sample of post-9/11 caregivers. In comparing caregivers from WWP with KP post-9/11 caregivers, it became apparent that WWP caregivers were more likely to be female and more likely to be caring for someone with a VA disability rating (Table 1.2). IPF was again used to create weights that were applied to the WWP respondents to account for differences between the groups. Variables used in the IPF procedure included caregiver characteristics (age, sex, the interaction of age and sex, and household income), care recipient characteristics (whether the care recipient had ever deployed to a war zone, his or her medical condition, whether the medical condition was related to military service, and his or her VA disability rating).[3]

With weighting, we were able to successfully increase the number of post-9/11 military caregivers in our sample from 133 to 414 without changing the distribution of other covariates from the original probability-based sample (from KP).[4] The distribution of characteristics of caregivers and care recipients from the original WWP sample, the original post-9/11 KP sample, and the blended sample with weights is shown in Table 1.2.

To summarize, by blending data from two sources, a probabilistic and a convenience-based sample, we have created a study of 1,129 military caregivers (including 414 post-9/11 caregivers) that is nationally representative of military caregivers in the United States. In addition, we have a comparison group of 1,828 civilian caregivers that is nationally representative of civilian caregivers in the United States. This makes the current study the largest and only nationally representative survey of military caregivers to date. Further, this represents one of the largest nationally representative surveys of civilian caregivers of adults. We have also recruited 1,163 non-caregivers to discern how caregivers and non-caregivers differ on identical questions tapping domains of health and well-being, family relationships, and job and work characteristics. A description of the total sample is presented in Table 1.3.

---

[3]  The IPF procedures also included a series of five "early technology adopter" characteristics (e.g., tendency to look for what is new when shopping; DiSogra et al., 2011).

[4]  Of the final weights for post-9/11 caregivers, approximately one-third are attributed to WWP, which results in a 50-percent increase in the effective sample size.

Table 1.2
Summary Characteristics of Post-9/11 Military Caregiver Respondents from WWP, Before and After Weighting

| | Benchmark Values | Characteristics of Military Caregiver Respondents from WWP—Unweighted | | Characteristics of Post-9/11 Military Caregivers Respondents from KP+WWP—After Weighting | |
|---|---|---|---|---|---|
| | Percentage | N | Percentage | Percentage | Standard Error (SE) |
| Caregiver sex | | | | | |
| Male | 44.5 | 17 | 6.1 | 40.7 | 5.7 |
| Female | 55.5 | 264 | 94.0 | 59.3 | 5.7 |
| Caregiver age | | | | | |
| 18–30 | 38.7 | 67 | 23.8 | 37.1 | 5.2 |
| 31–55 | 48.3 | 187 | 66.5 | 49.2 | 5.2 |
| 56–65 | 7.9 | 24 | 8.5 | 8.3 | 2.1 |
| 66–80 | 5.2 | 3 | 1.1 | 5.3 | 2.0 |
| 81+ | 44.5 | 67 | 23.8 | | |
| Household income | | | | | |
| <138% federal poverty level (FPL) | 19.8 | 60 | 21.4 | 19.7 | 4.2 |
| 138–249% FPL | 13.8 | 72 | 25.6 | 15.1 | 2.5 |
| 250%+ FPL | 66.3 | 149 | 53.0 | 65.2 | 4.6 |
| Care recipient disability rating | | | | | |
| No rating | 43.68 | 31 | 11.1 | 41.2 | 5.5 |
| 0% | -- | -- | -- | -- | -- |
| 10–20% | 9.3 | 4 | 1.4 | 8.6 | 3.7 |
| 30–40% | 13.0 | 12 | 4.3 | 12.1 | 3.7 |
| 50–60% | 5.4 | 28 | 10.1 | 6.0 | 1.7 |
| 70%+ | 28.0 | 201 | 72.8 | 31.7 | 3.9 |

## Limitations of Our Survey Approach

All research studies have limitations, and ours is no exception. First, there are design limitations. Our sampling strategy may miss caregivers and care recipients either erroneously or by design. Erroneous omissions occur if persons who are invited but refuse to participate in the KP sample differ from those who do participate, or if the KP sampling strategy unknowingly misses segments of the population. By design, we know that the KP sample excluded care recipients and caregivers living in institutions like long-term care facilities or nursing homes, as well as those who are homeless. We also only invite one participant per household; although that participant is invited to report about caregivers in his or her network, we are only gaining insight from the one person

Table 1.3
Summary Characteristics of RAND Survey of Military Caregivers

|  | Military Caregivers | | Civilian Caregivers | | Non-Caregiving Controls | |
|---|---|---|---|---|---|---|
|  | n | Weighted % | n | Weighted % | n | Weighted % |
| TOTAL | 1,129 | 100 | 1,828 | 100 | 1,163 | 100 |
| Care recipient era of service | | | | | | |
| Post-9/11 | 414 | 36.7 | N/A | N/A | N/A | N/A |
| Pre-9/11 | 715 | 63.3 | N/A | N/A | N/A | N/A |
| Caregiver sex | | | | | | |
| Male | 270 | 41.4 | 586 | 40.3 | 439 | 46.0 |
| Female | 855 | 58.6 | 1,242 | 59.7 | 724 | 54.0 |
| Caregiver age | | | | | | |
| 18–30 | 160 | 20.4 | 198 | 16.3 | 172 | 20.1 |
| 31–55 | 498 | 45.3 | 661 | 44.0 | 382 | 43.5 |
| 56–65 | 266 | 19.8 | 561 | 22.6 | 283 | 16.7 |
| 66–80 | 179 | 13.2 | 366 | 15.1 | 285 | 18.0 |
| 81+ | 21 | 1.3 | 42 | 2.0 | 41 | 1.7 |
| Caregiver race /ethnicity | | | | | | |
| White, non-Hispanic | 843 | 68.3 | 1,369 | 63.6 | 957 | 70.9 |
| Black, non-Hispanic | 84 | 12.5 | 170 | 15.0 | 69 | 10.6 |
| Other, non-Hispanic | 46 | 5.5 | 53 | 6.6 | 25 | 4.9 |
| Hispanic | 97 | 12.2 | 167 | 12.9 | 87 | 12.4 |
| Multiple, non-Hispanic | 54 | 1.5 | 69 | 2.0 | 25 | 1.3 |

NOTE: Military caregiver numbers across categories do not routinely add up to 1,129 because of missing data on characteristics of WWP respondents.

who participates in the survey. Finally, although we were very specific in our eligibility criteria for defining care recipients and caregivers, the definition is still somewhat subjective. Persons may be eligible for our survey as a caregiver, but did not think they met our criteria for many reasons.

We produced weights to blend samples from KP reports provided by care recipients and caregivers, as well as between KP and WWP. These weights were based on a select set of variables. To the extent that there remain differences between the groups on unobserved variables uncorrelated with those used in our weighting strategy, there may remain lingering differences between groups that may bias our estimates.

There are also limitations associated with the measures used in our analyses. All surveys that rely on self-report are limited by biases in how survey respondents answer questions. Social desirability bias occurs when people do not report truthfully in favor of providing the response that they believe to be "socially desirable." While this type of bias is reduced by administering surveys online, it still may exist and affect how people report on sensitive issues such as depression symptoms, relationship quality, or even time spent caregiving. In other instances, survey respondents may not provide accurate information. In the current survey, this is especially pertinent for items in which caregivers are reporting about care recipients (e.g., the care recipient's VA disability rating or medical conditions) or care recipients are reporting about caregivers (e.g., the caregiver's income). However, this may also occur if we are asking about events that may have occurred in the past and respondents cannot properly recall the information.

With respect to measures of health and well-being, we ask caregivers and care recipients to report whether the care recipient has certain medical conditions. We cannot confirm diagnoses, and this bias may lead to either underestimates (e.g., care recipients are clinically depressed but do not report being so because the condition is undiagnosed) or overestimates (caregivers report that the care recipient is depressed but the care recipient may not meet diagnostic criteria). Finally, our clinical measures of depression are likely to capture most of those with depression, but some who do not meet diagnostic criteria may also be identified as cases (i.e., false positives). Finally, we ask questions that tap issues such as physical functioning, relationship quality, and parenting; these are multidimensional and complex, and our measures are admittedly crude measures of these more nuanced constructs.

## Past Environmental Scans of Caregiver Support Programs

In an effort to understand and array the landscape of available programs that support military caregivers, we conducted an environmental scan of available military caregiver support resources, activities, and programs within the United States. In reviewing the existing literature on support for military caregivers, we found no comprehensive assessment of programs and resources specifically for this population. While there are several web-based resource links available through governmental and nongovernmental organizations that list federal and state policies, as well as web-based resources that identify available programs and services for caregivers (e.g., resource directories), we only found a few previous studies that have attempted to array the types of services available for civilian caregivers (often referred to as family caregivers in the literature). Where they exist, those efforts tend to focus on programs that serve caregivers for individuals over the age of 60 or on the provision of respite services specifically.

Some studies have tried to look at the provision of programs under the Administration on Aging (AoA), which is now part of the Administration for Community Living (ACL) within the Department of Health and Human Services (HHS), or focused on services within a certain state. For example, one environmental scan of caregiver support services in the state of California aimed to inform the National Family Caregiver Support Program (Whittier, Scharlach, and Dal Santo, 2005). Another study assessed respite services offerings and use in Ohio (Ohio Respite Coalition, undated). In addition, as part of the Older Americans Act (OAA), the AoA collects performance data and reports annually on OAA programs' efforts to improve services for caregivers. These reports discuss processes and outcomes within AoA programs, but do not capture the performance or availability of services offered outside of AoA programs.

We also identified an environmental scan of the availability of respite services. However, the scope of this study was programs offered in Canada (Dunbrack, 2003). In the United States, the Center for Disability and Aging Policy Lifespan Respite Care Program offers competitive grants to eligible agencies in 30 states and the District of Columbia. With the grant funding, states have established or enhanced their respite infrastructures through an assortment of activities and assessments. Some of the assessments include environmental scans to better understand available respite programs and family caregiver needs within the states (ACL, undated).

## RAND's Environmental Scan of Caregiver Support Programs

While the studies referenced in the prior section offer some insight into the availability of caregiver services in specific regions or areas, no prior study has examined the spectrum of services offered for military caregivers within the United States on a national level. Thus, our objective was to identify a broad range of programs, resources, and services (not limited to respite services) that would be available to military caregivers.

As part of our initial search, we identified a number of directories that assemble names, phone numbers, and websites of entities that may provide resources for military caregivers. While these directories are helpful starting points for caregivers, they do not provide detailed information about the depth and breadth of services offered for caregivers. Thus, we crafted a strategy that would reach beyond existing directories and facilitate a more robust accounting of exactly what these groups do in support of military caregivers. To identify organizational entities that provide services to military caregivers, we used a multipronged approach that included web searches, sorting through the National Resource Directory, consultations with nonprofit staff and subject matter experts, attendance at relevant meetings and events, and snowball sampling among service organizations (i.e., organizations were asked about, and referred us to, other organizations they knew of that offered programs and services to military caregivers). The search continued until we reached saturation, the point at which additional searches revealed no new entities. Data collection for this study component began on July 1, 2013, and ended on October 15, 2013.

In addition to reviewing and abstracting publicly available information about organizations and programs that support caregivers, we conducted interviews with the organizations that offered services involving *direct or intensive interaction* with caregivers. We will later describe the services prompting inclusion of an organization or program in our environmental scan (and our full inclusion and exclusion criteria are described in Appendixes D and G). Through our efforts, we identified a total of 127 organizations that appeared to meet our criteria. Of those, seven were interviewed and later determined ineligible because they did not meet our criteria. Of the remaining

120 entities that we included in our environmental scan, we sought to interview personnel at 108 of them (12 entities were identified after the interview period ended). A small number of organizations did not respond (n = 19) or declined to participate (n = 8). For entities that did not respond, declined, or were discovered after the interview period (n = 39), we developed descriptions of them based on publicly available information and were thus able to include them in this report.

A total of 81 distinct organizational entities were interviewed. Using a semistructured interview protocol, we gathered information to supplement the publicly available information about programs that support caregivers. We asked a series of questions to understand the history, origin, funding source, and objective of the programs. We also asked detailed questions about eligibility criteria, types of services offered, mode/mechanism of delivery, and whether any data had been gathered to assess the impact of the program on caregivers. More details about our methods and the results of the scan can be found in Appendixes D and E, respectively. Descriptions of the organizations and programs can also be found in Appendix H.

Based upon the data gathered through these interviews, we were able to catalog and describe the available resources, services, and programs across a number of dimensions. Moving forward in this report, we use the term "program" to refer to the broad set of activities implemented by organizations to support caregivers. To characterize the nature of programs, we created ten key categories and one "other" category to distinguish among caregiving support programs. Categorizing programs in this manner allowed us to understand how programs distribute across the categories, describe the range of services offered within each category, and examine how they compare to the observed and reported needs of caregivers. Caregivers' needs are multidimensional, and our program categorization was crafted to align across this spectrum. We note that while some programs offer services that fit into multiple categories, others offer distinct services that may fulfill unique caregiver needs. Figure 1.3 overlays the common caregiver categories with the dimensions of caregiver needs that they cover. Specifically, the outer ring represents the different caregiving needs, reflecting the multiple dimensions or domains of issues and needs that caregivers may face (e.g., psychological, financial, spiritual). The inner wheel represents the different types of services that the programs might offer. We portray this as a wheel to enable one to see that different types of programs (helping hand, mental health care, etc.) might address different dimensions of needs (psychological, financial, etc.), however, programs can have multiple benefits and as such, the slices of the inner wheel that reflect the types of services are not fixed— they can also slide to cover the different dimensions noted in the outer wheel.

### Program Offerings

Our framework for categorizing the organizations that provide caregiver resources and programs is based primarily upon the services they offer. We set criteria that, to be included in our inventory, an organization provided direct or intensive interaction with

**Figure 1.3**
**Caregiver Support Program Categories**

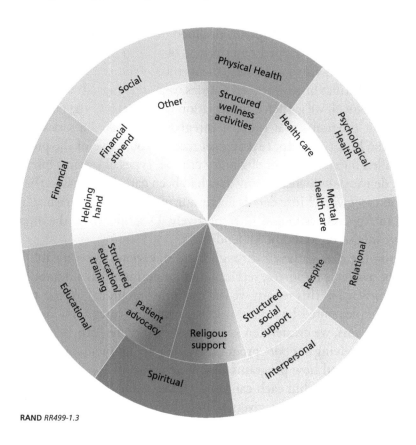

caregivers if it offered at least one of the following eight "common caregiving services" or "nonstandard" health or mental health care. In this context, "nonstandard" refers to the delivery of these types of health care services outside of traditional payment or delivery systems and/or that are designed for and offered specifically to caregivers.

Common caregiving services include:

- **Respite care:** Care provided to the service member or veteran by someone other than the caregiver in order to give the caregiver a short-term, temporary break
- **Patient advocate or case manager:** An individual who acts as a liaison between the service member or veteran and his or her care providers, or who coordinates care for the service member or veteran
- **Helping hand:** Direct support such as loans, donations, housing support, transportation assistance, or legal guidance, excluding assistance (legal or otherwise) with VA claims or appeals
- **Financial stipend:** Compensation for a caregiver's time devoted to caregiving activities and/or for loss of wages due to one's caregiving commitment

- **Structured social support:** Online or in-person support groups for caregivers or military family members (which may incidentally include caregivers) that are likely to assist with caregiving-specific stresses or challenges
- **Religious support:** Religious- or spiritual-based guidance or counseling
- **Structured wellness activities:** Organized activities such as fitness classes or stress relief lessons that focus on improving mental or physical well-being
- **Structured education or training:** In-person or online classes, modules, or webinars, or manuals or workbooks that involve a formalized curriculum (rather than ad hoc information) related to caregiving activities.

Nonstandard clinical care includes:

- **Health care:** Health care that is (1) offered outside of routine or traditional channels such as common government or private-sector payment and delivery systems, or (2) offered specifically to caregivers
- **Mental health care:** Mental health care that is (1) offered outside of routine or traditional channels such common government or private-sector payment and delivery systems, or (2) offered specifically to caregivers.

Individual organizations may offer only one program or service; others may offer multiple programs and services. In the following chapters, we will discuss how the array of programs and resources within and across these service categories compares to observed needs of caregivers. To provide an overview of the caregiver resources landscape as well as a frame of reference for the comparisons in future chapters, we provide a summary of the resources identified through our scan by category in the following sections.

As shown in Figure 1.4, of the caregiver-serving organizations that we identified, the most common type of services offered were structured social support (n = 53) or helping hand (n = 52). Very few of the organizations offered financial stipends (n = 3),[5] religious support (n = 4), health care (n = 4), or respite care (n = 9).

The ten program categories can be further grouped based on the goals of the services each provide. We created four such categories based upon the area of caregiver need they primarily address. These categories are not mutually exclusive, as some services may have multiple goals:

- services aiding caregivers to provide better care (patient advocacy or case management and structured education or training)

---

[5]  As discussed in Table 1.4, each military service has a Wounded Warrior program that administers the DoD Special Compensation for Assistance with Activities of Daily Living (SCAADL) benefit; because they are administering the same stipend, they are counted only once.

**Figure 1.4**
**Services Offered to Military Caregivers by Organizations Identified in the RAND Environmental Scan**

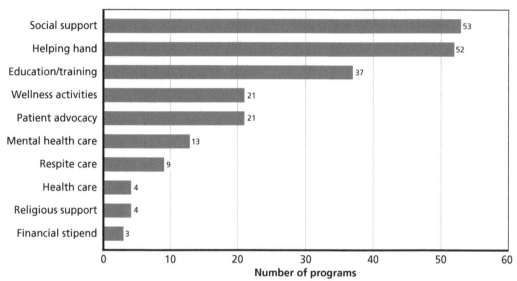

NOTE: An organization may offer various programs that span multiple categories.
RAND RR499-1.4

- services addressing caregiver health and well-being (respite care, health and mental health care, structured social support, and structured wellness activities targeting caregivers solely)
- services addressing caregiver family well-being (structured wellness activities targeting care recipients and their family caregivers or family members of caregivers, religious support network, and a "helping hand")
- services addressing income loss (financial stipend).

As Figure 1.5 demonstrates, 53 organizations (44 percent) aid caregivers by helping them provide better care, while only three (representing less than 5 percent of all organizations) address income loss.

### Operational Characteristics and Tax Status Designations of Caregiver Support Organizations

As we mentioned earlier, our protocol to gather information about the available programs and resources included an assessment of the history, origin, and tax determination status of the program or organization. Characterizing these features for programs and organizations offers important context for understanding the potential long-term sustainability of programs (discussed further in Chapter Four). For example, examining the maturity and potential reach of the programs and/or organizations and the priority of the caregiving population within their own mission might reveal whether

**Figure 1.5**
**Organizations Offering Caregiving Service, by Goal**

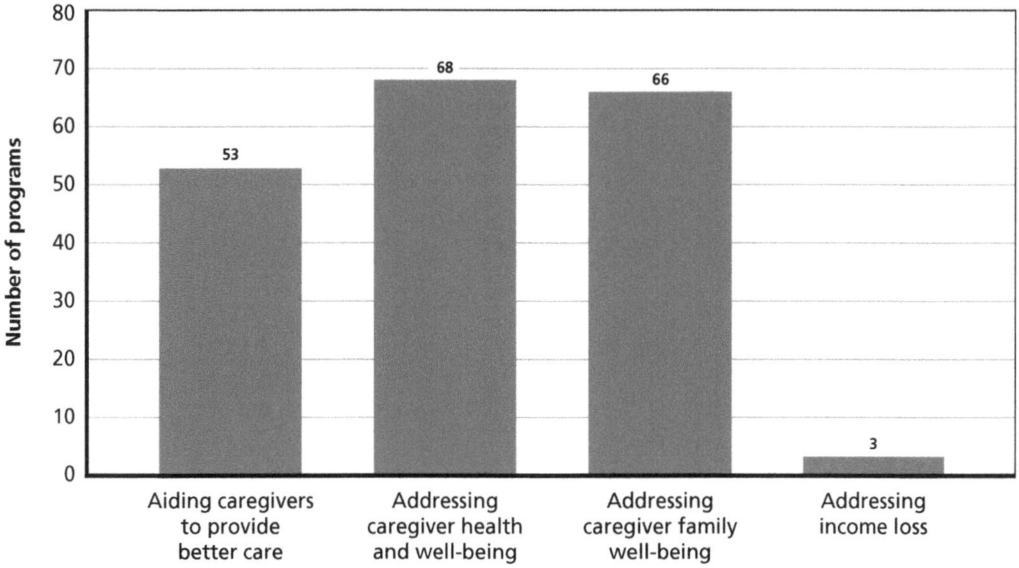

RAND RR499-1.5

programs have deep roots or whether they are new services, potentially vulnerable to changing priorities or interest areas. It also informs an understanding of how programs distribute across the government and nongovernment sectors.

Of the programs and resources identified in our scan, the majority (80 percent) were implemented by nonprofit organizations. Government-sponsored programs comprised 12 percent, and private, for-profit programs comprised 8 percent (Figure 1.6).

**Nonprofit Organizations.** About one-third of the nonprofit organizations serving military caregivers have been in existence for more than ten years. These organizations are generally ones that serve military personnel, veterans, and their families, and provide services to caregivers incidentally (roughly one-third are specifically targeted to caregivers—defined, again, as those for which caregivers are a stated or substantial part of the organization's reason for existence, as demonstrated by its mission, goals, and activities). They have a national or international scope, and provide services that are not specific to a certain illness or injury. Examples of these programs include the American Red Cross, which offers structured caregiver education; Armed Services YMCA, which provides a range of assistance, including structured social support and structured wellness activities; Cause (Comfort for America's Uniformed Services), which offers wellness activities such as massage and Reiki; and Public Counsel Center for Veterans Advancement, which provides legal representation.

**Private, For-Profit Organizations.** Half of the private, for-profit organizations serving military caregivers have been in existence for more than ten years, but there

**Figure 1.6**
**Tax Designation of Organizations Identified in the RAND**
**Environmental Scan**

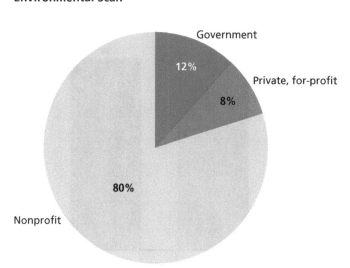

RAND RR499-1.6

are so few of these organizations that it means only five have existed for this long. All of the private, for-profit organizations are geared specifically toward caregivers, and none has military caregivers as its specific target audience. They also have a national or international scope, and provide services that are not specific to a certain illness or injury. Examples of these programs include AgingCare.com and VeteranCaregiver. com, which provide online social support, and *Today's Caregiver*, a magazine and website (Caregiver.com) that hosts conferences providing educational sessions on caregiving and caregiver support.

**Government-Owned/Operated.** The programs and resources specifically for caregivers of current or former military personnel that we identified as being administered by government organizations tend to be newer than the nonprofit or private, for-profit organizations: a majority of these have been in existence for between five and ten years. Of these 14 military caregiver programs sponsored by government organizations, 13 are specifically geared to military personnel, three are specific to caregivers, and 11 serve caregivers incidentally. They tend also to have a national or international scope, and two of these programs are geared toward a specific illness or injury type, specifically TBI or mental illness. One example of these programs is the VA Program of Comprehensive Assistance for Family Caregivers, which provides a wide range of services, including respite care, helping-hand (travel) assistance, a financial stipend for caregivers, caregiver training, and structured social support through its Peer Support Mentoring Program. Other organizations include the military services' "wounded warrior" programs, which provide nonclinical case management and facilitate helping-hand (travel) and financial assistance, specifically the Department of Defense's (DoD's) SCAADL benefit (described in Table 1.4).

We also examined the type of caregiving services offered by the tax designation of the organization implementing them. Figure 1.7 shows the proportion of organizations within each tax status designation category offering different services. Private, for-profit organizations are characterized primarily by offering structured social support (70 percent) and structured education and training (50 percent). In contrast, nonprofit organizations are characterized by also offering structured social support (42 percent) in addition to helping-hand services (48 percent) and are the primary providers of structured wellness activities. A greater share of government organizations offer patient advocates or case managers (n = 11) and are the primary providers of financial stipends (n = 2). We provide more information on caregiving services by tax designation status in Appendix E.

### Limitations of Our Approach to the Environmental Scan

Like our survey approach, our environmental scan also has limitations worth noting. First, there are likely to be organizations providing support services to caregivers that were not included in the scan. Notably, those organizations that do not make materials publicly available would likely be excluded, as could smaller organizations that operate at a very local level. Second, while we took necessary steps to ensure that the information we ascertained from organizations we interviewed was correct, we relied on publicly available information for 39 organizations for which we were unable to confirm

**Table 1.4**
**Examples of Federal Programs That Support Military Caregivers**

| Program | Description |
|---|---|
| Medicaid home- and community-based service programs | • State-run programs include standard services (case management, home-maker, home health aide, personal care, adult day health services, habilitation, and respite care).<br>• States vary in whether services are eligible for nonelderly care recipients, caregivers who are nonfamily members, and caregivers who receive a stipend. |
| DoD programs for military caregivers | • Each service branch has a WWP that offers patient-advocacy and helping-hand services for caregivers for wounded, ill, or injured service members.<br>• *SCAADL* financial stipends are available for service members who served post-9/11; have permanent, catastrophic injuries; are in outpatient care; and have a designated primary caregiver who provides assistance with at least one specified ADL. |
| VA programs for military caregivers | • *Aid and attendance* (i.e., pension) benefits are available to veterans of any period of war who requires such support.<br>• *VA Caregiver Support Program* offers respite care, social support services, and training to eligible caregivers for veterans of all eras.<br>• *Program of Comprehensive Assistance for Family Caregivers* is available to eligible post-9/11 caregivers. Services include a monthly stipend, coverage for travel expenses, access to health insurance, mental health care, and additional training and respite care. |

**Figure 1.7**
**Services Offered to Military Caregivers by Organizational Tax Designation**

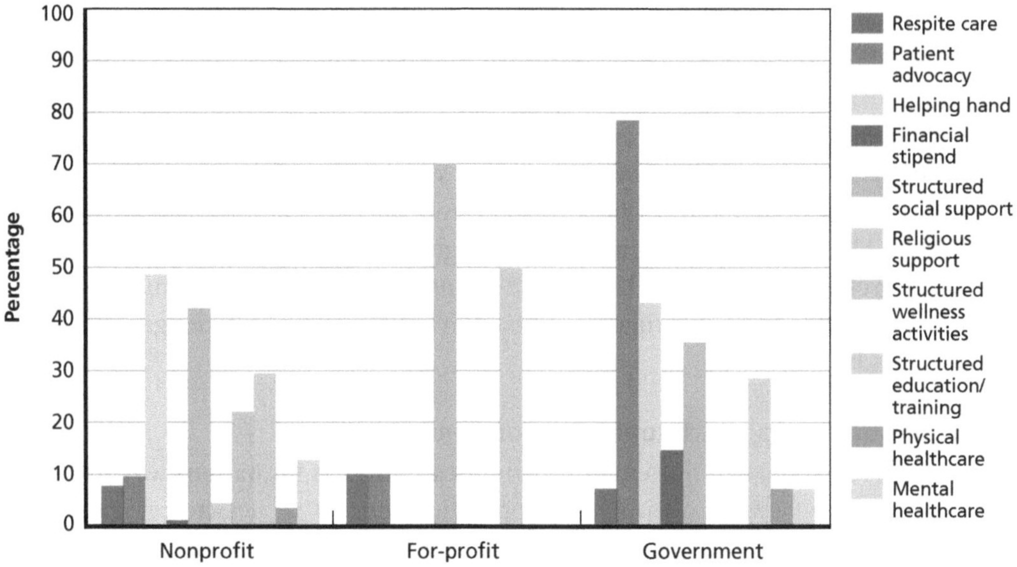

RAND RR499-1.7

accuracy. Third, our categorizations are crude and were created to facilitate analysis. There is great heterogeneity in the types of services offered within the same category (e.g., structured social support) across organizations. We attempt to highlight some of this diversity. Moreover, some programs existed on the boundaries of these categories, and classifying them was not a straightforward endeavor. In such instances, we discussed these classifications as a team to reach a consensus on the most appropriate classification. Finally, our scan occurred over four months in the summer and fall of 2013. As such, it represents a snapshot of the environment at that point of time: Programs that are included in the current scan evolve or shutter, and new programs are created that would not be included.

### Review of Federal and State Policies to Support Caregivers

Several federal and state policies exist to support caregivers in the United States. These policies serve as an important backdrop and context for how specific support programs operate and serve the population of caregivers broadly and military caregivers specifically. We review these policies in greater detail in Appendix F and refer to them throughout the report as relevant.

Many policies that support caregivers have emanated from initiatives designed to serve and address the needs of aging and elderly populations, such as those programs offered through HHS's ACL and Centers for Medicare and Medicaid Services (CMS), and/or those facilitated through the OAA, such as the National Family Caregiver Program; or policies to support the disabled population such as benefit protections provided through the Department of Labor (DoL) and the Americans with Disabilities Act (ADA). Caregivers also benefit from provisions outlined under the Family and Medical Leave Act (FMLA) that enable continued employment and benefit provision while providing support to a family member for medical reasons. Other policies and programs have grown from efforts to improve access to and quality of health care, such as the Affordable Care Act, which may extend health care coverage opportunities for individuals serving as caregivers, and increase system accountability for serving vulnerable populations. Collectively, these policies have fostered a growing awareness of the importance and value of informal caregiving, as well as increasing opportunities for employment protections (for example, through DoL policies and programs), income replacement (for example, through CMS Medicaid Home and Community Based Services waivers and stipend programs; see Table 1.4), and access to health insurance (through the Affordable Care Act). Efforts to collate and advance policies on family caregiving in the United States have been led by nonprofit organizations such as the Family Caregiver Alliance (FCA), the NAC, and the Rosalynn Carter Institute for Caregiving (RCI). Additional information about these relevant examples of caregiver support programs can be found in Appendix F.

For military caregivers, concerns about their well-being and needs prompted new federal policies as well. In recent years, several pieces of federal legislation have been enacted to establish or improve the benefits of caregivers of veterans. The National Defense Authorization Acts (NDAAs) of 2008 and 2010 made amendments to the FMLA that expanded the protections afforded to military caregivers and established new benefits, such as the DoD SCAADL, which provides monthly compensation to offset income loss among caregivers caring for a catastrophically ill or injured service member (see Table 1.4). Additionally, the Caregivers and Veterans Omnibus Health Benefits Act of 2010 (CVOHSA) established the Program of Comprehensive Assistance for Family Caregivers within the VA to provide services supplemental to those already offered through the VA, including respite care, travel assistance, caregiving training, a financial stipend, and a Peer Support Mentoring Program for eligible caregivers caring for veterans who served after September 11, 2001.

In addition to these federal policies and programs, many of which are run or administered through the states, there are state-based policies and programs that serve caregivers. There is great variability across states in terms of the number and nature of policies to support caregivers, but generally these policies have either expanded federal programs to cover additional populations (for example, to clarify the inclusion of disease-specific groups or expand age-eligibility criteria) or to supplement available programs, particularly around long-term or hospice care. Military caregivers may benefit from these provisions and services depending on specific eligibility criteria; for example, based upon the age of care recipient.

In our review of these policies, we identified 147 state administered programs that support caregivers either directly or incidentally. Only 62 of these programs were available to support care recipients, or the caregivers of care recipients, with a minimum age of 18 or 21 years; the remainder had much higher minimum age requirements (typically, over 60 years). These programs are distributed across 40 states, leaving many caregivers of individuals under the age of 60 without access to state-based support programs depending on where they reside (Appendix F provides a map of the United States highlighting which states offer programs to care recipients as young as 21). Within those 40 states, seven states (13.7 percent) have programs that are family-caregiver specific, 19 states (37.3 percent) have programs that pay family members to provide care, and 23 states (45.1 percent) have programs with no cap in respite care. We will refer to these programs throughout the remainder of the report where they are deemed relevant to supporting military caregivers' specific needs.

Readers with additional questions or interests in specific provisions for benefits and programs afforded by these federal and state policies are directed to Appendix F.

# CHAPTER TWO

# Critical Lifelines: The Role and Contributions of Military Caregivers

## Introduction

At its core, the social ecological framework of caregiving has the care recipient and his or her caregiver. This chapter focuses primarily on this relationship, and is divided into four sections. In the first section, we estimate the number of caregivers to quantify the magnitude of caregiving, and military caregiving in the United States. The next two sections focus on characteristics of the caregiver and the care recipient. In the final section, we discuss the types of tasks that caregivers perform as part of their caregiving duties and the time that performing these duties takes. Throughout these sections, we integrate information from our environmental scan of available programs to describe how understanding the characteristics of caregivers and care recipients can affect eligibility for, and use of, programs. Where possible, we also provide some examples of how these programs serve various caregivers and care recipients.

## Estimating the Number of Caregivers in the United States

Estimating the number of caregivers in the United States is an essential first step in describing this population. Documenting the size of this population helps policymakers and program officials better understand the target population they intend to serve, and facilitates an assessment of the impact that caregiving has on society. The probabilistic sample drawn from KP enables us to identify the proportion of households in the United States in which a military caregiver resides. We estimate that there are 5,499,253 military caregivers nationally, or that military caregivers comprise 1.75 percent of the U.S. population (or 2.3 percent of the population of adults over the age of 18).[1] There is very little error (SE = 322,141) with this estimate.

---

[1]   Assuming a total U.S. population of 313.9 million and a total adult population of 240.1 million.

We also estimate that there are 1,900,498 (SE = 198,754) veterans or service members in the U.S. household population currently relying on caregiving support;[2] of these, 294,640 (SE = 87,002) veterans or service members both rely on caregiving support and are also caregivers to other adults themselves. In other words, 15 percent of military care recipients are also providing caregiving support for another individual. (For this study, all of these veterans were classified only as military care recipients and not asked about their caregiving duties.)

## Key Finding

There are 5.5 million military caregivers in the United States. Approximately 20 percent (1.1 million) are caring for persons who served post-9/11.

Using our survey results, we can also estimate the number of civilian caregivers to care recipients over the age of 18. We estimate that there are 16,865,682 civilian caregivers of adults in the United States (SE = 446,333; 95 percent confidence interval: 15,990,869 to 17,740,495). In other words, 5.4 percent of the U.S. population (7.0 percent of the adult population) currently serves as a caregiver to a civilian over the age of 18 years. The combined military and civilian figures suggest that there are 22.6 million caregivers of adults: 7 percent of the U.S. population and 9.4 percent of the population of adults. Details of our enumeration procedure are provided in Appendix C.

While our estimate provides new insight into the magnitude of caregiving in the United States today, it is worth noting that 22.6 million is comparable to prior estimates of caregivers in the United States (FCA, undated b).[3] As described in Chapter One, our methods for estimating the number of caregivers most likely produces an underestimate, as the methods for conducting the survey excluded certain groups of individuals from our screening procedure. Importantly, our methods only captured individuals currently serving as caregivers (between August and October 2013). Thus, we exclude those who previously served as caregivers and are no longer serving in this role because the care recipient no longer needed caregiving for any number of reasons: improved health, death, the caregiver no longer being able to provide the required care, or a changed relationship between the caregiver and care recipient (a further description of the latter two explanations is provided in Chapter Four).

---

[2]   This is also a conservative estimate of the number of ill and injured veterans and service members receiving caregiving support, as it excludes those outside of our sampling frame (i.e., those individuals currently living in an institution, financially compensating a professional caregiver, or who are homeless).

[3]   Specifically, NAC and AARP (1997) and Arno, Levine, and Memmott (1999). It is lower than the estimate of 65.7 million provided by NAC and AARP (2009) and by Fox and Brenner (2012); possible reasons for this large difference are provided in Appendix C.

## Care Recipients' Era of Service

Today's living veterans span multiple eras of service. As a consequence, military caregivers provide aid and support to veterans from multiple generations. As veterans age, they may develop age-related medical or physical limitations that increase their need for external assistance. However, younger veterans from more recent eras of service also experience emotional and physical disabilities as a result of war- or deployment-related trauma.

Prior to the RAND Survey of Military Caregivers, most of what was known about this population derived from the NAC study *Caregivers of Veterans—Serving on the Homefront* (2010). That study generally presented aggregate statistics for all veteran caregivers, regardless of when the person for whom they were caring served in the military. Our survey of military caregivers estimates that post-9/11 military caregivers make up 19.6 percent of all military caregivers (Figure 2.1). This means that roughly 1,075,461 Americans (or 0.3 percent of the U.S. population; 0.5 percent of U.S. adults) are post-9/11 military caregivers. We hypothesized that this group of caregivers would be different from pre-9/11 military caregivers in their demographic characteristics, and that these differences may affect their access and use of available programs and services. Thus, for most of the remainder of the report, we provide estimates for post-9/11 and pre-9/11 military caregivers separately, and compare both to our representative sample of civilian caregivers.

It is important to note that not all military care recipients served during a period of war. While we have grouped care recipients (and their caregivers) according to their reported era of service, the United States experienced long periods of peacetime in which many military personnel achieved veteran status. According to VA statistics, 73 percent

**Figure 2.1**
**Era of Service of Military Care Recipients
in the United States**

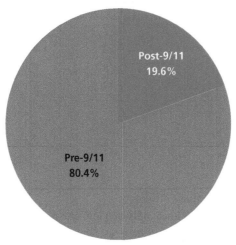

of living veterans are considered war veterans, though all did not necessarily deploy (VA, 2013a). In our survey, 61 percent of post-9/11 care recipients and 48 percent of pre-9/11 care recipients had deployed to a war zone, though this difference was not statistically significant (see Table 2.1).

## Impact of Era of Service on Program Eligibility

The era of service and deployment history of military care recipients is important because it often defines eligibility for federal and state benefits, public and private programs, and services for both the veteran and his/her caregiver. While most organizations we identified reported that they serve military caregivers of all eras, 13 of the 120 programs for military caregivers offer services only to those caring for service members and veterans who served in OEF, OIF, or OND (referred to as post-9/11). Many of these organizations were founded by service members and veterans who served in the post-9/11 era and their families and/or their caregivers. All of the caregiver programs exclusive to post-9/11 populations have been founded since 2003, and all these programs are run by nonprofit organizations. In interviews, several of these programs' representatives expressed a desire to extend services to caregivers of service members and veterans of all eras but said they were unable to do so because of limited resources and other restrictions.

The two most prominent and recent government programs for military caregivers serve only post-9/11 care recipients and caregivers by legislative mandate. DoD's

Table 2.1
**Military Characteristics of Care Recipients in the United States**

|  | Post-9/11 Care Recipients | | Pre-9/11 Care Recipients | |
|---|---|---|---|---|
|  | Percentage | SE | Percentage | SE |
| Deployed to a war zone[a] | 60.7 | 5.7 | 48.4 | 2.9 |
| Current military status[b] |  |  |  |  |
| Currently serving—active duty | 12.5 | 4.0 | 0.0 | 0.0 |
| Currently serving—reserve | 8.7 | 2.7 | 0.1 | 0.1 |
| Veteran | 79.2 | 4.5 | 99.9 | 0.1 |
| History of service[c] |  |  |  |  |
| Army | 63.9 | 5.0 | 55.6 | 2.9 |
| Navy[b] | 8.4 | 2.4 | 20.8 | 2.4 |
| Air Force | 11.3 | 2.7 | 17.3 | 2.3 |
| Marine Corps | 18.5 | 4.3 | 11.0 | 2.0 |

[a] No evidence of a statistically significant difference.

[b] Indicates statistically significant differences between pre- and post-9/11 care recipients.

[c] Total may not add up to 100 percent because care recipients may have previously served in more than one service branch.

SCAADL benefit is a financial stipend to post-9/11 service members meeting eligibility criteria who are receiving caregiver support with at least one ADL. The VA Program of Comprehensive Assistance for Family Caregivers supplements services offered to caregivers of veterans from all eras through the VA Caregiver Support Program. Specifically, while caregivers from all eras can receive aid and attendance benefits (a pension for veterans who require assistance with ADLs), respite care, social support services, and training, the VA Program of Comprehensive Assistance for Family Caregivers provides supplementary services to eligible post-9/11 caregivers, including a monthly stipend, coverage for travel expenses, access to health insurance, mental health counseling, and additional training and respite care. Senate Bill 851, introduced in April 2013, proposes to increase the eligibility of this program to include pre-9/11 military caregivers as well. Our estimates suggest that currently 66 percent of post-9/11 military caregivers (i.e., 709,805) are eligible for the program; applying the same criteria to pre-9/11 military caregivers, 35 percent (i.e., 1.5 million) may be eligible under the proposed expansion.

## Characteristics of Military Caregivers

Having quantified the number of military caregivers in the United States, we now turn to describing this population in more detail. We begin this section with a description of how caregivers and care recipients are related to one another and the impact that this relationship has on program eligibility. We then describe military caregivers with respect to sociodemographic characteristics, their history of military service, the duration of time that they have spent caregiving, and their caregiving network. Throughout this section, we also highlight how the characteristics of military caregivers affect their eligibility for services offered by those programs we identified in the environmental scan.

### Relationship of Caregivers to Care Recipients

Caregivers are traditionally thought to be spouses, parents, children, or other close family of the care recipient. In fact, many definitions of "caregiver" use the family connection or relationship with the care recipient to define the term (e.g., "family caregiver"). Our survey methods did not restrict participation to only those caregivers who were "related" to their care recipient: thus, we can examine patterns of relationships to care recipients within

### Key Finding

33 percent of all post-9/11 military caregivers are spouses of the care recipient; 25 percent are the care recipients' parents; and fewer than 10 percent are care recipient's children. In comparison, 36 percent of pre-9/11 and civilian caregivers are children of the care recipient. Across groups, between 12 and 23 percent of caregivers are not related to the care recipient.

our populations of interest. Though there is certainly overlap, post-9/11 military caregivers, pre-9/11 military caregivers, and civilian caregivers vary in how they are related to the people for whom they are providing care. Of post-9/11 military caregivers, 33 percent are spouses of the person they are caring for, whereas only roughly one quarter of pre-9/11 military and 16 percent of civilian caregivers are spouses of the care recipient. One-quarter of post-9/11 military caregivers are parents of the care recipient. In contrast, only 10 percent of civilian caregivers are the care recipient's parents and even fewer pre-9/11 military caregivers are parents. Alternatively, more than one-third of pre-9/11 military and civilian caregivers are the care recipient's children (an additional 10 percent are caring for a grandparent, aunt, or uncle), relative to only 6 percent among post-9/11 military caregivers. It is also noteworthy that roughly 15 percent of pre-9/11 military and civilian caregivers are friends and neighbors, a group that accounts for almost one-quarter of post-9/11 caregivers (Table 2.2).

Just under half of post-9/11 and civilian caregivers live with the care recipient, compared with fewer (39 percent) pre-9/11 military caregivers (see Table 2.2).

**Table 2.2**
**Relationship of Caregivers to Care Recipients in the United States**

| Relation to Care Recipient | Post-9/11 Care Recipients | | Pre-9/11 Care Recipients | | Civilian Caregiver Recipients | |
|---|---|---|---|---|---|---|
| | % | SE | % | SE | % | SE |
| Spouse, partner, or significant other | 33.2* | 4.0 | 22.3* | 2.1 | 15.7 | 1.2 |
| Parent | 25.1 | 3.9 | 1.5 | 0.6 | 10.2 | 1.0 |
| Child | 5.8* | 3.2 | 36.5 | 2.7 | 36.1 | 1.7 |
| Other family | 9.8 | 3.5 | 19.4 | 2.5 | 21.5 | 1.6 |
| Grandparent | 0.4 | 0.3 | 0 | 0 | 0 | 0 |
| Grandchild | 0 | 0 | 7.1 | 2.0 | 6.3 | 1.1 |
| Sibling | 4.3 | 3.1 | 6.6 | 1.5 | 5.7 | 0.9 |
| Sibling-in-law | 0.1 | 0.1 | 1.4 | 0.6 | 1.1 | 0.3 |
| Former spouse, partner, or significant other | 0.1 | 0.1 | 1.0 | 0.4 | 0.9 | 0.3 |
| Uncle/aunt | 0.2 | 0.1 | 0 | 0 | 0 | 0 |
| Nephew/niece | 0.8 | 0.7 | 2.4 | 1.0 | 4.1 | 0.8 |
| Other | 3.8 | 1.9 | 0.9 | 0.4 | 3.4 | 0.6 |
| Friend or neighbor | 23.4* | 5.6 | 15.7 | 2.2 | 12.6 | 1.3 |
| Other | 2.8 | 1.8 | 4.6 | 1.2 | 3.9 | 0.8 |
| Lives with care recipient | 49.1 | 5.1 | 38.7* | 2.7 | 45.5 | 1.8 |

* Statistically significant difference in proportion reporting the specific relationship versus not that relationship relative to civilian caregivers. Significance tests were only conducted for (1) spouse, partner, or significant other; (2) child; (3) friend or neighbor; and (4) lives with care recipient.

## The Impact of Relationship Status on Program Eligibility

The caregiver's relation to the care recipient can determine eligibility for services and benefits. Most of the military caregiver support programs identified in the environmental scan are geared to serve the care recipient (i.e., military personnel and veterans), and many only serve caregivers incidentally; they offer services primarily for service members and veterans, and expand eligibility to include family members. Thus, caregivers tend to become eligible for these services only to the degree that they are related to eligible veterans and service members. This is particularly evident in programs that offer structured wellness and social support activities.

One example of such a program is Sportsmen's Foundation for Military Families, which offers wellness retreats for veterans and their families featuring various outdoor activities (a full description can be found in Appendix H). The logic behind the retreats is that injured veterans who participate are empowered by these outdoor activities and sharing this empowering experience with their families helps them strengthen their family bonds. Thus, the activity itself is focused on service members and veterans. However, since family caregivers attend as well and receive some benefits from participating, programs consider the caregiver part of the population served. While attending these events may benefit caregivers, they generally participate as a caregiver supporting the service member or veteran rather than as the target population. Of the programs analyzed, 88 focused on the military population specifically, of which 71 programs served caregivers incidentally, similar to Sportsmen's Foundation for Military Families. Thus, only about 15 percent of the programs in the scan serve military caregivers as a stated or substantial target population. Again, we consider organizations to be caregiver "specific" if caregivers are a stated or substantial part of the organization's reason for existence, as demonstrated by its mission, goals, and activities.

Even for programs that offer services specifically for caregivers, eligibility is more often determined by being a member of the care recipient's family (traditionally defined as a first-degree relative) rather than by being a caregiver. Only a handful of programs described serving both family members and caregivers as separate groups, and more programs list families in their eligibility criteria than caregivers. Many programs described a great deal of overlap in their definition of military families and caregivers. Some consider the populations as one and the same, assuming that all families provide some caregiving to their military member, or that all informal caregivers are family members. Dozens of programs list families as their target population (and not caregivers), but they provide services to both families and caregivers. Thus, these organizations consider caregivers as a subgroup of family members.

An additional complicating factor in separating and serving the overlapping family and caregiver groups is that the definition of caregivers continues to evolve. Some programs recognize that families and caregivers fall outside of the traditionally defined relationships. These programs recognize that military families and caregivers can include extended family members such as grandparents, aunts, and uncles; and those outside of the family, like friends and neighbors. Both government and non-profit programs are working to redefine their eligibility criteria to include the broader range of individuals who care for service members and veterans. For example, the DoD Office of Warrior Care Policy specifically emphasizes that there is not a typical military caregiver and that many service members have multiple caregivers inside and outside of their families. In providing care to service members, this office aims to reach the entire military caregiver community of family, friends, and neighbors. Another program, CarePages.com, facilitates an online community of caregivers, family, and friends. Through personalized websites, CarePages members can relate their stories, post photos, and update friends and family instantly. In turn, the caregiver network is expanded and more people share in the social support offered.

As a means to facilitate inclusion in caregiver services, some programs, including veteran service organizations, have offered auxiliary membership to families. This has encouraged additional groups—such as spouses and family members, nondeployed veterans, veterans of other eras, and civilian supports—to be a more active part of the community of veterans and their families. For example, the Military Order of the Purple Heart has a Ladies Auxiliary that is made up of mothers, wives, sisters, widows, daughters, stepdaughters, granddaughters, and legally adopted female lineal descendants of Purple Heart recipients, even if the Purple Heart recipient is not a member of the Military Order. The Ladies Auxiliary collaborates with the Military Order to provide assistance, comfort, and aid to veterans and their families; their activities also facilitate bonding and structured social support among the women who participate.

As another way to encourage inclusion, many programs do not specify eligibility criteria for services. For many of these programs, the services they offer (especially structured social support and training) serve a broader definition of caregivers, including friends, neighbors, and extended family members. For instance, AGIS does not specify eligibility criteria for its services. The AGIS website enables caregivers to create Family Care Groups, which are free, personal, private web pages that help caregivers to organize family and friends around caregiving needs. These Family Care Groups facilitate collaboration and communication among an inclusive group of caregivers.

### Demographics and Military Characteristics of Caregivers

With respect to sociodemographic characteristics (e.g., sex, age, race/ethnicity, and education level), civilian and pre-9/11 caregivers are more similar to each other than either are to post-9/11 caregivers. Descriptive characteristics are provided in Table 2.3. Importantly, among all groups, roughly 40 percent of caregivers are men. This differs from most prior research, drawn largely from convenience-based samples, which suggests that the overwhelming majority (i.e., more than 90 percent) of military caregivers are females (see the "Differences Between Male and Female Caregivers" box). As might be expected, post-9/11 military caregivers tend to be younger than pre-9/11 military and civilian caregivers. On the other hand, 25 percent of pre-9/11 military

Table 2.3
Demographic Characteristics of Caregivers in the United States

| | Post-9/11 Caregivers | | Pre-9/11 Caregivers | | Civilian Caregivers | |
|---|---|---|---|---|---|---|
| | Percentage | SE | Percentage | SE | Percentage | SE |
| Sex[a] | | | | | | |
| Male | 40.7 | 5.7 | 41.8 | 2.9 | 40.3 | 1.8 |
| Female | 59.3 | 5.7 | 58.2 | 2.9 | 59.7 | 1.8 |
| Age[b] | | | | | | |
| 18–30 | 37.1 | 5.1 | 10.7 | 2.3 | 16.3 | 1.7 |
| 31–55 | 49.2 | 5.1 | 43.0 | 2.9 | 44.0 | 1.8 |
| 56–65 | 8.3 | 2.1 | 26.4 | 2.3 | 22.6 | 1.3 |
| 66–80 | 5.3 | 2.0 | 17.8 | 1.9 | 15.1 | 1.1 |
| 81+ | | | 2.1 | 0.6 | 2.0 | 0.4 |
| Race/ethnicity[b] | | | | | | |
| White, non-Hispanic | 57.3 | 5.4 | 74.6 | 2.6 | 63.6 | 1.9 |
| Black, non-Hispanic | 10.3 | 3.7 | 13.8 | 2.3 | 15.0 | 1.5 |
| Other, non-Hispanic | 9.7 | 3.4 | 3.1 | 1.0 | 6.6 | 1.2 |
| Hispanic | 20.7 | 5.1 | 7.2 | 1.5 | 12.9 | 1.4 |
| Multiple, non-Hispanic | 2.0 | 0.5 | 1.2 | 0.3 | 2.0 | 0.4 |
| Highest level of education[a] | | | | | | |
| High school | 24.0 | 6.2 | 35.6 | 3.3 | 41.8 | 1.9 |
| Some college | 39.6 | 5.5 | 35.3 | 2.9 | 32.0 | 1.6 |
| College | 21.2 | 3.9 | 18.4 | 2.2 | 15.5 | 1.1 |
| Post-college | 15.3 | 3.4 | 10.8 | 1.6 | 10.8 | 0.9 |
| Household income[b] | | | | | | |
| < 138% FPL | 19.7 | 4.2 | 16.7 | 2.1 | 27.7 | 1.7 |
| 138–249% FPL | 15.1 | 2.5 | 12.5 | 1.9 | 17.5 | 1.4 |
| > 250% FPL | 65.2 | 4.6 | 70.8 | 2.6 | 54.8 | 1.8 |
| Residence[a] | | | | | | |
| Lives in a Metropolitan Statistical Area | 85.5 | 3.9 | 82.2 | 2.5 | 84.4 | 1.3 |

NOTE: Metropolitan Statistical Area is defined by the Office of Management and Budget as an area with "at least one urbanized area of 50,000 or more population, plus adjacent territory that has a high degree of social and economic integration with the core as measured by commuting ties."

[a] No evidence of a statistically significant difference.

[b] Statistically significant differences in the distributions between groups.

caregivers are nonwhite, relative to roughly 40 percent of civilian and post-9/11 military caregivers.[4]

---

[4]  The difference between nonwhite pre-9/11 military caregivers relative to civilian caregivers is significant (odds ratio [OR] = 0.6; 95-percent confidence interval [CI]: 0.4, 0.8), while that between post-9/11 military caregivers

## Differences Between Male and Female Caregivers

Past studies of caregivers, and especially of military caregivers, have shown that the overwhelming majority of caregivers are females. We find nearly 40 percent of post-9/11 military caregivers are men. We asked: *How are post-9/11 military male caregivers different from their female counterparts?*

- **They are their care recipient's friend:** 50 percent of male caregivers are friends or neighbors of the care recipient; 51 percent of female caregivers are the care recipient's spouse.
- **More than one-quarter previously served in the armed forces:** 28 percent of male caregivers, relative to 14 percent of female caregivers, have served in the armed forces (though this difference is not significant).
- **Half spend more than eight hours a week providing care:** 46 percent of male caregivers spend more than eight hours per week providing care; significantly more female caregivers (71 percent) spend more than eight hours.
- **They perform fewer caregiving tasks:** Male caregivers assist with an average of 0.8 ADLs and 3.2 IADLs; female caregivers assist with an average of 1.1 ADLs and 4.3 IADLs (differences in IADLs is significant; no evidence of a difference in ADLs).
- **Their care recipient is less likely to be married:** 44 percent of male caregivers are caring for someone who has never been married, significantly more than the 29 percent of female caregivers who are caring for someone who has never been married.
- **Their care recipient is less likely to have a mental illness:** 36 percent of male caregivers are caring for someone with a mental illness, significantly fewer than the 84 percent of female caregivers.

---

relative to civilian caregivers is not (OR = 1.3; 95-percent CI = 0.8, 2.1).

There were no statistically significant differences between groups with respect to educational attainment; however, with respect to household income, civilian caregivers are less likely to be at more than 250 percent of the federal poverty level (FPL), relative to both post-9/11 and pre-9/11 military caregivers.[5] Roughly 85 percent of caregivers across all groups live in a metropolitan area. Marital status and labor force participation are discussed in more detail in Chapter Three.

Civilian caregivers and pre-9/11 military caregivers also look similar with respect to their own prior personal military history. Roughly 10 percent had previously served in the armed forces and 2–3 percent had deployed. In contrast, 20 percent of post-9/11 military caregivers previously served in the military and 8 percent had deployed (Figure 2.2). Less than 1 percent of all caregivers across categories are currently serving in the military (data not shown).

**Figure 2.2**
**Military Characteristics of Caregivers in the United States**

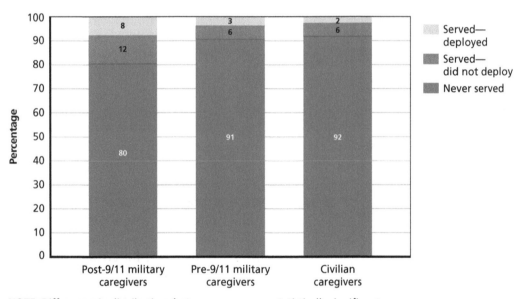

NOTE: Differences in distributions between groups are statistically significant.
RAND RR499-2.2

---

5   For post-9/11 military caregivers relative to civilian caregivers, OR = 1.5, 95-percent CI = 1.0, 2.4; for pre-9/11 military caregivers relative to civilian caregivers, OR = 2.0; 95-percent CI = 1.5, 2.7.

## Duration of Caregiving

The length of time an individual provides caregiving may be an important factor in understanding the impact that caregiving has on his or her own outcomes. Prior studies have shown that the duration of caregiving may have an effect on income loss and reported financial burden (NAC and AARP, 2009; AARP Public Policy Institute, 2011). In our assessment, there is no statistical difference in the duration of caregiving across post-9/11 military, pre-9/11 military, and civilian caregivers. Approximately 85 percent of civilian and pre-9/11 military caregivers and 92 percent of pre-9/11 military caregivers have been serving in the role for more than one year; between 10 and 16 percent have been serving in the role for 11 years or longer. These data suggest that caregivers have been serving for shorter periods of time than has been previously reported: in the NAC study on military caregiving, for example, 30 percent of caregivers of veterans had been caring for the veteran for 10 years or more (NAC, 2010).

## Key Finding

Only 47 percent of post-9/11 military caregivers have a caregiving network, relative to 71 percent of pre-9/11 military caregivers and 69 percent of civilian caregivers.

## Caregiving Network

Some caregivers are fortunate to have a network of family members and friends who help them provide caregiving assistance. Understanding the size and composition of this network helps identify the number of additional informal support mechanisms that are potentially available to support the caregiver and care recipient, but also informs the potential ripple effect or cascade of caregiving impacts beyond the primary caregiver. While approximately two-thirds of pre-9/11 military caregivers and civilian caregivers reported having such a support network, less than half of all post-9/11 military caregivers had one—a difference that is statistically significant (Figure 2.3).

Among those with a social support network, post-9/11 military caregivers had a mean network size of 1.0 additional informal caregiver to help care for the care recipient (SE = 0.1), while pre-9/11 military and civilian caregivers had larger networks (for pre-9/11 military caregivers, mean [M] = 1.5, SE = 0.1; for civilian caregivers, M = 1.4, SE = 0.1).[6] Post-9/11 caregivers also reported being significantly more challenged obtaining services to help them as caregivers (e.g., 21 percent reported being extremely challenged obtaining these services, compared with 10 and 12 percent for pre-9/11 and civilian caregivers, respectively) and with finding neighbors, friends, or family members to help with caregiving tasks (e.g., 26 percent were extremely challenged versus 16 and 20 percent for pre-9/11 and civilian caregivers, respectively).

---

[6]  In a bivariate Poisson regression model, the coefficient estimate for post-9/11 military caregivers among those with a support network was −0.4 (p < 0.01).

**Figure 2.3**
**Presence of Caregiving Support Networks Among Caregivers**

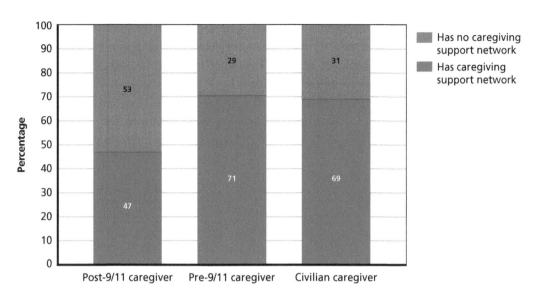

NOTE: For post-9/11 military caregivers relative to civilian caregivers, OR = 2.5; 95% CI = 1.6, 3.9. There was no evidence of a statistically significant difference between pre-9/11 military caregivers relative to civilian caregivers.
RAND RR499-2.3

To understand the extent to which children under the age of 18 were called upon to perform caregiving support, we examined whether the network of caregivers contained any members that included children under 18, such as the caregiver's or care recipient's own children or grandchildren. Thirty-nine percent of post-9/11 caregivers, 23 percent of pre-9/11 caregivers, and 27 percent of civilian caregivers reported having a child under 18 who lived with them. However, fewer than 5 percent of caregiver networks reported included someone under 18.[7] On the other hand, 28 percent of civilian caregiving networks and 35 percent of pre-9/11 military caregiving networks included someone over age 65, though only 9 percent of post-9/11 caregivers with a network had someone over 65 in it (data not shown). Consistent across all groups, when caregivers and care recipients were related to each other and had a network of support, 90 percent of these networks contained at least one additional family member, and between 15 and 24 percent had a friend in their caregiver network (data not shown).

---

[7]  Some studies have estimated that there are 1.3–1.4 million children between 8 and 18 serving as caregivers (NAC and UHF, 2005). To explore the issue of children serving as caregivers, we selected caregivers who were parents of one or more of children under 18 listed in their caregiving network and asked them a series of questions assessing their child's role in caregiving and potential impacts of caregiving. However, very few respondents had children who met this criteria (n = 16: 13 post-9/11 caregivers, three pre-9/11 caregivers, and no civilian caregivers); this low number prevented us from quantifying the number of children serving as caregivers, describing the caregiving tasks they perform, or estimating potential consequences they face as a result of caregiving.

## The People Military Caregivers Care For

In the previous section, we defined post-9/11 and pre-9/11 military caregivers based on characteristics of their care recipients' era of service. Recall, care recipients were labeled post-9/11 as long as they separated from military service after September 11, 2001, regardless of whether they deployed after 9/11 or whether they also served before 2001. As previously discussed (and presented in Table 1.1), 61 percent of post-9/11 care recipients had deployed to a war zone (relative to 48 percent of pre-9/11 care recipients), and 21 percent of post-9/11 military care recipients were still serving in the armed forces. In the section that follows, we further describe characteristics of care recipients across demographic characteristics, their VA disability rating status, the types of conditions they have, and their level of current functioning.

### Demographics

Aside from a care recipient's gender—roughly 85 percent of post-9/11 and pre-9/11 military care recipients are male, compared with 32 percent of civilian care recipients—pre-9/11 and civilian care recipients look more similar to each other than either group looks to post-9/11 care recipients. These characteristics are illustrated in Table 2.4. Similar to caregivers themselves, post-9/11 care recipients are more likely to be younger and nonwhite, and to have a higher level of educational attainment. Across all care recipients (i.e., post-9/11, pre-9/11, and civilian), between 5 and 12 percent of care recipients live in a residential facility, with a significantly greater proportion of pre-9/11 care recipients living in a facility.

### VA Disability Rating

Veterans who have a service-connected disability are eligible to received disability compensation and priority enrollment in the VA health care system. Of those veterans who apply for benefits, the VA uses a disability evaluation process and applies specific criteria to determine the "average detriment to earning capacity" resulting from a disability connected to, or aggravated by, active service. This is quantified in a disability rating determined by the veterans' medical assessments, time in service and combat, and other factors. Disability ratings are scored on a 0–100 percent scale and the VA uses the score to determine entitlement for compensation and other benefits and services. In our survey, we asked military caregivers and veterans to report whether their care recipient had a VA disability rating and if so, what the value was.

Two times as many (58 percent) of post-9/11 care recipients have a disabil-

> ### Key Finding
>
> 58 percent of post-9/11 military care recipients have a VA disability rating; 32 percent have a rating of 70 percent or higher. An additional 38 percent have applied for a disability rating, 80 percent of which are still under review.

**Table 2.4**
**Demographic Characteristics of Care Recipients in the United States**

| | Post-9/11 Care Recipients | | Pre-9/11 Care Recipients | | Civilian Care Recipients | |
|---|---|---|---|---|---|---|
| | Percentage | SE | Percentage | S.E | Percentage | 95% CI |
| Sex* | | | | | | |
| Male | 85.3 | 3.0 | 84.3 | 2.0 | 31.8 | 1.7 |
| Female | 14.7 | 3.0 | 15.7 | 2.0 | 68.2 | 1.7 |
| Age* | | | | | | |
| 18–30 | 46.2 | 5.1 | -- | -- | 12.4 | 1.3 |
| 31–55 | 47.9 | 5.1 | 12.4 | 1.8 | 20.3 | 1.5 |
| 56–65 | 6.0 | 3.6 | 19.2 | 2.3 | 13.8 | 1.3 |
| 66–80 | -- | -- | 30.9 | 2.6 | 23.3 | 1.5 |
| 81+ | -- | -- | 37.5 | 2.7 | 30.1 | 1.6 |
| Race/Ethnicity* | | | | | | |
| White, non-Hispanic | 52.0 | 5.3 | 71.6 | 2.7 | 65.9 | 1.9 |
| Black, non-Hispanic | 9.2 | 3.4 | 14.8 | 2.3 | 14.1 | 1.4 |
| Other, non-Hispanic | 2.9 | 1.6 | 3.3 | 1.1 | 6.1 | 1.1 |
| Hispanic | 31.5 | 5.7 | 7.8 | 1.5 | 11.8 | 1.3 |
| Multiple, non-Hispanic | 4.4 | 1.7 | 2.5 | 0.8 | 2.1 | 0.4 |
| Highest Level of Education* | | | | | | |
| High school | 31.0 | 5.1 | 55.0 | 2.8 | 66.4 | 1.7 |
| Some college | 54.0 | 5.1 | 25.8 | 2.4 | 18.8 | 1.4 |
| College | 10.6 | 2.3 | 8.7 | 1.3 | 9.2 | 0.9 |
| Post-college | 4.4 | 1.8 | 10.5 | 1.5 | 5.6 | 0.8 |
| Household Income* | | | | | | |
| < 138% of FPL | 29.1 | 5.0 | 28.7 | 2.9 | 47.4 | 2.0 |
| ≥ 138% and < 250% FPL | 21.4 | 4.7 | 21.1 | 2.6 | 20.2 | 1.6 |
| ≥ 250% FPL | 49.5 | 5.4 | 50.2 | 3.1 | 32.3 | 1.7 |
| Lives in Residential Facility* | 8.1 | 4.4 | 12.9 | 2.1 | 8.1 | 0.8 |

* Significant differences between groups.

ity rating compared with pre-9/11 care recipients (30 percent); similarly, two times as many (32 percent) of post-9/11 care recipients have a rating of 70 percent or higher compared with pre-9/11 care recipients (15 percent) (Figure 2.4). This difference is largely accounted for by having deployed to a war zone; as shown in Figure 2.5, the proportion of those who have deployed is generally greater at higher levels of disability—for example, 88 percent of post-9/11 military care recipients with a disability rating of 70 percent or above have deployed, relative to 43 percent of post-9/11 care recipients who have no disability rating. After accounting for deployment, pre-9/11

Figure 2.4
VA Disability Rating for Post- and Pre-9/11 Military Care Recipients

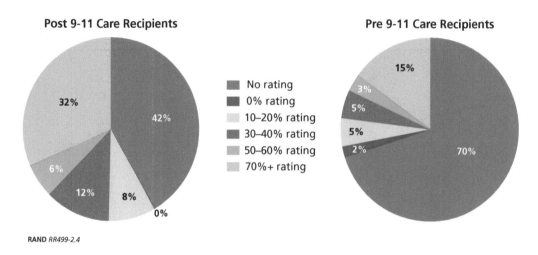

RAND RR499-2.4

Figure 2.5
Proportion of Military Care Recipients by Disability Rating Who Have Deployed

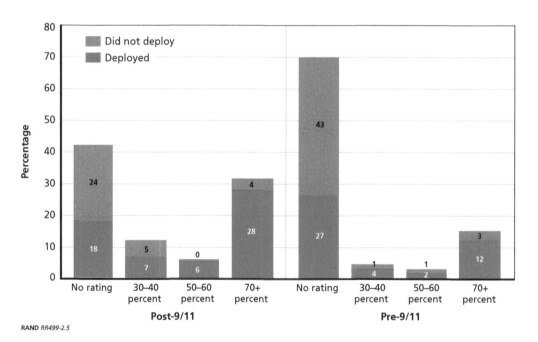

RAND RR499-2.5

military care recipients actually have greater odds of having a disability rating, meaning that among care recipients who have not deployed, there are more pre-9/11 care recipients than post-9/11 care recipients with a rating.

Of post-9/11 care recipients without a VA disability rating, 38 percent had applied for a rating and one out of five of these applications were denied (the remainder are still under review). Sixteen percent reported that they plan to apply but have not yet done so. Among pre-9/11 care recipients without a rating, 5 percent had applied and close to three-quarters of those applications were denied. Twelve percent of pre-9/11 care recipients reported that they plan to apply but have not yet done so (data not shown). These findings are consistent with VA data indicating an increase in the number and proportion of veterans receiving disability compensation over the past decade (VA, 2012). According to the VA, a greater proportion of post-9/11 veterans have sought benefits and services through the VA compared with prior-era veterans. This shift may be attributable to increased outreach provided by the VA and transition assistance for service members as they leave military service.

### Veteran Characteristics That Affect Program Eligibility

Eligibility for caregiving services and programs may vary depending on the characteristics of the care recipient. This occurs in the civilian caregiving environment, where the care recipient's age and disease condition may define eligibility for specific benefit programs and services. In our scan of policies and programs, we found that the same may apply to military caregivers, whose eligibility for federal and state caregiver programs would be determined based on the age or condition of the care recipient (for example, there are programs to support caregivers of individuals with brain injury as well as programs for those providing care to individuals over the age of 60 years through CMS, as described in Appendix F). With respect to the programs identified in our scan, excluding the VA, several programs use VA disability ratings, honorable discharge status, or require that care recipients have combat-era service as eligibility criteria for the services they provide. Though they use these criteria to determine eligibility, programs have identified challenges with this approach. They cite concerns over the backlog in processing disability claims within the VA, which has received much recent policy attention. While veterans wait for their determinations, their caregivers may not be eligible for programs and services. Thus, in the circumstances where VA disability ratings are the main eligibility criteria, veterans and their families and caregivers may have to wait to receive services.

There are two other potential issues with using discharge status and combat-related service as eligibility criteria. The first issue is that veterans with dishonorable discharge statuses and noncombat-related service and their caregivers are ineligible for services. As a result, their needs may go unmet. Second, veterans and their caregivers may be required by some programs to show or obtain the appropriate documentation (in a Certificate of Release or Discharge from Active Duty, generally referred to as a "DD-214") that proves honorable discharge status and combat-related service. For those who do not have their DD-214 documentation, services may be delayed while they navigate the system to obtain a copy. While some programs have acknowledged the frustrations associated with relying on disability ratings and discharge status, several continue to use them as eligibility criteria.

Conversely, some programs that cited challenges with the rigidity in eligibility criteria for determining caregiver services have adopted flexible criteria to meet caregivers' diverse needs. Caregivers' circumstances range greatly, and—in some cases—are not easily categorized. For this reason, many programs determine eligibility for services on a case-by-case basis. For example, some decisions about offering financial and helping-hand assistance are determined by assessment teams and case workers, and are based on assessments of the individual circumstances rather than a set list of eligibility criteria. The Gary Sinise Foundation builds custom "smart homes" for veterans and their families. Veterans do not need to have a specific injury or illness to be selected to receive such a home as part of the "Building for America's Bravest" initiative. Rather, Gary Sinise hand-selects veterans and their families after careful review of their experiences and needs. Likewise, Easter Seals New Hampshire Military and Veterans Services offers helping-hand financial support for veterans, service members, and their families, without a set criteria for their service eligibility. Programs feel that having more flexibility in determining eligibility for services allows them to serve veterans and caregivers who may not receive services otherwise.

In some instances, caregivers who are eligible for a program may be aware of the program and the services it offers, but are not aware that they qualify for services. This challenge of outreach and education about program eligibility was noted by several of our interviewees in the environmental scan. For example, Army Emergency Relief noted that many soldiers and their families in the Army community are aware that this organization provides emergency relief but often do not know they are eligible for the assistance. This lack of awareness of eligibility criteria reportedly exists despite a range of outreach efforts, including notification through chain of command, staff visits to installations, mailings to retirees, social media, and visits to mobilizing reserve units.

## Types of Conditions and Relation to Military Service

To understand more about the care recipient's need for caregiving assistance, we assessed the types of conditions that care recipients experience and whether the condition was related to their military service. Understanding the nature of their conditions can be informative for designing support programs and providing benefits to their caregivers. This information was ascertained directly from respondents (either caregivers or military care recipients) who were provided with a list of 18 medical conditions and asked to indicate whether they/their care recipient had been diagnosed as having each.[8]

---

[8] The 18 conditions included the most common medical conditions among veterans (VA, 2011a) as well as other common medical conditions (e.g., cancer, dementia). Respondents wrote in other conditions or diagnoses, which were coded by a registered nurse/research assistant and, where possible, grouped into our analytic categories along with the other structured responses.

Before discussing whether differences in conditions are attributable to age or deployment to a war zone, we present crude, unadjusted prevalence estimates across groups. By our assessment, the most prevalent category of conditions among all care recipients was a problem that impaired physical movement: For post-9/11 care recipients, 74 percent had limiting back pain (58 percent of pre-9/11 care recipients and 53 percent of civilian care recip-

## Key Finding

64 percent of post-9/11 military care recipients have a mental health or substance use disorder; nearly 50 percent of all post-9/11 military care recipients have depression, twice as many as their civilian and pre-9/11 military counterparts.

ients also had back pain; see Table 2.5). However, the next most prevalent category for post-9/11 military caregivers was a mental health or substance use disorder: 52 percent had PTSD, 46 percent had major depressive disorder, and 15 percent had a substance use disorder (64 percent of post-9/11 care recipients had at least one of these conditions). In contrast, 36 percent of pre-9/11 and 33 percent of civilian care recipients had a mental health or substance use disorder, though it is notable that between 25 and 30 percent of care recipients in both groups had depression. The second most prevalent condition category among pre-9/11 and civilian care recipients were chronic conditions: 77 percent of pre-9/11 care recipients and 63 percent of civilian care recipients had hypertensive vascular disease, cancer, or diabetes, relative to 35 percent of post-9/11 care recipients. A similar proportion (57 percent) of pre-9/11 and post-9/11 care recipients had problems with hearing and vision, higher than reported among civilian care recipients (38 percent). Conversely, 30 percent of pre-9/11 and civilian care recipients had a neurological condition (multiple sclerosis, Parkinson's disease, or dementia), relative to just 6 percent of post-9/11 care recipients. Twenty percent of post-9/11 care recipients had a TBI, whereas only around 10 percent of pre-9/11 and civilian care recipients did.

We tested whether differences in medical conditions between groups of care recipients were driven by (a) having a history of deployment to a war zone or (b) the care recipient's age. After accounting for war-zone deployment, post-9/11 military care recipients still had greater probability of having a TBI and mental health or substance use disorder relative to civilian care recipients, whereas pre-9/11 military care recipients were more likely than civilian care recipients to have a hearing or vision problem and a chronic condition. After adjusting for the care recipient's age, post-9/11 care recipients were more likely to report a mental health or substance use disorder, a hearing or vision problem, and a physical impairment relative to civilian care recipients; pre-9/11 military care recipients had significantly elevated rates of mental health or substance use, hearing and vision, chronic, and physical impairment relative to civilian care recipients. Civilian care recipients remained more likely to have chronic conditions relative

**Table 2.5**
**Medical Conditions of Care Recipients in the United States**

| | Post-9/11 Care Recipients | | Pre-9/11 Care Recipients | | Civilian Care Recipients | |
|---|---|---|---|---|---|---|
| | Percentage | SE | Percentage | SE | Percentage | SE |
| Traumatic brain injury (TBI) | 20.3[a] | 2.8 | 10.0 | 1.9 | 9.9 | 1.2 |
| Problems with hearing or vision | | | | | | |
| Tinnitus (ringing of ears) | 37.1 | 4.7 | 20.3 | 2.1 | 9.9 | 1.2 |
| Hearing loss | 39.5 | 4.7 | 49.2 | 2.9 | 30.3 | 1.7 |
| Blindness | 10.2 | 4.1 | 7.5 | 1.4 | 8.8 | 1.0 |
| Any problem with hearing or vision | 56.8[a,b] | 5.2 | 56.2[a,b] | 2.9 | 38.1 | 1.8 |
| Disabilities that impair physical movement | | | | | | |
| Amputation | 3.9 | 1.2 | 2.2 | 0.7 | 3.4 | 0.8 |
| Paralysis or spinal cord injury | 15.0 | 4.3 | 6.3 | 1.3 | 6.8 | 1.0 |
| Back pain | 73.6 | 4.4 | 57.6 | 2.8 | 52.8 | 1.8 |
| Limited motion or other knee impairment | 42.4 | 5.1 | 45.4 | 2.9 | 39.0 | 1.8 |
| Traumatic arthritis | 17.9 | 3.5 | 27.2 | 2.6 | 23.5 | 1.6 |
| Any disability that impairs physical movement | 80.3[b] | 4.2 | 75.2[b] | 2.4 | 66.2 | 1.7 |
| Chronic condition | | | | | | |
| Hypertensive vascular disease | 26.5 | 4.4 | 59.1 | 2.9 | 44.1 | 1.8 |
| Cancer | 4.6 | 1.7 | 26.4 | 2.5 | 15.6 | 1.3 |
| Diabetes | 14.8 | 4.8 | 31.3 | 2.6 | 28.2 | 1.7 |
| Any chronic condition | 34.5[a] | 4.9 | 77.2[a,b] | 2.5 | 63.2 | 1.8 |
| Neurological conditions | | | | | | |
| Multiple sclerosis | 1.0 | 0.7 | 1.2 | 0.5 | 2.3 | 0.6 |
| Parkinson's disease | 0.5 | 0.4 | 5.3 | 1.0 | 3.9 | 0.7 |
| Dementia | 2.0 | 0.8 | 26.4 | 2.6 | 22.9 | 1.5 |
| Any neurological condition | 5.5[a,b] | 1.4 | 31.2 | 2.6 | 29.4 | 1.6 |
| Mental health and substance use | | | | | | |
| PTSD | 52.0 | 5.4 | 15.7 | 2.1 | 7.7 | 1.0 |
| Major depressive disorder | 45.7 | 5.0 | 26.5 | 2.5 | 29.1 | 1.7 |
| Substance use disorder | 15.4 | 3.8 | 9.1 | 1.7 | 6.0 | 0.8 |
| Any mental health or substance use | 64.0[a,b] | 5.7 | 36.1[b] | 2.7 | 33.3 | 1.7 |

[a] Statistically significant difference from civilian care recipients controlling for history of deployment to a war zone.

[b] Statistically significant difference from civilian care recipients controlling for age. Tests were only conducted for TBI and "any condition" in each of the five groups.

to post-9/11 care recipients after adjustment for a history of deployment, and more likely to have a neurological condition relative to post-9/11 care recipients after adjustment for both history of deployment and age.

**Figure 2.6**
**Proportion of Medical Conditions Related to Military Service**

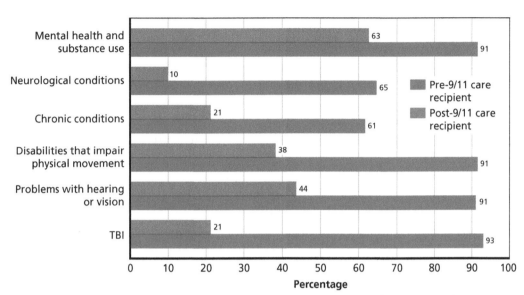

NOTE: All differences between pre-9/11 and post-9/11 care recipients except for neurological conditions
are significant after controlling for history of deployment to a war zone.
RAND RR499-2.6

Across disease categories, post-9/11 care recipients were more likely to have conditions related to their military services than pre-9/11 care recipients (Figure 2.6). Ninety-
three percent of post-9/11 care recipients with TBI, 91 percent of those with vision and
hearing problems, 91 percent of those with physical impairment, and 91 percent of those
with a mental health or substance use problem indicated that the condition was related to
their military service. (The proportions for pre-9/11 military caregivers were 21 percent,
44 percent, 38 percent, and 63 percent, respectively.) All differences between post-9/11
and pre-9/11 care recipients except for neurological conditions remained significant even
after controlling for a history of deployment to a war zone. In fact, across all disease categories except mental health or substance use, half or fewer of pre-9/11 veterans with the
conditions attributed the condition to their military service.

## Disease-Specific Programs

In the U.S. health care system, one's diagnosis or disease condition typically determines
the services and/or interventions that are required or recommended. Moreover, programs are sometimes created to provide services specifically to individuals with certain
conditions. Some of these programs also support caregivers of individuals with such
conditions, and were therefore included in our environmental scan. We reviewed the
full range of caregiver support programs included in our scan to understand whether

they are oriented toward or restricted to caregivers of individuals with specific conditions. We found that six of the 120 programs identified in our scan were aimed solely at providing services to caregivers for those with specific conditions. We also found a range of programs with broad eligibility criteria (not disease-specific) that offer specific initiatives (e.g., modules within educational programs) focused on certain conditions.

Table 2.6 outlines programs aimed *solely* at providing services to caregivers for those with specific diseases. These six disease-specific programs offer services to caregivers for individuals with two categories of conditions: mental health issues, and brain injury or cognitive disability. As already described, mental health issues are disproportionately prevalent among post-9/11 military care recipients; thus, focus on this disease category seems appropriate.

As shown in Table 2.6, five programs that provide disease-specific services offer *structured education or training*. Three of these programs are TBI-specific, and two focus on mental health issues. As described later in this chapter, such training programs may be helpful for certain caregivers, since caring for physical issues and cognitive or mental issues presents unique challenges (e.g., Etters, Goodall, and Harrison, 2008; Degeneffe, 2001). One example of a disease-specific program, Brain Injury Alliance (BIA) of Colorado, provides TBI-specific training that offers information and skills pertaining to cognitive rehabilitation and relational issues, including training on intimacy after a brain injury (for spousal caregivers). Educational programs focused

**Table 2.6**
**Programs Focused on Specific Diseases and Type of Caregiving Service Offered**

| Program Condition—Specific Focus | Name of Program | Education/Training | A Helping Hand | Structured Social Support | Patient Advocate or Case Manager | Structured Wellness Activities | Respite Care | Financial Stipend | Religious Support | Health Care | Mental Health Care |
|---|---|---|---|---|---|---|---|---|---|---|---|
| Mental health issues | National Alliance on Mental Illness (NAMI) Family-to-Family | X | | X | | | | | | | |
| | Support and Family Education (SAFE)—Mental Health Facts for Families | X | | X | | | | | | | |
| Brain injury and cognitive disability | American Veterans with Brain Injuries | | | X | | | | | | | |
| | Brain Injury Alliance (BIA) and BIA of Colorado | X | | X | | | | | | | |
| | Brain Injury Association of America | X | | X | | | | | | | |
| | Defense and Veterans Brain Injury Center | X | | | | | | | | | |

on mental health issues, including topics such as the experience of caring for someone with serious mental illness, the characteristics and causes of mental illnesses, and the impact of mental illness on the family.

Table 2.6 also illustrates that five disease-specific programs offer *structured social support*. Three of these programs are brain injury-specific, and two focus on mental health issues. Such support tends to emphasize issues pertaining to the condition(s) of focus. For example, SAFE's Mental Health Facts for Families program and NAMI's Family-to-Family program both organize support groups where caregivers discuss issues specific to caring for individuals with mental illness (more information on social support services is provided in Chapter Three).

The six disease-specific programs we identified do not offer services beyond structured education and training and social support. Specifically, these programs do not provide patient advocacy, structured wellness activities, respite, financial services, and health care services.

Some programs whose focus is not disease-specific offer distinct services targeted toward caregivers for individuals with certain conditions. Table 2.7 lists such programs identified in our environmental scan. These include such things as the American Red Cross Family Caregiving Course's Caring for a Loved One with Alzheimer's Disease or Dementia module, as well as FCA's Link2Care, which includes dementia-specific online resources and social support. However, this may not represent the entire range

**Table 2.7**
**General Caregiving Programs with Initiatives Focused on Specific Diseases**

| Organization | Organizational Initiative | Education/ Training | Structured Social Support |
|---|---|---|---|
| American Red Cross | Family Caregiving Course: *Caring for a Loved One with Alzheimer's Disease or Dementia* module | Alzheimer's | |
| Caregiver Action Network (CAN) | Coping with Alzheimer's web page/videos | Alzheimer's | |
| FCA | Link2Care | | Dementia |
| Hospice Foundation of America | Coping with Cancer at the End of Life Alzheimer's Disease and Hospice Care | Alzheimer's Cancer | |
| Shepherd's Centers of America | Support groups | | Stroke Alzheimer's Parkinson's |
| Strength for Caring | Cancer caregiver education | Cancer | |
| VA Caregiver Support Program | REACH VA | Alzheimer's Dementia Spinal cord injury | |
| Video Caregiving | Alzheimer's webpage/videos | Stroke Alzheimer's Cognitive disabilities | |

of disease-specific initiatives within our scan, since the full range of disease-specific options within organizations may not be widely visible, and since some initiatives may tailor themselves toward caregivers of individuals with certain illnesses in practice but not explicitly label them as such.

Like the disease-specific programs presented in Table 2.6, the disease-specific *initiatives* described in Table 2.7 only exist in two service domains: education and training or social support. In addition, most of the initiatives in Table 2.7 focus on conditions such as stroke, Alzheimer's disease, dementia, cancer, or Parkinson's disease, making them more relevant to pre-9/11 and civilian caregivers than post-9/11 military caregivers. This contrasts with the disease-specific *programs* identified in our environmental scan that focus on mental health issues or brain injury. The implications of these findings for military caregivers accessing these resources are unclear. On the one hand, caregivers of individuals with mental illness or TBI may locate disease-specific resources more easily since the programs offering these services are visibly labeled as disease-specific. These caregivers may learn about services to support themselves while seeking information specifically for themselves or, more likely, about providing care to the care recipient. On the other hand, caregivers of individuals with stroke, Alzheimer's disease, dementia, cancer, or Parkinson's disease may already be utilizing services from general caregiving organizations and may benefit from accessing disease-specific education or social support from the same source.

We also note that disease-specific programs and initiatives do not cover all of the most common disease conditions of military or veteran care recipients in the United States. For example, we did not find any disease-specific programs or initiatives focusing on tinnitus, hearing loss, vision problems, or certain disabilities that impair physical movement. Thus, it is likely that when caregivers of individuals with these injuries and illnesses seek services, they do so from programs offering general caregiving services rather than from those aimed at disease-specific populations.

### Functional Impairment

Regardless of the designation of specific conditions, an individual's need for caregiving assistance may depend in large part on his or her degree of functional impairment. To assess functional impairment among care recipients, we employed the World Health Organization Disability Assessment Schedule 2.0 (WHODAS-2). As described in more detail in Appendix A, the WHODAS-2 is a valid and reliable measure of disability status that, with 12 questions, assesses six domains of health and disability: cognition, mobility, self-care, getting along with others, daily life activities, and participation in community activities (Garin et al., 2010). The scale ranges from a low score of 0 (no impairment) to 48 (high impairment). The mean score for care recipients on the WHODAS is presented in Figure 2.7 and ranges from 33 for post-9/11 military care recipients to 36.5 for civilian care recipients. There is no statistical difference in mean scores between civilian and pre-9/11 military care recipi-

**Figure 2.7**
**Impairment (as Measured by the WHODAS) Among Care Recipients**

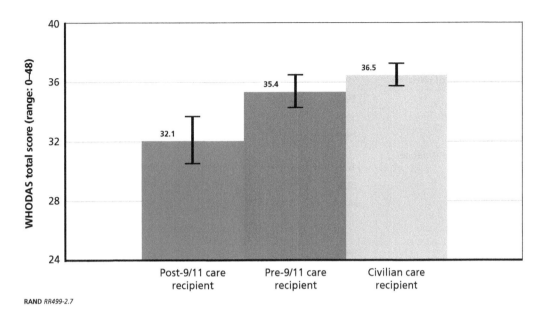

ents, nor between pre-9/11 and post-9/11 care recipients; however, the mean level of impairment is lower among post-9/11 military than it is for civilian care recipients.

## What Military Caregivers Do

### The Tasks Military Caregivers Perform

Prior studies have described the tasks that caregivers perform; these tasks are often grouped into two categories: activities of daily living (ADLs) and instrumental activities of daily living (IADLs). The series of tasks known as ADLs describe basic human functioning, including bathing, dressing, feeding, toileting, or using a wheelchair. As shown in Table 2.8, the proportion of caregivers that help with at least one ADL is the lowest among post-9/11 caregivers (44 percent), then pre-9/11 caregivers (54 percent), and is highest among civilian caregivers (64 percent). In fact, civilian caregivers report performing more ADLs than pre- and post-9/11 military caregivers even after accounting for whether the caregiver is a spouse or friend of the care recipient and the medical condition the care recipient has.[9] The most common ADL that all groups help with is

---

[9]  Multivariate Poisson regression models were estimated in which the number of ADLs that caregivers performed was the dependent variable and predicted by caregiver status (pre-9/11 military, post-9/11 military, civilian), dummy indicators of whether the caregiver was the care recipient's spouse or friend/neighbor, and dummy indicators of medical condition (TBI, problems with hearing or vision, disabilities that impair physical move-

**Table 2.8**
**ADLs and IADLs Performed by Military Caregivers**

| | Post-9/11 Military Caregivers | | Pre-9/11 Military Caregivers | | Civilian Caregivers | |
|---|---|---|---|---|---|---|
| | Percentage | SE | Percentage | SE | Percentage | SE |
| **ADLs** | | | | | | |
| Getting into/out of chair | 29.7 | 5.0 | 35.4 | 2.8 | 43.0 | 1.8 |
| Dressing | 19.7 | 3.8 | 28.9 | 2.5 | 38.7 | 1.8 |
| Toileting | 11.7 | 3.5 | 14.9 | 2.0 | 25.0 | 1.7 |
| Bathing | 18.8 | 3.6 | 22.0 | 2.1 | 35.8 | 1.8 |
| Dealing with incontinence/ diapers | 6.9 | 2.0 | 19.4 | 2.2 | 26.8 | 1.6 |
| Eating | 9.9 | 2.0 | 15.7 | 2.1 | 19.7 | 1.5 |
| Any ADL | 44.3* | 5.2 | 54.0* | 2.9 | 63.8 | 1.7 |
| **IADLs** | | | | | | |
| Taking medicines, pills, or injection | 39.0 | 4.8 | 37.6 | 2.7 | 46.5 | 1.8 |
| Managing finances | 60.5 | 5.3 | 55.6 | 2.9 | 63.6 | 1.8 |
| Grocery shopping | 52.0 | 5.3 | 73.1 | 2.4 | 74.1 | 1.6 |
| Housework | 58.8 | 5.1 | 67.1 | 2.7 | 72.0 | 1.7 |
| Preparing meals | 44.4 | 5.1 | 59.4 | 2.8 | 65.9 | 1.7 |
| Transportation | 39.5 | 5.0 | 69.0 | 2.7 | 75.8 | 1.6 |
| Arranging or supervising paid services | 14.0 | 2.2 | 32.8 | 2.6 | 40.7 | 1.8 |
| Coordinating medical care or rehabilitative services | 39.1 | 4.7 | 47.6 | 2.9 | 56.3 | 1.8 |
| Administering physical or medical therapies or treatments | 36.1 | 4.9 | 32.6 | 2.6 | 44.4 | 1.9 |
| Any IADL | 79.4* | 4.8 | 94.0 | 1.2 | 95.6 | 0.8 |

* Statistically significant difference from civilian caregivers. Tests of difference were only conducted for any ADL and any IADL.

getting into and out of chairs; many more civilian and pre-9/11 military caregivers help with dealing with incontinence/diapers and eating than post-9/11 military caregivers, of whom under 10 percent help with these tasks. On average, post-9/11 caregivers help with 1.0 ADLs (SE = 0.1), pre-9/11 caregivers help with 1.3 ADLs (SE = 0.1), and civilian caregivers help with 1.9 ADLs (SE = 0.1).

In addition, there are IADLs—those tasks required for noninstitutional community living, such as housework, meal preparation, transportation to medical appointments and

ment, chronic conditions, neurological conditions, and a mental health or substance use disorder). The coefficient estimate for post-9/11 military caregivers was −0.75 (p < 0.001) and for pre-9/11 military caregivers was −0.41 (p < 0.001).

community services, and health management and maintenance. Many more caregivers help with IADLs than with ADLs: 79 percent of post-9/11 military caregivers, 94 percent of pre-9/11 military caregivers, and 96 percent of civilian caregivers help with any IADL. On average, civilian caregivers assist with a total of 5.4 IADLs (SE = 0.1), while pre-9/11 military caregivers assist with an average of 4.8 IADLs (SE = 0.1), and post-9/11 military

## Key Finding

Post-9/11 military caregivers help with, on average, fewer ADLs and IADLs than civilian and pre-9/11 caregivers, even after accounting for the medical condition of the person for whom they are providing care.

caregivers assist with an average of 3.9 (SE = 0.3). Here again, civilian caregivers report performing more IADLs than both groups of military caregivers, even after accounting for the whether the caregiver is a spouse or friend of the care recipient, and the medical condition the care recipient experiences.[10]

Another way to examine caregivers' assistance with ADLs and IADLs is to examine the proportion of care *recipients* who need help with a given task and, of those, the proportion of their caregivers who perform this task. This presentation, shown for military care recipients and caregivers only in Table 2.9, shows that the greater proportion of pre-9/11 military caregivers who assist with ADLs and IADLs is driven by the needs of the people for whom they are caring. In other words, more pre-9/11 military care recipients need help with ADLs and IADLs than do post-9/11 care recipients. What is noticeable, however, is that when the care recipient needs help with an ADL or IADL, post-9/11 military caregivers generally provide this type of assistance. For example, one of the more extreme cases is that under 10 percent of post-9/11 military care recipients need assistance with incontinence and diapers, relative to 30 percent of pre-9/11 military caregivers. However, when such assistance is needed, 91 percent of post-9/11 military caregivers provide this assistance relative to 65 percent of pre-9/11 military caregivers.

We asked about three other tasks that are not necessarily characterized as ADLs or IADLs but that we identified as relevant in our review of the literature and the background research we performed in the first phase of this project: (1) remembering what the care recipient should be doing, (2) filling out paperwork related to benefits and compensation or legal issues, and (3) coping with stressful situations or avoiding triggers of anxiety or antisocial behavior. The results are shown in Figures 2.8 through 2.10.

Among all caregivers, there was no difference across groups in the proportion that reported that they helped the care recipient remember what she or he should be doing

---

[10] Multivariate Poisson regression models were estimated in which the number of IADLs that caregivers performed was the dependent variable and predicted by the same covariates listed in the previous footnote. The coefficient estimate for post-9/11 military caregivers was −0.35 (p < 0.001) and for pre-9/11 military caregivers was −0.15 (p < 0.001).

**Table 2.9**
**Activities of Daily Living That Caregivers Perform**

| | Care Recipient Needs Assistance | | | | Of Those Care Recipients Needing Such Support, Proportion of Caregivers Performing Tasks | | | |
| --- | --- | --- | --- | --- | --- | --- | --- | --- |
| | Post-9/11 Military Care Recipients | | Pre-9/11 Military Care Recipients | | Post-9/11 Military Caregivers | | Pre-9/11 Military Caregivers | |
| | Percentage | SE | Percentage | SE | Percentage | SE | Percentage | SE |
| **ADLs** | | | | | | | | |
| Getting into/out of chair | 33.2 | 5.0 | 37.8 | 2.8 | 89.4 | 4.9 | 93.8 | 1.8 |
| Dressing | 20.2 | 3.8 | 34.3 | 2.7 | 98.1 | 1.4 | 85.0 | 3.7 |
| Toileting | 12.1 | 3.5 | 18.9 | 2.2 | 97.5 | 1.8 | 79.5 | 5.1 |
| Bathing | 21.9 | 3.9 | 41.2 | 2.8 | 86.9 | 7.4 | 54.0 | 4.5 |
| Dealing with incontinence/diapers | 7.5 | 2.0 | 30.4 | 2.7 | 91.4 | 4.7 | 65.1 | 5.6 |
| Eating | 12.1 | 2.5 | 16.8 | 2.1 | 81.7 | 11.0 | 94.4 | 1.9 |
| **IADLs** | | | | | | | | |
| Taking medicines, pills, or injection | 40.3 | 4.8 | 45.0 | 2.8 | 97.2 | 1.5 | 83.7 | 3.3 |
| Managing finances | 62.4 | 5.3 | 65.5 | 2.7 | 97.5 | 2.0 | 85.0 | 2.9 |
| Grocery shopping | 54.3 | 5.2 | 79.3 | 2.1 | 97.2 | 1.4 | 92.3 | 1.7 |
| Housework | 61.3 | 5.1 | 76.2 | 2.4 | 96.3 | 1.9 | 88.2 | 2.0 |
| Preparing meals | 45.1 | 5.1 | 70.2 | 2.6 | 98.9 | 0.7 | 84.9 | 2.3 |
| Transportation | 41.4 | 5.0 | 74.7 | 2.5 | 95.4 | 3.4 | 92.5 | 2.1 |
| Arranging or supervising paid services | 16.8 | 2.7 | 45.2 | 2.9 | 83.9 | 7.8 | 72.9 | 4.4 |
| Coordinating medical care or rehabilitative services | 40.0 | 4.7 | 61.1 | 2.8 | 98.3 | 1.0 | 78.6 | 3.7 |
| Administering physical or medical therapies or treatments | 38.4 | 4.9 | 51.2 | 2.9 | 94.1 | 2.8 | 63.9 | 4.1 |

NOTE: Small sample sized impeded tests of differences between groups.

(roughly half of post-9/11, pre-9/11, and civilian caregivers). Civilian care recipients were more likely than post-9/11 care recipients to need help with paperwork (70 percent versus 58 percent) and pre-9/11 military caregivers were less likely than civilian caregivers to help with this task. Post-9/11 military care recipients were more likely to need assistance coping with stressful situations or avoiding triggers (76 percent versus 54–56 percent in the other groups), and their caregivers were more likely to perform this task (75 percent versus 49 and 53 percent among pre-9/11 and civilian caregivers, respectively). This last finding, that post-9/11 military caregivers were more likely than civilian caregivers to help the care recipient cope with stressful situations, remained, even after accounting for whether the care recipient had PTSD and the number of medical conditions the care recipient had, both of which were also associated with caregivers' likelihood of performing this task. Like the ADLs and IADLs, almost all post-9/11 caregivers helped their care recipient with these three tasks when such help was needed.

## Programs and Resources for Training Caregivers

The desire to capably and effectively perform caregiving may motivate caregivers to seek resources that will prepare them for the tasks. In our environmental scan, we explored the extent to which programs and resources were available to train caregivers for these types of tasks. We examined the provision of structured training, use of

**Figure 2.8**
**Care Recipient Needs Help Remembering**

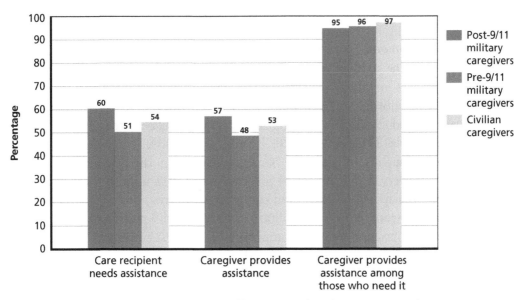

NOTE: No evidence of statistically significant differences was found among groups of care recipients needing assistance or caregivers providing such assistance. Differences in providing assistance among those who need it were not tested.
RAND RR499-2.8

**Figure 2.9**
**Care Recipient Needs Help Filling Out Paperwork**

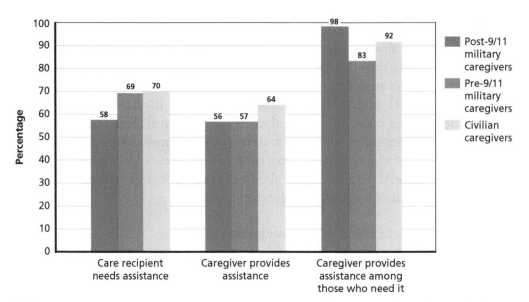

NOTE: Post-9/11 care recipients were significantly less likely than civilian care recipients to need assistance filling out paperwork; pre-9/11 caregivers were significantly less likely than civilian care recipients to provide such assistance. Differences in providing assistance among those who need it were not tested.
RAND *RR499-2.9*

patient advocates or case managers, and availability of informational resources about caregiving tasks.

### Structured Education and Training

In our scan, we define structured education or training as in-person or online classes, modules or webinars, or manuals or workbooks that involve a formalized curriculum (rather than ad hoc information) related to caregiving activities. Caregivers often report a need for structured education and training, and this need may be particularly great early in one's caregiving role (Tanielian et al., 2013; Smith et al., 2004). We discuss the efficacy and effectiveness of such trainings in the "Caregiver Training: The Evidence" box.

Among caregivers in our survey, 24 percent of post-9/11 military caregivers indicated that they participated in structured caregiving education or training in the past year, relative to 7 percent of pre-9/11 military caregivers and 9 percent of civilian caregivers. This may be because a greater proportion of post-9/11 military caregivers are more challenged by uncertainty about the medical aspects of their care recipients' medical condition: More than 34 percent of post-9/11 caregivers reported being extremely challenged by medical uncertainty, compared with 12 and 15 percent of pre-9/11 and civilian caregivers, respectively.

**Figure 2.10**
**Care Recipient Needs Help Coping with Stressful Situations**

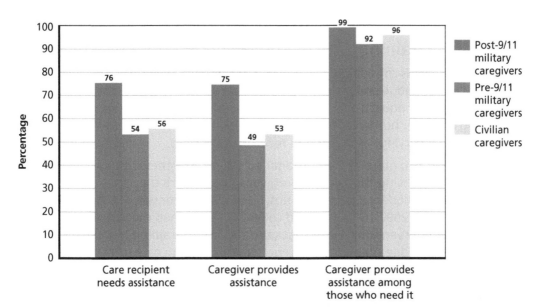

NOTE: Post-9/11 military care recipients were significantly more likely than civilian care recipients to need assistance coping with stressful situations, and post-9/11 caregivers were significantly more likely than civilian caregivers to provide such assistance. Differences in providing assistance among those who need it were not tested.
RAND RR499-2.10

Thirty-seven organizations in our environmental scan address the needs of caregivers specific to the caregiving tasks they may be expected to perform. To provide a useful overview of the educational activities for military caregivers, we categorized them based on the target populations: (1) caregiver specific vs. incidental and (2) military specific vs. incidental (Table 2.10). The education or training activities labeled as caregiver- or military-*specific* contain curricula specifically targeted toward these populations.[11]

A majority of the educational activities we identified in the environmental scan fell into the caregiver-specific category. This reflects that fact that education or training that is directly relevant to caregiving is likely to be labeled as such. That said, we still identified a number of educational activities that are likely to be useful to caregivers but that are targeted toward families or other populations rather than caregivers specifically. Although we did not analyze in detail the content of these educational activities, those which are both *caregiver*-specific and *military*-specific may be most likely to address the nuanced challenges that military caregivers face. We discuss each of these

---

[11] These categorizations differ slightly from similar categorizations that we applied to the organizational entities themselves. For example, a given *organization* may not be military specific (i.e., not specify a military population as a stated or substantial target population), but may offer caregiver *education* that has military-specific curricula.

## Caregiver Training: The Evidence

**Overview:** There is considerable evidence that caregiver training is effective for increasing knowledge and ability to provide care (Brodaty, Green, and Koschera, 2003; Sörensen, Pinquart, and Duberstein, 2002). Training is also effective in reducing caregiver burden and improving mental health outcomes, and has significant but varying results on care recipient symptoms.

**The Evidence:** Two meta-analyses examined the effectiveness of caregiver training for improving the lives of caregivers and the care they provide to care recipients (Brodaty, Green, and Koschera, 2003; Sörensen, Pinquart, and Duberstein., 2002). Sörensen and colleagues examined the average effects of 38 intervention studies that used structured training to increase caregiver knowledge of, and competence with, providing care (also known as psychoeducational interventions). When caregivers were tested immediately after the intervention or at a later follow-up, psychoeducational training programs produced large increases in caregiver knowledge and ability to provide care. These effects held even when limiting the analysis to just the more rigorous studies analyzed (i.e., randomized designs, n = 19 studies). Smaller effects for psychoeducational training were found for reducing burden and depressive symptoms among caregivers. Brodaty and colleagues analyzed the results of 30 studies (21 of which were randomized control trials) examining the effects of psychoeducational training for caregivers whose care recipients had dementia. Their analysis revealed that training led to increases in caregiver knowledge, improved caregiver mood, and decreased caregiver psychological distress, but they did not find a significant effect on caregiver burden. More recent randomized control trials have found similar effects of psychoeducational training on caregiver well-being for those caring for cancer patients (Hudson et al., 2013; Waldron et al., 2012).

**Limitations:** Most of the extant research on caregiver training has been conducted on caregivers of older care recipients who are frail (i.e., in poor health) and/or have dementia. There is scant research on caregivers of care recipients with severe mental illness. In addition, most studies have examined the short-term effects of caregiver training, and more research is needed to understand the long-term effectiveness of this type of intervention (Hudson et al., 2013).

**Table 2.10**
**Education and Training Activities by Target Populations**

| | Military Specific | Military Incidental |
|---|---|---|
| Caregiver-Specific | Blue Star Families<br>Defense and Veterans Brain Injury Center<br>DoD Office of Warrior Care Policy<br>Easter Seals, in conjunction with:<br>  • USO<br>  • VA Caregiver Support Program<br>Hospice Foundation America<br>MBP Consulting<br>Military Officer's Association of America<br>Navy-Marine Corps Relief Society Financial<br>  Assistance<br>Operation Homefront<br>RCI<br>Well Spouse Association | CAN<br>Caregiverhelp.com<br>Caregiver Video Series: Walking on Eggshells<br>FCA<br>Home Instead Senior Care<br>National Council on Aging–Building Better<br>  Caregivers<br>National Hospice and Palliative Care<br>  Organization<br>NAMI Family-to-Family<br>Share the Care<br>Shepherd's Centers of America<br>Strength for Caring<br>Today's Caregiver<br>Terra Nova Films and Video Caregiving<br>American Red Cross (Family Caregiving<br>  Course) |
| Caregiver-Incidental | American Red Cross (Reconnection<br>  Workshops)<br>Association of the United States Army,<br>  Family Readiness Directorate<br>BIA of Colorado<br>Coming Home Project<br>Compass Retreat Center<br>Military Child Education Coalition<br>Wounded Warrior Project® | AARP<br>Brain Injury Association of America<br>Patient Advocate Foundation<br>SAFE |

four categories, beginning with activities that are both caregiver- and military-specific (i.e., the upper left quadrant of Table 2.10).

Caregiver- and military-specific education is offered by 11 organizations, including large organizations such as the VA Caregiver Support Program (under a contract with Easter Seals, Atlas Research, and others) and the United Service Organizations (USO), also in conjunction with Easter Seals and Atlas Research. Caregivers of eligible post-9/11 *veterans* are required to complete the VA Caregiver Support Program's "core curriculum" training as a prerequisite for applying to the VA's Program of Comprehensive Assistance for Family Caregivers. The training offers several modules relevant to aspects of military caregiving: caregiver self-care, home safety, caregiver skills, managing challenging behaviors, personal care, and resources. The training includes 4.5 hours of content delivered online in English or Spanish. The USO offers similar trainings, but targeted toward caregivers of *active-duty* service members. The training is a series of four in-person sessions. The core session focuses on the importance of the caregiving role and what caregivers can do for themselves to ensure that they maintain a balanced lifestyle. Three additional sessions highlight managing challenging behaviors such as TBI and PTSD, managing caregiver stress, and parent-child communication.

Several other caregiver- and military-specific training activities exist as well. For example, The Elizabeth Dole Foundation partnered with the Military Officer's Association of America by providing funding for the organization to create a caregiver guide: "Tips for Lifelong Caregiving." This online tool aims to assist caregivers of wounded, ill, and injured service members and veterans with issues such as medical-disability insurance and benefits programs, guardianship and fiduciary matters, estate planning, and a range of other legal and financial matters. The American Bar Association and United States Automobile Association provided assistance and expertise on content development. In addition, RCI offers Operation Family Caregiver, a training program designed to improve caregivers' problem-solving capabilities, reduce levels of depression, and improve overall quality of life. Individual sessions are led by a caregiving coach who works one on one with the caregiver face to face or via telephone or the Web. The Defense and Veterans Brain Injury Center is another organization providing training specifically to military caregivers, offering a curriculum targeted toward caregivers of veterans with TBI. A handful of other organizations also offer caregiver- and military-specific education, as shown in the upper left quadrant of Table 2.10.

As shown in the other three quadrants of Table 2.10, a range of organizations provide education or training relevant to military caregivers but not targeted specifically toward them. These offerings are broad and diverse and include caregiver-specific educational activities offered by organizations such as CAN, FCA, and American Red Cross. It also includes military-specific educational activities through organizations such as the Coming Home Project, Military Child Education Coalition, and WWP. The format and delivery of these educational activities ranges greatly, from online modules to in-person sessions at retreats.

Though caregiving trainings have proven effective as referenced previously, the effectiveness of the specific programs offered to military caregivers is unknown. Several of these organizations reported collecting evaluation data on their training programs; however, most of these assessments were neither formalized nor rigorous assessments of the impact on task performance. They focused largely on caregiver satisfaction with the program rather than short-term outcomes such as increased knowledge and caregiving competencies or long-term outcomes such as caregiver burden.

### Patient Advocacy and Case Management

A particularly salient task that caregivers identified in our earlier work was their role as an advocate and case manager for their care recipient (Tanielian et al., 2013). Patient advocacy or case management involves an individual acting as a liaison between the care recipient and his or her health care or benefit providers, or coordinating (medical or nonmedical) services for the care recipient. Although these services are targeted toward meeting the needs of the service member or veteran rather than the caregiver, the caregiver is frequently involved with and can benefit from case management services. Thus, we consider patient advocacy or case management to be a "common caregiving service."

We asked caregivers about the challenges they faced in obtaining medical care and other assistance for their care recipient, challenges that could be ameliorated through having additional support in advocacy and case management. We found that when controlling for sociodemographic differences among the groups, post-9/11 caregivers reported significantly greater challenges obtaining medical care or other assistance for their care recipients than did pre-9/11 and civilian caregivers (the average rating on a four-point scale was 2.6 vs. 2.0 and 2.1, respectively). About 21 percent of post-9/11 caregivers reported that they were extremely challenged with obtaining medical care for their care recipients, compared with 9 percent of pre-9/11 caregivers and 12 percent of civilian caregivers. Ratings by pre-9/11 caregivers and civilian caregivers did not significantly differ.

In our scan, we found that a range of the identified organizations (21) provide some type of patient advocacy or case management services. The most prominent sources of patient advocacy or case management for wounded, ill, and injured military personnel are the Federal Recovery Care Coordination Program, DoD's "wounded warrior" programs, which reside within each military service,[12] and the VA's OEF/OIF/OND Care Management Program. Each has a slightly different focus but can usually be accessed through either the DoD or VA treatment setting. For example, the VA's program is housed within VA medical centers and includes clinical case management, while the "wounded warrior" programs focus on nonmedical case management for seriously injured, wounded, or ill service members. The Federal Recovery Care Coordination Program is a joint DoD and VA program that was designed to complement these services and ensure continuity and warm hand-offs between federal health care systems. Seriously wounded, ill, or injured service members or veterans are automatically assessed during their acute care in federal health care settings for enrollment in these programs.

Aside from federal programs, there exists a range of other nonprofit or community organizations that assist with case management. These organizations vary in their emphasis, with some focused heavily on clinical care and others on nonmedical benefits. Many are available to veterans nationally, although a handful of programs have a statewide focus. For example, the Virginia Wounded Warrior Program provides case management and care coordination for veterans and family members seeking health care or behavioral health care in Virginia. Likewise, Iraq and Afghanistan Veterans of America's case management and referral services connect veterans with a range of resources and benefits, and are operational in New York and California. Some organizations, such as WWP, assist caregivers in accessing a range of benefits and services *for themselves*, rather than simply for their care recipient. The full range of programs focused on patient advocacy or case management is listed in Appendix E.

Overall, almost 22 percent of caregivers indicated that, in the past year, they used an advocate or case manager for their care recipients. Controlling for sociodemo-

---

[12] The "wounded warrior" programs are the Army Wounded Warrior Program, Marine Corps Wounded Warrior Regiment, Navy Wounded Warrior Safe Harbor, Air Force Warrior Wounded Warrior Program, and Special Operations Command's Care Coalition.

graphic characteristics, significantly more post-9/11 caregivers indicated that they used an advocate or case manager in the past year than did pre-9/11 and civilian caregivers (31 percent vs. 21 and 20 percent, respectively). Civilian caregivers did not significantly differ from pre-9/11 caregivers in their use of an advocate or case manager.

### The Time Military Caregiving Takes

The NAC and AARP define five levels of caregiving based upon the amount of hours spent each week providing care, and the burden of care associated with helping with activities of daily living (NAC and AARP, 2004). In the following section, we discuss how caregivers vary in the amount of time spent per week providing different types of support.

We asked caregivers to estimate the time they spend each week performing caregiving duties. On average, post-9/11 and civilian caregivers spend comparable time each week performing these duties, and more time than pre-9/11 military caregivers (see Figure 2.11). However, fewer post-9/11 (12 percent) and pre-9/11 (10 percent) military caregivers spend more than 40 hours per week caregiving than civilian caregivers (17 percent); 8 percent of civilian caregivers reported spending more than 80 hours per week caregiving. In the 2010 NAC survey, more than a third of caregiver respondents (43 percent) reported spending at least 40 hours per week helping their veteran, which is significantly different than our survey results. This difference may be related to the reliance in the NAC survey on caregivers engaged in support programs.

**Figure 2.11**
**Hours per Week Spent Caregiving**

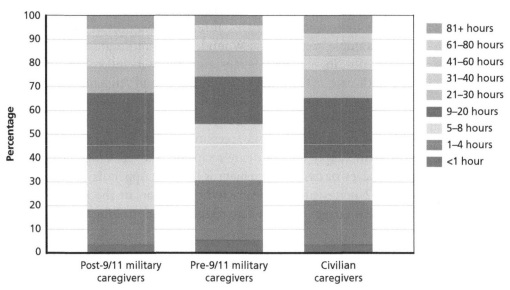

RAND RR499-2.11

We estimated regression models to discern the drivers of time spent caregiving. Even after accounting for the tasks caregivers perform (i.e., number of ADLs and IADLs), the number of people in the caregiver's caregiving network, whether the caregiver is the care recipient's spouse or neighbor, and the number of medical conditions the care recipient has, pre-9/11 military caregivers still spend less time per week caregiving than post-9/11 and civilian caregivers. Aside from the number of medical conditions the care recipient has, all other variables are associated with time spent caregiving in the ways we would expect, and all are significant even after adjustment (Table 2.11). For example, time spent caregiving increases with the number of ADLs and IADLs that caregivers perform, and—importantly—whether the caregiver is the care recipient's spouse. In fact, even after adjustment, spouses spend on average 14 hours more per week caregiving than nonspouses (p < 0.001). On the other hand, time spent caregiving is lessened by the number of people in a caregiver's caregiving network, and is on average four hours less per week for caregivers who are friends or neighbors of the care recipient (p = 0.016).

We also asked caregivers to report how much time each person in their caregiving network spends performing caregiving tasks, and added up these hours to present a total time spent caregiving for the same care recipient. This procedure yielded generally the same pattern of results (Figure 2.12): 35 percent of civilian care recipients receive more than 40 hours of care per week, relative to roughly 30 percent of both post-9/11 and pre-9/11 care recipients.

**Table 2.11**
**Predictors of Time Spent Caregiving Among Post-9/11 Caregivers, Pre-9/11 Caregivers, and Civilian Caregivers**

| Predictor | Unadjusted Associations β (p-value) | Adjusted Associations β (p-value) |
|---|---|---|
| Post-9/11 caregiver (vs. civilian caregiver) | 1.98 (0.26) | 1.09 (0.49) |
| Pre-9/11 caregiver (vs. civilian caregiver) | −6.06 (0.001) | −4.17 (0.001) |
| Number of ADLs caregiver assists with | 4.20 (<0.001) | 2.36 (<0.001) |
| Number of IADLs caregiver assists with | 3.26 (<0.001) | 2.34 (<0.001) |
| Number of people in caregiver network | −2.13 (<0.001) | −1.62 (<0.001) |
| Caregiver is the care recipient's spouse | 15.97 (<0.001) | 13.61 (<0.001) |
| Caregiver is the care recipient's friend or neighbor | −11.22 (<0.001) | −3.56 (0.016) |
| Number of medical conditions care recipient has | 1.81 (<0.001) | 0.47 (0.117) |

NOTE: β = Ordinary Least Square regression model coefficient. Regression models were estimated with post-stratification weights.

**Figure 2.12**
**Hours per Week Spent Caregiving by Caregiver's Network**

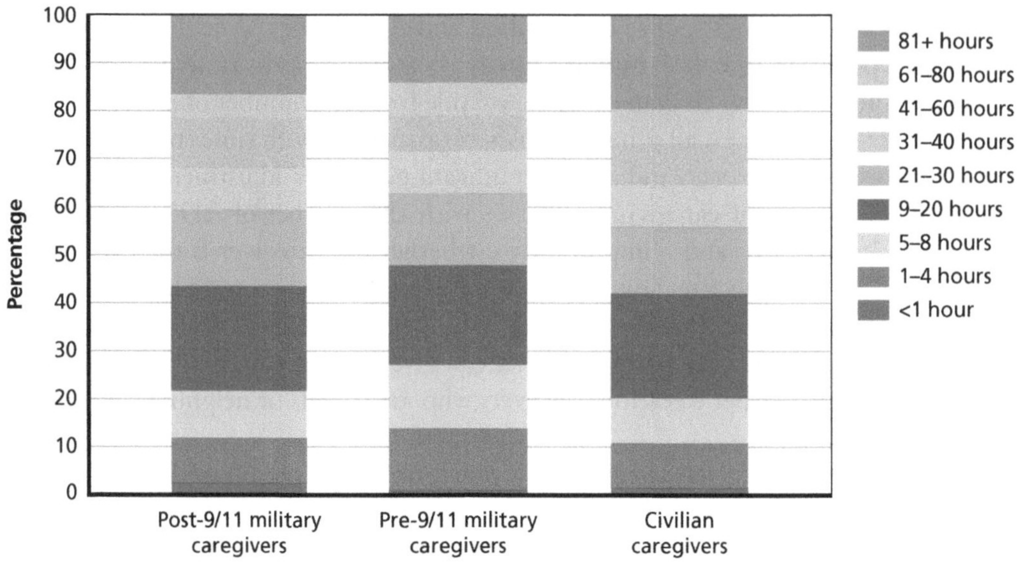

## Summary

There are 5.5 million military caregivers in the United States; 20 percent caring for an individual who served in the military post-9/11—a trait that certain caregiver support programs require for program eligibility, including the VA's Program of Comprehensive Assistance for Family Caregivers and DoD's SCAADL. In general, pre-9/11 military caregivers look more similar to civilian caregivers than they do to post-9/11 military caregivers. Post-9/11 military caregivers are unique from these other groups of caregivers in that they are more likely to be spouses and friends of the care recipient than children of the care recipient. Post-9/11 military caregivers are younger and more likely to be of a minority race/ethnicity. They are also more likely to have previously served in the military themselves, but are less likely to have a caregiving support network.

Like the people who are caring for them, in general, pre-9/11 military care recipients look more similar to civilian care recipients than they do to post-9/11 military care recipients. Aside from their sex, post-9/11 military care recipients differ from these other groups in sociodemographic characteristics (e.g., younger, more likely to be non-white). Post-9/11 care recipients are more likely than pre-9/11 care recipients to have a VA-service-connected disability rating; almost a third of post-9/11 care recipients have a rating of 70 percent or higher. Even though they are more likely to have a disability rating, it is noteworthy that post-9/11 care recipients have slightly better functioning than the other care recipient groups. Their medical conditions are also different: All groups report having limiting back pain, but a greater proportion of post-9/11 care recipients has a mental health or substance use disorder not solely attributed to their history of deployment to a war zone, and greater shares of pre-9/11 and civilian care recipients have chronic and neurological conditions, due largely (but not entirely) to their older age. There are a handful of programs for caregivers that focus on specific conditions, with two programs geared specifically to those providing care to persons with mental health issues, and several programs for those supporting individuals with forms of dementia.

Military caregivers perform a variety of tasks to support their care recipients. While post-9/11 military caregivers perform fewer ADLs and IADLs than pre-9/11 and civilian caregivers, this is largely attributable to their care recipients requiring less assistance with these types of tasks. Nonetheless, civilian and post-9/11 military caregivers report roughly the same time per week caregiving; regardless of their era of service, however, spouses spend the most time caregiving per week.

In our earlier qualitative work, military caregivers highlighted the importance of their role in providing patient advocacy and case management for their care recipient in an effort to obtain necessary medical care and services for their loved one. The current survey reveals that post-9/11 caregivers reported being significantly more challenged in this area than did pre-9/11 or civilian caregivers. We identified 21 programs that support military caregivers by providing patient advocacy or case management services; however, only 22 percent of caregivers reporting using these services. While these programs are often oriented toward facilitating the care of the care recipients, gaining the assistance of formal case managers may lower the burden that caregivers face. We also found that post-9/11 caregivers rated these services significantly more helpful than did other caregivers.

A number of programs exist to train and orient caregivers to these tasks, and training caregivers has been shown to be effective, though none of the current trainings we identified are evaluating the effectiveness of their training on reducing caregiver burden. Around a quarter of post-9/11 military caregivers have participated in such trainings, more than pre-9/11 and civilian caregivers. In general, these trainings vary in technical aspects (i.e., duration, modality), and some offer specific skills for certain disease categories. Though practical information on caregiving is contained in each, most also contain content to help caregivers balance their caregiving responsibilities with the hope that such behaviors will stave off any deleterious consequences associated with caregiving. The next chapter expands upon such consequences in greater detail.

# Understanding and Addressing Caregiver Needs: The Risks and Consequences of Caregiving and Programs to Mitigate Them

## Introduction

Past research has documented adverse impacts of caregiving on caregivers in a wide array of life domains, including physical health, mental health, familial relationships and parenting, employment, and finances (NAC and AARP, 2009; NAC, 2010; Pinquart and Sörensen, 2003b). However, most of the available research on caregivers has been conducted on convenience samples of civilian caregivers. Little, if any, research has assessed the impacts of caregiving in a probability-based sample of military caregivers, leaving the true nature and extent of these impacts ambiguous.

In this chapter, we address this gap, comparing post-9/11 caregivers, pre-9/11 caregivers, and civilian caregivers to non-caregivers on several health and psychosocial outcomes. We compare these groups without and with adjustment for sociodemographic characteristics, such as age and sex, to better understand the effect of caregiving status on functioning independently of these potential confounds. We also examine the effects of different aspects of the caregiving context described in Chapter Two—such as the nature of the care recipient's disabilities, degree of the care recipient's impairment, and time spent caregiving—on caregivers' functioning.

In light of past research, we expected that all three groups of caregivers would report lower levels of functioning than non-caregivers, with and without adjustment for sociodemographic characteristics. We also expected that the post-9/11 caregivers would have poorer functioning than pre-9/11 caregivers and civilian caregivers for three primary reasons. First, the adoption of a caregiving role before old age is less normative and more unexpected, which may increase the difficulty of coping with the stress of caregiving. Second, providing care to a post-9/11 care recipient, most of whom are relatively young, means that the caregiver can likely expect to provide care for a long time, perhaps for the rest of the care recipient's life. Thus, post-9/11 caregivers are likely to bear the burden of caregiving for an extended duration. Third, relative to pre-9/11 and civilian care recipients, nearly twice as many post-9/11 care recipients had a mental health condition, and there are more than double the proportion of post-9/11 military care recipients with a mental health condition than pre-9/11 military and civilian care recipients with dementia (see Chapter Two). In past research, caregivers of care recipients with conditions of which behavioral problems are a hallmark characteristic (e.g., dementia) have experienced more negative mental health outcomes than caregivers of care recipients with other types of conditions (Pinquart and Sörensen, 2003b).

## Health and Well-Being of Military Caregivers

### Physical Health

In past research, military caregivers reported negative effects of becoming a caregiver on physical health in the areas of sleep deprivation (77 percent), "strains, aches, or pains" (63 percent), increased blood pressure (33 percent), and "generally getting sick more often" (27 percent) (NAC, 2010). In our study, caregivers report similar health issues as a result of caregiving: for example, between one-third and one-half of caregivers report sleep disturbances as a result of caregiving,[1] and between 20 and 30 percent report that caregiving causes physical strain.[2] In addition, just over a quarter of post-9/11 caregivers (28 percent) reported that they were extremely challenged by their own physical health, mental health, or well-being, compared with 13 percent of pre-9/11 and civilian caregivers.

Findings from other research in which caregivers' physical health has been compared with a control group of non-caregivers have also been consistent with the notion that caregiving adversely affects physical health, although the difference between caregivers' and non-caregivers' physical health appears to be of fairly small magnitude (Pinquart and Sörensen, 2003a).

We assessed physical health by asking respondents to rate their general health and report the extent to which they experience various role limitations due to problems with their physical health. As shown in Figure 3.1, post-9/11 caregivers reported the worst general health and the greatest degree of physical impairment, and non-caregivers reported the best general health and the least amount of physical impairment.

To determine whether the groups of caregivers differed significantly from the non-caregiver control group on general health and role limitations due to physical health, we estimated regression models for each outcome. As shown in Table 3.1, all three groups of caregivers reported significantly worse general health and more role limitations due to physical health than did non-caregivers.

Because several sociodemographic differences between the groups of caregivers and non-caregivers may account for the observed differences on general health and role limitations due to physical health, e.g., pre-9/11 caregivers tend to be older than non-

---

[1]   Fifty-five percent of post-9/11 military caregivers, 33 percent of pre-9/11 military caregivers, and 32 percent of civilian caregivers reported sleep disturbances as a result of caregiving.

[2]   Twenty-nine percent of post-9/11 military caregivers, 21 percent of pre-9/11 military caregivers, and 23 percent of civilian caregivers reported physical strain as a result of caregiving.

**Figure 3.1**
**General Health and Role Limitations Due to Physical Health Among Post-9/11 Caregivers, Pre-9/11 Caregivers, Civilian Caregivers, and Non-Caregivers (n = 3,869)**

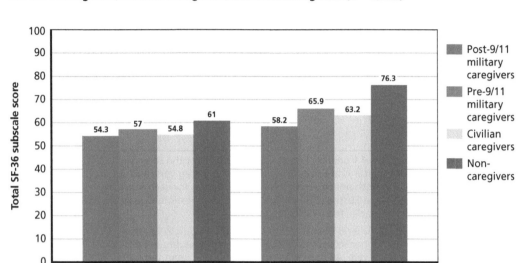

NOTE: General health scores and role limitations due to physical health are subscales from the SF-36 (Short Form 36, a quality-of-life measure discussed in Appendix A), and range from 0 to 100, where higher scores indicate higher general health and fewer role limitations due to physical health, respectively.
RAND *RR499-3.1*

caregivers (see Table 2.3), we compared the groups on these outcomes while adjusting for several sociodemographic characteristics.[3] As shown in Table 3.1, similar patterns of differences between the groups of caregivers and non-caregivers were demonstrated after adjustment for these characteristics: post-9/11 caregivers and civilian caregivers had significantly worse general health than non-caregivers, and all three groups of caregivers had significantly more role limitations due to physical health than non-caregivers. In other words, after accounting for the differences in groups by core sociodemographic variables, post-9/11 military caregivers' general health was six points lower than non-caregivers (on a 100-point scale), civilian caregivers scored four points lower than non-caregivers, and there was no evidence of a difference between pre-9/11 military caregivers and non-caregivers. These differences were even greater for role limitations, where post-9/11 military caregivers scored 20 points lower, civilian caregivers scored 11 points lower, and pre-9/11 military caregivers scored nine points lower than non-caregivers. Thus, it appears that the observed group differences in general health

---

[3]   Unless otherwise indicated, all adjusted multivariate regression models described in this chapter include the following core set of sociodemographic characteristics as predictors: respondent's history of military service, sex, age, race/ethnicity, marital status, household size and income, highest level of education, and residence in a major metropolitan area.

**Table 3.1**
**The Effect of Caregiver Status on General Health and Role Limitations Due to Physical Health, Unadjusted and Adjusted for Sociodemographic Characteristics (n = 3,869)**

| Caregiver Status[a] | General Health | | Role Limitations Due to Physical Health | |
|---|---|---|---|---|
| | Unadjusted B (SE) | Adjusted B (SE) | Unadjusted B (SE) | Adjusted B (SE) |
| Post-9/11 military caregiver | −6.7(2.7)[b] | −6.4(2.5)[b] | −18.1(3.9)[b] | −19.7(3.9)[b] |
| Pre-9/11 military caregiver | −4.0(1.8)[b] | −2.6(1.7) | −10.4(2.7)[b] | −8.7(2.6)[b] |
| Civilian caregiver | −6.2(1.4)[b] | −4.1(1.3)[b] | −13.0(2.2)[b] | −11.0(2.2)[b] |
| Non-caregiver | — | — | — | — |

[a] The joint (i.e., three degrees of freedom) F-tests of significance for the three dummy-coded indicators corresponding to post-9/11 military caregivers, pre-9/11 military caregivers, and civilian caregivers were significant at $p < .01$ in both unadjusted and adjusted models for each outcome: general health: unadjusted ($F[3, 3834] = 6.94$); adjusted ($F[3, 3821] = 4.20$); role limitations due to physical health: unadjusted($F[3, 3826] = 14.99$; adjusted ($F[3, 3814] = 13.06$).

[b] $p < .01$. Scores on the SF-36 General Health and Role Limitations due to Physical Health subscales range from 0 to 100, where higher scores indicate higher general health and fewer role limitations due to physical health, respectively. All parameter estimates were computed with post-stratification weights in SAS PROC SURVEYREG. The core set of sociodemographic characteristics was included in the adjusted multivariate model.

and role limitations due to physical health cannot simply be attributed to sociodemographic differences.

### Health Care Coverage and Utilization

To understand how well caregivers' health care needs are met (or not), we asked respondents several questions about their health care coverage and utilization. As shown in Table 3.2, nearly one-third of post-9/11 caregivers reported a lack of health care coverage such as "health insurance, prepaid plans such as health maintenance organizations, or government plans such as Medicare or Indian Health Services." In contrast, roughly 20 percent of pre-9/11 caregivers, civilian caregivers, and non-caregivers lack health care coverage, a proportion comparable to rates of uninsured adults in the United States before the Affordable Care Act (Henry J. Kaiser Family Foundation, 2013).

Past research on military caregivers indicates that they may be inclined to postpone or completely forgo medical care for themselves due to the demands of caregiving (Tanielian et al., 2013). In the NAC (2010) study, over half of military caregivers (58 percent) reported "delaying/skipping your own doctor/dentist appointments" as a result of becoming a caregiver. Delving more deeply into caregivers' patterns of health care utilization, we found that slightly more than a quarter of post-9/11 caregivers reported not having a usual source of medical care, i.e., a "doctor's office, clinic, health center, or other place that you usually go if you are sick or need advice about your health." Approximately half as many pre-9/11 caregivers, civilian caregivers, and non-caregivers did not have a usual source of medical care.

Among pre-9/11 caregivers, civilian caregivers, and non-caregivers without a usual source of medical care, the top three reasons for not having a usual source of care were the cost of care or lack of health insurance, lack of health problems that warrant medical attention, and postponing or "not getting around to" seeking medical care. Post-9/11 military caregivers also endorsed lack of health problems that warrant medical attention and postponing or "not getting around to" seeking medical care in their top three reasons. Among post-9/11 caregivers and non-caregivers,

## Key Finding

Nearly one-third of post-9/11 military caregivers lack health care coverage, twice that of non-caregivers as well as civilian and pre-9/11 military caregivers; similar patterns emerge for not having a regular source of medical care. The leading reason for not having a regular source of care is that post-9/11 caregivers think they do not need it.

lack of need of medical care was the most commonly endorsed reason, whereas, among pre-9/11 and civilian caregivers, the cost of care or lack of health insurance was the most commonly endorsed reason. At first glance, it may seem counterintuitive that post-9/11 caregivers, who were most likely to lack health care coverage, were least likely to endorse lack of health care coverage as a reason for not having a usual source of care. However, this finding is less counterintuitive when considering that post-9/11 caregivers are relatively young and so may be least likely to have medical conditions that would prompt them to seek out a usual source of care. This explanation is consistent with the finding that lack of health problems that warrant medical attention was post-9/11 caregivers' most commonly endorsed reason for not having a usual source of care.

Perhaps because they were less likely to have health care coverage and a usual source of medical care, post-9/11 military caregivers were more likely to have visited the emergency department or urgent care clinic than their counterparts. Just over 40 percent of post-9/11 caregivers had visited the emergency room or an urgent care clinic at least once in the past year, whereas between one-fourth and one-third of pre-911 caregivers, civilian caregivers, and non-caregivers had done so. Between 14 and 20 percent of respondents in the four groups reported that their last routine medical checkup, i.e., a general physical exam, had occurred more than two years ago.

### Programs That Offer Nonstandard Health Care for Caregivers

Many spouse caregivers, particularly of those who retired from the armed forces, are insured through the DoD's TRICARE program or are eligible to receive care through the VA if they enrolled in the VA Program of Comprehensive Assistance for Family Caregivers. Nevertheless, service members and families who have not qualified for, or are in the process of qualifying for, VA benefits or who are not accessing TRICARE

**Table 3.2**
**Health Care Coverage and Utilization of Post-9/11 Caregivers, Pre-9/11 Caregivers, Civilian Caregivers, and Non-Caregivers**

| | Post-9/11 Caregivers (n = 353) | Pre-9/11 Caregivers (n = 525) | Civilian Caregivers (n = 1,828) | Non-Caregivers (n = 1,163) |
|---|---|---|---|---|
| | Percentage (SE) | | | |
| Does not have health care coverage | 32.4(6.7) | 17.6(2.4) | 22.6(1.7) | 18.6(2.1) |
| Does not have a usual source of health care | 28.2(6.2) | 12.0(2.2) | 13.7(1.4) | 13.8(1.8) |
| Reasons for no usual source of health care among those without a usual source[a] | | | | |
| Too expensive/no insurance | 7.9(3.0) | 50.3(9.8) | 47.2(5.6) | 28.3(6.2) |
| Don't need a doctor/haven't had any health care problems | 37.7(14.9) | 22.1(8.1) | 27.0(5.2) | 44.5(6.9) |
| Put it off/didn't get around to it | 23.6(10.8) | 10.3(4.0) | 13.6(3.5) | 21.7(6.1) |
| Don't know where to go | 3.2(1.7) | 9.5(7.0) | 8.2(3.0) | 4.7(2.3) |
| Previous doctor is not available/moved | 15.8(7.7) | 4.0(2.8) | 7.0(1.8) | 5.2(2.3) |
| Don't like/trust/believe in doctors | 2.9(2.3) | 1.4(1.1) | 6.5(1.9) | 2.1(1.1) |
| No care available/care too far away, not convenient | 0.25(0.26) | 4.6(3.0) | 2.5(1.3) | 0.74(0.56) |
| Other | 10.6(6.8) | 16.8(6.4) | 9.6(2.8) | 3.0(1.4) |
| Number of visits to hospital emergency room or urgent care in the past year | | | | |
| 0 | 57.5(5.6) | 70.8(2.9) | 66.9(1.8) | 72.8(2.1) |
| 1 | 12.6(4.0) | 13.8(2.1) | 17.1(1.4) | 15.3(1.7) |
| 2 or more | 29.9(4.9) | 15.4(2.4) | 16.0(1.4) | 11.9(1.6) |
| Time since last routine medical checkup | | | | |
| Less than one year | 61.2(5.6) | 73.2(2.7) | 66.2(1.8) | 67.3(2.3) |
| One year or more but less than two years | 18.9(4.0) | 12.7(2.2) | 15.2(1.3) | 14.6(1.7) |
| Two or more years ago | 20.0(4.7) | 14.1(2.0) | 18.5(1.5) | 18.1(2.0) |

NOTE: All percentages and standard errors reported in the table were estimated with post-stratification weights.

[a] For the percentages of respondents in each group who reported reasons for not having a usual source of care, the denominators (i.e., the number of respondents who reported not having a usual source of care) were: post-9/11 military caregivers (n = 63), pre-9/11 military caregivers (n = 58), civilian caregivers (n = 194), and non-caregivers (n = 128).

insurance (specifically, those in the National Guard or reserves) may be subject to a significant health care burden.

For military caregivers not covered by these health benefits, only a handful of programs offer access to health coverage outside the realm of traditional care benefits available for Americans. Four organizations identified in our environmental scan offered "nonstandard" *physical health* care or payment for care. For example, the Air Warrior Courage Foundation provides financial assistance for nonmilitary dependent caregivers and family members to obtain medical and dental care. The Patient Advocate

Foundation offers limited assistance with expenses such as medication copayments, although this assistance is designed to supplement individuals who are already insured. Military caregivers may also be able to access funds from a range of organizations that provide emergency financial assistance (as discussed later), which may then be applied to medical bills. However, emergency financial assistance programs are typically not designed to provide ongoing payment for health care.

### Mental Health

The impact of caregiving on mental health has been the subject of research for many years. The higher prevalence of depression among caregivers relative to non-caregivers was documented in a quantitative review of research on depression among caregivers of older adults and non-caregivers (i.e., meta-analysis); indeed, among other health-related and psychosocial outcomes examined, it was the outcome on which the differences between caregivers and non-caregivers were of greatest magnitude (Pinquart and Sörensen, 2003a).

According to one conceptual model, caregivers' mental health is directly affected by the stress and burden of caregiving, such as the caregiver's activity restrictions, which are in turn determined by the demands of caregiving, such as the number of ADLs and IADLs with which the caregiver provides assistance and time spent caregiving (Pearlin et al., 1990; Pearlin, 1994). Empirical research to date has provided some support for this conceptual model. For example, the demands of caregiving and caregiving stress have been shown to predict increases in depression over time (Beach et al., 2000). In addition, negative health outcomes have been much more commonly reported by military caregivers who have a higher burden of care relative to those with a lower burden of care (NAC, 2010).

Consistent with past research, our findings indicated that caregivers had higher levels of mental health problems than non-caregivers (see Figures 3.2 and 3.3). Of particular import, nearly 40 percent of post-9/11 caregivers met criteria for probable major depressive disorder (MDD). This prevalence was nearly four times higher than that of non-caregivers, whose rate of probable MDD closely resembled that of the U.S. adult general population (i.e., 10 percent).[4] Probable MDD was roughly twice as common among pre-911 caregivers and civilian caregivers as in non-caregivers. The NAC (2010) study of military caregivers found a higher prevalence of depression among military caregivers (63 percent), a discrepancy possibly due to differences in the convenience versus probabilistic sampling strategy or measures used to assess probable depression.[5]

---

[4]  In the Behavioral Risk Factor Surveillance Survey, a nationally representative study of the general U.S. population that used the same measure of depression and cutoff for determining probable MDD as this study, the rate of probable MDD was 8.6 percent (Kroenke et al., 2009).

[5]  The NAC's measure of depression consisted of a single question about whether the caregiver had experienced depression "as a result of becoming a caregiver," whereas our measure of depression, which is based on the Diagnostic and Statistical Manual of Mental Disorders (DSM-IV) diagnostic criteria for MDD, assessed the occur-

**Figure 3.2**
**Probable Major Depressive Disorder Among Post-9/11 Caregivers, Pre-9/11 Caregivers, Civilian Caregivers, and Non-Caregivers**

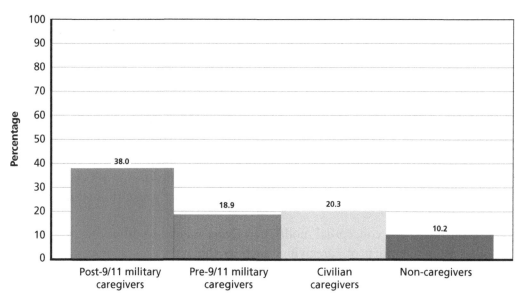

NOTE: Probable MDD was determined with a cutoff of 10 or higher on the eight-question Patient Health Questionnaire (PHQ-8) (Kroenke et al., 2009).
RAND RR499-3.2

A similar pattern of results was observed for anxiety, which was most severe among post-9/11 caregivers and least severe among non-caregivers (we do not assess probable generalized anxiety disorder, but rather present an aggregate continuous measure of anxiety symptoms). Pre-9/11 caregivers and civilian caregivers reported levels of anxiety that fell in between those of non-caregivers and post-9/11 caregivers.

We estimated regression models to test the significance of the effect of caregiver status on probable MDD and anxiety unadjusted and adjusted for sociodemographic characteristics. As shown in Table 3.3, caregiver status had a significant effect on both probable MDD and anxiety. Specifically, all three groups had significantly higher odds of probable MDD and significantly greater levels of anxiety than did non-caregivers.

Because several sociodemographic differences between the four groups described in Chapter Two may account for the observed differences in probable MDD and levels of anxiety, we compared the groups on probable MDD and anxiety while adjusting for the core set of sociodemographic characteristics. As shown in Table 3.3, differences between the three groups of caregivers and non-caregivers on probable MDD

---

rence of depressive symptoms over the past two weeks. In addition, the NAC study estimate is based on a convenience sample, and convenience samples of caregivers have been found to inflate the magnitude of problems (Pinquart and Sörensen, 2003b).

**Figure 3.3**
**Anxiety Symptoms Among Post-9/11 Caregivers, Pre-9/11 Caregivers, Civilian Caregivers, and Non-Caregivers**

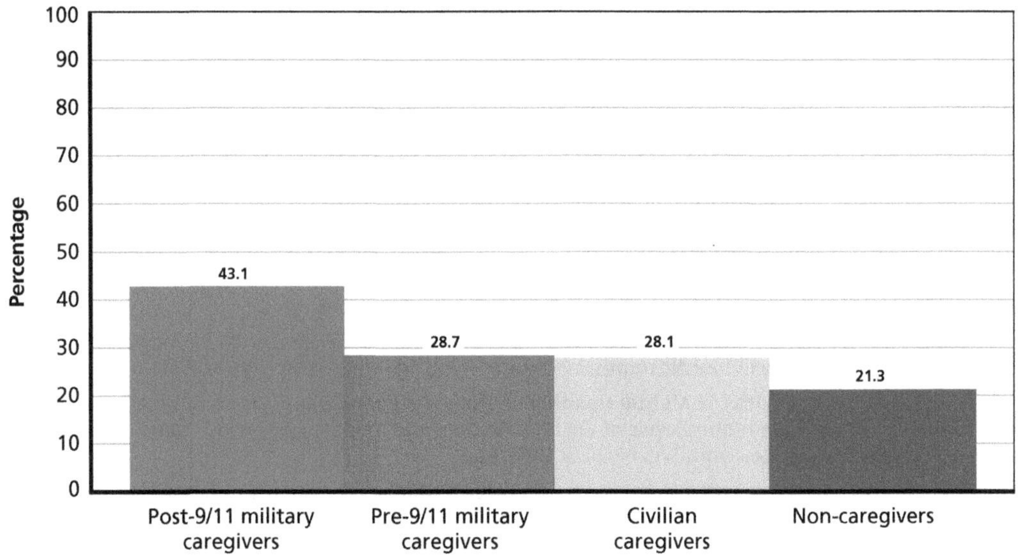

NOTE: Anxiety was measured with the Mental Health Inventory anxiety subscale, which ranges from 0 to 100. Higher scores indicate higher levels of anxiety.
RAND RR499-3.3

and anxiety persisted after adjustment for sociodemographic characteristics. Post-9/11 military caregivers had roughly five times the odds of meeting criteria for probable depression and scored an average of 19 points higher on anxiety symptoms than non-caregivers, even after accounting for sociodemographic differences; pre-9/11 military and civilian caregivers had twice the odds of meeting criteria for probable depression and scored between six and eight points higher on the anxiety scale. Thus, it appears that the observed group differences in mental health status cannot simply be attributed to sociodemographic differences among the groups.

In light of caregivers' elevated rates of probable MDD, which could not be explained by sociodemographic differences between caregivers and non-caregivers, we examined the effects of various aspects of the caregiving context on probable MDD among caregivers. We selected aspects of the caregiving context whose theoretical or empirical importance has been highlighted in past research on caregivers' mental health. These factors included characteristics of the relationship between the caregiver and care recipient likely to influence caregiving demand, such as whether the caregiver lives with the care recipient; indicators of the care recipient's severity of impairment; caregiving activities, such as time spent caregiving; and help received from other caregivers. We estimated unadjusted and adjusted models in which probable MDD was regressed on these contextual factors and the core set of caregivers' sociodemographic

**Table 3.3**
**The Effect of Caregiver Status on Probable MDD and Anxiety, Unadjusted and Adjusted for Sociodemographic Characteristics (n = 3,869)**

| Caregiver Status[c] | Probable MDD[a] | | Anxiety[b] | |
|---|---|---|---|---|
| | Unadjusted | Adjusted | Unadjusted | Adjusted |
| | OR (95% CI) | OR (95% CI) | B (SE) | B (SE) |
| Post-9/11 caregiver | 5.4(3.0, 9.6)* | 4.9(2.6, 9.3)* | 21.8(3.8)* | 18.9(3.7)* |
| Pre-9/11 caregiver | 2.0(1.3, 3.2)* | 2.2(1.4, 3.5)* | 7.4(2.0)* | 8.3(2.0)* |
| Civilian caregiver | 2.2(1.5, 3.3)* | 2.2(1.5, 3.2)* | 6.8(1.6)* | 6.4(1.6)* |
| Non-caregiver[d] | — | — | — | — |

* $p < .001$. All parameter estimates were computed with post-stratification weights. The core set of sociodemographic characteristics was included in adjusted multivariate models for probable MDD and anxiety.

[a] Probable MDD was determined with a cutoff of 10 or higher on the PHQ-8 and was modeled as a binary dependent variable in logistic regression models with SAS PROC SURVEYLOGISTIC.

[b] Anxiety was measured with the Mental Health Inventory anxiety subscale, which ranges from 0 to 100. Higher scores indicate higher levels of anxiety. Anxiety was modeled as a continuous dependent variable in regression models with SAS PROC SURVEYREG.

[c] Caregiver status was represented in the model by three dummy-coded binary indicators with non-caregivers serving as the reference category. The joint (i.e., three degrees of freedom) Wald chi-square tests of significance for the three dummy-coded indicators were significant at $p < .0001$ in unadjusted and adjusted models of probable MDD: unadjusted ($x^2 = 34.9$); adjusted ($x^2 = 27.9$). The joint F-tests for the three-dummy coded indicators were significant at $p < .001$ in unadjusted and adjusted models of anxiety: unadjusted (F[3, 3839] = 15.0); adjusted (F[3, 3826] = 13.0).

[d] Parameter estimates for the non-caregiver group were not generated because it was the reference category in regression models.

characteristics, as well as whether caregivers have children under 18 in their household. The full list of predictors and their effects on probable MDD in unadjusted and adjusted regression models are shown in Table 3.4.

Several characteristics of caregivers were significantly associated with probable MDD in unadjusted models. Higher odds of probable MDD were found among caregivers who provided care to a post-9/11 care recipient, were female and younger, had a lower level of education, lower income, and at least one child under 18 residing in their household. Aspects of the caregiver's relationship to the care recipient that indicate greater involvement in the care recipient's life, such as being the spouse or partner of the care recipient (vs. a friend, neighbor, or other nonrelative), living with the caregiver, and being the care recipient's primary caregiver, were also associated with higher odds of probable MDD.

As expected, indicators of the severity of the care recipient's injuries and impairment were significantly associated with probable MDD in unadjusted models: Higher odds of probable MDD were found among caregivers who assist care recipients who are more severely impaired in their daily functioning, have more medical conditions, and have at least one psychological or neurological condition of which behavioral problems

**Table 3.4**
**Predictors of Probable MDD Among Post-9/11 Caregivers, Pre-9/11 Caregivers, and Civilian Caregivers (n = 2,412)**

| Predictor | Unadjusted Associations OR (95% CI) | Adjusted Associations OR (95% CI) |
|---|---|---|
| Caregiver characteristics | | |
| Post-9/11 caregiver[a] (vs. civilian caregiver) | 2.40(1.45, 3.98)* | 1.81(0.96, 3.40) |
| Pre-9/11 caregiver (vs. civilian caregiver) | 0.91(0.65, 1.29) | 0.97(0.64, 1.46) |
| Sex | 0.68(0.49, 0.95)* | 0.70(0.46, 1.06) |
| Age | 0.98(0.97, 1.00)* | 0.98(0.97, 0.99)* |
| Race/ethnicity/demographic[b] | | |
| Hispanic | 1.34(0.79, 2.27) | 1.30(0.68, 2.51) |
| Non-Hispanic black | 0.54(0.32, 0.91)* | 0.53(0.29, 0.94)* |
| Non-Hispanic other | 1.05(0.46, 2.39) | 1.37(0.59, 3.20) |
| Non-Hispanic mixed race | 1.28(0.68, 2.42) | 1.06(0.48, 2.34) |
| Married or living with partner | 0.87(0.64, 1.18) | 0.92(0.61, 1.39) |
| Highest level of education | 0.85(0.73, 0.98)* | 0.85(0.72, 1.01) |
| Household income | 0.95(0.92, 0.98)* | 0.96(0.92, 1.00)* |
| Household size | 0.99(0.90, 1.08) | 0.82(0.71, 0.95)* |
| Residence in major metropolitan area | 0.91(0.60, 1.39) | 1.08(0.68, 1.72) |
| Children under 18 in household | 1.48(1.06, 2.06)* | 1.40(0.90, 2.18) |
| History of military service[c] | 1.31(0.84, 2.04) | 1.76(1.03, 3.02) |
| Relationship between caregiver and care recipient | | |
| Romantic partner (vs. nonrelative)[d] | 2.57(1.58, 4.18)* | 1.52(0.74, 3.12) |
| Family member (vs. nonrelative) | 1.40(0.90, 2.18) | 1.46(0.85, 2.50) |
| Live together | 1.91(1.41, 2.60)* | 1.06(0.67, 1.68) |
| Primary caregiver | 1.67(1.24, 2.25)* | 1.51(0.95, 2.40) |
| Degree and type of care recipient's disability[e] | | |
| Severity of impairment | 1.02(1.01, 1.04)* | 1.02(0.99, 1.04) |

**Table 3.4, cont.**

| Predictor | Unadjusted Associations OR (95% CI) | Adjusted Associations OR (95% CI) |
|---|---|---|
| Total number of medical conditions | 1.21(1.13, 1.29)* | 1.08(1.00, 1.16) |
| Psychological or neurological condition (incl. TBI) | 2.24(1.59, 3.15)* | 1.35(0.90, 2.01) |
| Caregiving activities | | |
| Time spent caregiving | 1.23(1.15, 1.31)* | 1.18(1.06, 1.30)* |
| Time since became caregiver | 1.07(0.95, 1.20) | 0.98(0.84, 1.15) |
| Number of ADLs with which caregiver helps | 1.07(1.00, 1.15) | 0.93(0.83, 1.04) |
| Number of IADLs with which caregiver helps | 1.05(0.99, 1.11) | 0.94(0.86, 1.02) |
| Helps care recipient cope with stressful situations or avoid "triggers" of anxiety or antisocial behavior | 2.37(1.69, 3.32)* | 1.51(1.02, 2.22)* |
| Help from other caregivers | | |
| Number of other caregivers | 0.96(0.87, 1.07) | 1.13(0.99, 1.29) |
| Time spent by other caregivers | 1.00(1.00, 1.01) | 1.00(1.00, 1.01) |

NOTE: Logistic regression models were estimated with post-stratification weights.

[a] Caregiver status was represented by two dummy-coded indicators for post-9/11 and pre-9/11 caregivers, with civilian caregivers as the reference category. The two degree-of-freedom Wald chi-square tests for the two dummy coded indicators was significant at p < .05 only in the unadjusted model: $x^2$ = 12.87.

[b] Race/ethnicity was represented by four dummy-coded indicators, with non-Hispanic white as the reference category. Although the binary indicator for non-Hispanic black race/ethnicity was significant at p < .05 in unadjusted and adjusted models, we did not interpret this because the joint degree of freedom test for race/ethnicity was not significant in either the unadjusted or the adjusted model.

[c] Caregiver's history of military service was significant in unimputed adjusted models, but because it was not significant in the imputed model and had a very small magnitude of effect, we did not interpret it as significant.

[d] Type of relationship between the caregiver and care recipient was represented by two dummy-coded indicators for spouse or partner and other family member, with nonrelatives (e.g., friends and neighbors) as the reference category. The two degree-of-freedom Wald chi-square test for the two dummy-coded indicators was significant at p < .05 only in the unadjusted model: $x^2$ = 17.89.

[e] Severity of the care recipient's impairment was assessed with the WHODAS-2. Psychological or neurological condition was a binary indicator for TBI, dementia, PTSD, depression, or substance use vs. none of these.

are a hallmark characteristic (e.g., TBI, dementia, PTSD, depression, or substance use). Finally, caregiving demands, such as time spent caregiving and helping the care recipient cope with behavioral problems, were also significantly associated with probable MDD.

Many of the characteristics and experiences that were significant in unadjusted models ceased to be significant in the adjusted multivariate model, including caregiver status. The following characteristics of caregivers continued to predict greater odds of probable MDD: younger age, non-Hispanic white race/ethnicity, and lower household income. Lower household size, which was not significant in unadjusted models, became a significant predictor of greater odds of probable MDD in the adjusted model. The key aspects of the caregiving context that predicted greater odds of probable MDD were the amount of time spent caregiving and helping the care recipient cope with behavioral problems. Both of these aspects of the caregiving context may be particularly challenging for caregivers to navigate, thereby increasing the stress and strain of caregiving and precipitating depression. Caregivers who face these challenges may require more support and resources to help them cope with the medical comorbidities of their care recipients, reduce time spent caregiving, and effectively respond to the behavioral symptoms of their care recipients.

## Key Finding

The elevated proportion of post-9/11 military caregivers with depression may be accounted for by the time this group spends caregiving and helping care recipients cope with stressful situations or avoid triggers of anxiety or antisocial behavior.

### Mental Health Care Utilization

We also asked about the receipt of specialty mental health care in the past year, i.e., whether the respondent had "seen or talked to a mental health professional such as a psychiatrist, psychologist, psychiatric nurse, or clinical social worker." The services received from a mental health professional include the prescription of psychotropic medication, provision of psychotherapy ("talk" therapy) or counseling, or both. As shown in Table 3.5, roughly 30 percent of post-9/11 caregivers have seen a mental health specialist, making this group nearly four times more likely than non-caregivers and roughly twice as likely as civilian and pre-9/11 military caregivers to have accessed this care. Roughly 15 percent of pre-9/11 military and civilian caregivers had seen a mental health specialist, making them 1.5 to 2 times as likely as non-caregivers to have received this care. In a separate question, caregivers were asked about their receipt of psychological counseling from a "trained health care professional" in the past year.[6]

---

[6] Data on this survey item are not available for non-caregivers because it was included in a series of questions designed to provide information about resources used by caregivers.

## Key Finding

Roughly two-thirds of caregivers with probable depression have not received care from a mental health professional in the past year; over 80 percent of those who have sought care have found such care to be helpful.

The proportions of both groups of military caregivers and civilian caregivers who had received psychological counseling in the past year were very similar to the proportions who reported having received specialty mental health care, which includes but is not limited to counseling.[7] In all three groups of caregivers, at least 80 percent of respondents rated the counseling they had received as "somewhat helpful" or "very helpful."

Respondents who reported having seen a mental health professional were asked how many visits they had made to a mental health professional in the past year. Among recipients of mental health services, post-9/11 caregivers appear to be getting a higher "dose" of mental health treatment than the other groups. Of those who had seen a mental health professional, a little over 40 percent of post-9/11 caregivers listed at least eight visits, whereas roughly 25 percent of pre-9/11 caregivers, civilian caregivers, and non-caregivers reported at least eight visits (see Table 3.5).

To gauge unmet need for mental health services, we examined mental health service utilization among the subgroup of respondents who met criteria for probable MDD. Among these respondents, rates of mental health services utilization were higher than when considered among all caregivers in all groups except for post-9/11 caregivers. However, across the four groups, at least two-thirds of respondents with probable MDD reported not having received mental health services in the past year. While it is possible that some of these respondents had only recently developed depressive symptoms and had not yet had an opportunity to pursue treatment, these findings suggest that many respondents in need of mental health services may not be receiving them.

### Programs That Offer Nonstandard Mental Health Care for Caregivers

For mental health care needs specifically, services may be available to caregivers (depending on their eligibility) at Vet Centers, at VA medical centers, and through linkage to community resources if they are part of the VA Program of Comprehensive Assistance for Family Caregivers. In addition to the VA services, 12 organizations

---

[7] Although it might be expected that the respondents who reported having received psychological counseling in the past year would be a subset of those who had received any type of mental health care from a mental health professional, this was not the case: Of the 2,713 military and civilian caregivers, there were 68 (2.51 percent) who reported having received psychological counseling from a "trained health care professional" and who reported not having seen or talked to a mental health professional in the past year. We believe this is likely due to respondents interpreting "trained health care professionals" to include health care professionals who are not mental health care specialists, e.g., primary care providers.

**Table 3.5**
**Mental Health Care Utilization of Post-9/11 Caregivers, Pre-9/11 Caregivers, Civilian Caregivers, and Non-Caregivers**

| | Post-9/11 Caregivers (n = 353) | Pre-9/11 Caregivers (n = 525) | Civilian Caregivers (n = 1,828) | Non-Caregivers (n = 1,163) |
|---|---|---|---|---|
| | Percent (SE) | | | |
| | **All Respondents** | | | |
| Received care from a mental health professional in past year | 30.8(5.0) | 14.5(2.2) | 15.4(1.3) | 8.0(1.4) |
| Number of visits to mental health professional in past year out of those who received care[a] | | | | |
| 1–3 | 33.4(7.9) | 56.5(8.3) | 37.8(4.4) | 35.2(8.5) |
| 4–7 | 23.4(6.4) | 22.4(6.6) | 35.0(4.5) | 36.2(9.1) |
| 8 or more | 43.3(9.8) | 21.2(6.9) | 27.1(4.0) | 28.6(8.0) |
| Received psychological counseling from a trained health care professional in the past year[b] | 29.5(5.2) | 14.4(2.4) | 13.0(1.3) | -- |
| Counseling somewhat or very helpful[c] | 84.1(6.9) | 94.0(4.8) | 94.2(1.9) | -- |
| | **Respondents with Probable MDD** | | | |
| Received care from a mental health professional in past year | 32.9(7.5) | 34.6(6.9) | 30.4(3.7) | 19.4(6.4) |
| Number of visits to mental health professional in past year out of those who received care[d] | | | | |
| 1-3 | 31.9(8.6) | 48.8(13.6) | 26.1(6.5) | 40.7(17.3) |
| 4-7 | 27.6(9.4) | 21.3(10.5) | 36.9(7.4) | 41.2(20.1) |
| 8 or more | 40.5(9.5) | 29.9(13.3) | 37.0(7.3) | 18.1(9.6) |
| Received psychological counseling from a trained health care professional in past year[b] | 47.8(9.6) | 25.1(6.0) | 27.6(3.7) | -- |
| Counseling somewhat or very helpful[e] | 85.2(7.8) | 96.1(3.9) | 90.6(4.1) | -- |

[a] For number of visits to mental health professional in past year among respondents who had received care, the denominators (i.e., number of respondents who had received care) for each group were: post-9/11 military caregivers (n = 140), pre-9/11 military caregivers (n = 76), civilian caregivers (n = 283), non-caregivers (n = 87).

[b] Data on this survey item are not available for non-caregivers because it was included in a series of questions designed to provide information about resources used by caregivers.

[c] For helpfulness of psychological counseling received in the past year among respondents who had received psychological counseling, the denominators (i.e., number of respondents who had received counseling) for each group were: post-9/11 caregivers (n = 129), pre-9/11 caregivers (n = 68), civilian caregivers (n = 240).

[d] Denominators (i.e., number of respondents with probable MDD who had received care) for each group were: post-9/11 caregivers (n = 67), pre-9/11 caregivers (n = 27), civilian caregivers (n = 102), non-caregivers (n = 21).

[e] Denominators (i.e., number of respondents with probable MDD who had received counseling) for each group were: post-9/11 caregivers (n = 68), pre-9/11 caregivers (n = 25), civilian caregivers (n = 94).

identified in the environmental scan provide or pay for mental health care for military caregivers. Organizations such as Give an Hour and The Soldier's Project link family members and loved ones with private therapists in their region who volunteer their time and expertise. Similarly, The Camaraderie Foundation and Courage Beyond offer

**Key Finding**

Twelve organizations identified in the environmental scan provide or pay for *mental health* care for military caregivers.

financial assistance to qualified military family members or caregivers to pay for private therapy sessions. Organizations such as the Armed Services YMCA, FCA, Strategic Outreach to Families of All Reservists, and Military and Family Life Consultant Joint Family Support Assistance Program also offer payment for counseling services, but these services tend to be limited by factors such as geographic location (see the "Geographic Availability of Caregiver Support" box) and population served, or the type of counseling offered (e.g., nonmedical counseling only). Moreover, many organizations facilitating access to mental health care are designed to supplement the mental health benefits offered by DoD or the VA, and thus offer a limited number of counseling sessions.

### Self-Reported Effects of Caregiving

Military and civilian caregivers were asked about the negative and positive effects of caregiving. To assess the negative effects of caregiving, respondents reviewed a variety of ways in which caregiving may have adversely affected their lives and endorsed those who applied to them.

Figure 3.4 displays the items on this list and their rates of endorsement by post-9/11 military caregivers, pre-9/11 military caregivers, and civilian caregivers. Across the areas of impact assessed, rates of endorsement ranged from a high of 65 percent (emotional adjustments reported among post-9/11 military caregivers) to 32 percent (being confined, e.g., caregiving restricts free time or visiting with family and friends, reported among post-9/11 military caregivers). In addition to experiencing emotional adjustments, more than half of post-9/11 caregivers reported changes in personal plans (62 percent) and being upset by the care recipient's behavior (55 percent). Changes in personal plans and changes from the care recipient's former self were the two most commonly endorsed effects among pre-9/11 military and civilian caregivers, with nearly half of each group endorsing each of these (changes in personal plans: 48 percent of pre-9/11 military caregivers, 47 percent of civilian caregivers; changes from the care recipient's former self: 48 percent for both pre-9/11 military and civilian caregivers).

In addition to the mental and physical burden of caregiving, caregivers may derive psychological benefits from the care they provide. Caregivers may develop pride in their ability to navigate the challenges of caregiving or feel a greater sense of purpose and meaning from helping someone else (Kramer, 1997). Positive health effects of providing care to a disabled spouse over the age of 65 have been documented in a longitudinal study of caregivers in which increases in help provided over time predicted decreases in anxiety and depression (Beach et al., 2000). To assess positive psychological benefits of caregiving, caregiver respondents were

## Geographic Availability of Caregiver Support

Most of the programs for military caregivers are either national in scope or national with local offices, branches, or events. The latter reflect national programs that have a distinct and localized presence in selected communities across the country. Often these programs tailor services to the needs of these local communities. Some programs have international scopes and serve service members, veterans, and their families and caregivers when overseas, which can be especially helpful given the added stresses that are sometimes associated with living abroad. Many of the programs with local offices, branches, or events offer in-person services like mental health care, structured training and education, and structured social support activities. Many internationally and nationally focused programs also offer in-person services, and many are able to reach a wider geographically located population by leveraging the Internet to provide services online. For example, many programs use webinars and Skype to provide training and mental health services to caregivers from the comfort of their homes.

The smallest group of programs is locally focused. These localities vary in size from regions to states to counties: for example, the Virginia Wounded Warrior program only serves Virginia residents, and the Wounded Heroes Fund only serves veterans in Kern County, California.

**Figure 3.4**
**Adverse Impacts of Caregiving Self-Reported by Post-9/11 Military Caregivers, Pre-9/11 Military Caregivers, and Civilian Caregivers**

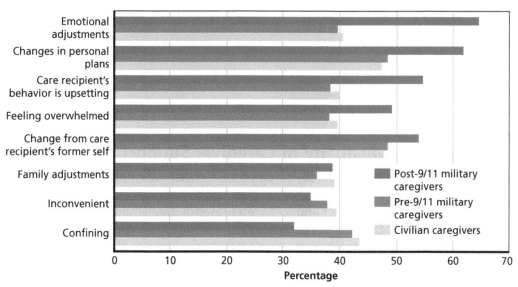

RAND RR499-3.4

asked four questions about how much they had benefited psychologically and experienced personal growth as a result of being a caregiver. On a scale that ranged from 4 to 16, where higher scores indicate higher levels of self-perceived personal growth from caregiving, all three groups of caregivers reported similar levels of personal growth on average: post-9/11 caregivers (M = 12.0, SE = 0.32), pre-9/11 caregivers (M = 11.4, SE = 0.23) and civilian caregivers (M = 11.0, SE = 0.14). Thus, in general, caregivers in the current study did report psychological benefits from serving as caregivers.

## Other Programs to Address Caregiver Health and Well-Being

We described the nonstandard clinical health and mental health care available to military caregivers in previous sections. A range of other services are available to support the overall health and well-being of military caregivers (not specific to addressing particular problems) as well. These include providing respite care, structured social support, and structured wellness activities for caregivers. Caregivers may also benefit from a range of referral sources designed to aid them in identifying organizations that provide these various services. The number of programs identified in our environmental scan that offer these services is shown in Table 3.6.

Table 3.6
**Services to Address Caregiver Well-Being**

| Resources to Assist in Providing Better Care | Total Programs |
| --- | --- |
| Respite care | 9 |
| Structured social support | 53 |
| Structured wellness activities | 21 |

### Respite Care

Respite care, defined as short-term, temporary relief during which a trained individual tends to the individual for whom the caregiver is caring, can be a critical service. It permits caregivers to dedicate time to themselves and tend to their own needs. Respite care has typically been defined to include a range of services that allow for "the temporary provision of care for a person with" a disability "at home or in an institution by people other than the primary caregiver" (Lee and Cameron, 2004). This care may be provided in a "center-based day program;" care recipients are transported to and cared for at a location away from home for a few hours at a time. Respite care may also be provided in the care recipient's home with or without the primary caregiver present, or in an institution for an extended period of time (e.g., while the primary caregiver goes away on vacation) (Gottlieb and Johnson, 2000).

In general, studies have found that uptake of respite care tends to be relatively low. Past studies of caregivers have found that roughly 10 to 15 percent of caregivers use respite care (NAC, 2010; NAC and AARP, 2004; Alzheimer's Association and NAC, 2004). One review of respite care for caregivers of care recipients with dementia found that between one-third and one-half of caregivers decline respite care when it is offered to them (Gottlieb and Johnson, 2000). Our study indicates that a much greater proportion of caregivers—27 percent—have used formal or informal respite care services. In our survey, after adjusting for sociodemographic differences between groups, the proportion of caregivers using these services did not significantly differ between pre-9/11, post-9/11, and civilian caregivers.

Although roughly a quarter of military caregivers use respite care, such offerings are seldom offered by the organizations identified in our environmental scan. Only nine organizations provide such assistance. This excludes programs providing wellness services such as trips to day spas or retreats, which are sometimes broadly or inaccurately termed "respite;" such activities were only included in our definition of respite care if they specifically provided respite care *in addition to* these other services. Our definition here is consistent with the VA's definition of respite care (VA, 2013c)

The VA Caregiver Support Program is one example of a program that provides respite care. The program offers an array of respite care services, including up to 30 days of respite care per year. VA respite care is offered in a range of settings, both in and out of the home. For example, the VA's Homemaker and Home Health Aide Program

## Respite Care: The Evidence

**Overview:** Although there is some tentative support for the notion that respite care benefits caregivers' well-being, the poor quality of the studies conducted to date makes it difficult to draw firm conclusions regarding the efficacy of respite care.

**The Evidence:** For caregivers of those with dementia, care offered at center-based programs has been shown to decrease caregivers' subjective burden in a few studies (Cox, 1997; Kosloski and Montgomery, 1993; Montgomery and Borgatta, 1989). Positive effects of respite care on caregivers in the form of reductions in worry/strain, overload, depressive affect, and anger were found in one of the more rigorously designed studies; caregivers for people with dementia who used center-based day programs at least twice a week for three and 12 months were compared with a matched control group (Zarit et al., 1998). However, null effects of respite care provided at center-based programs on depression of caregivers of people with dementia were reported in other studies (Cox, 1997; Gottlieb and Johnson, 2000; Lawton, Brody, and Saperstein, 1989). Moreover, enthusiasm for the observed benefits of respite care on caregivers must be tempered by the small magnitude of effects in the few studies that have documented statistically significant, positive effects of respite care on caregiving (Gottlieb and Johnson, 2000). Similarly, respite care has evidenced beneficial effects of small magnitude on burden, mental health, and physical health of caregivers of frail older people, which includes but is not limited to older people with dementia (Mason et al., 2007; Shaw et al., 2009).

**Limitations:** Most of the extant research on respite care has been conducted on caregivers of older care recipients who are frail (i.e., in poor health) and/or have dementia. There is scant research on caregivers of care recipients with severe mental illness, despite recognition of the importance of studying the unique respite needs of this population (Jeon, Brodaty, and Chesterton, 2005). There is consensus that the field suffers from a deficit of rigorous studies assessing the effects of respite care on the well-being of caregivers and care recipients (Gottlieb and Johnson, 2000; Jeon, Brodaty, and Chesterton, 2005; Lee and Cameron, 2004; Mason et al., 2007; McNally, Ben-Shlomo, and Newman, 1999; Shaw et al., 2009).

provides home health aides to visit the veteran and assist with personal care needs like bathing and dressing, and the Skilled Home Care service arranges for in-home medical professionals who care for *homebound* veterans. Similarly, the VA Home Hospice Care program provides in-home respite care during the advanced stages of a veteran's terminal disease. Finally, the VA Adult Day Health Care Centers provide a social environment for veterans outside the home, while facilitating an opportunity for caregiver respite.

A small handful of other organizations offer respite care for veterans and their families. Notably, Easter Seals operates the Legacy Corps program in conjunction with AmeriCorps and the University of Maryland. Legacy Corps trains AmeriCorps volunteers to provide respite care and then arranges for the care to be offered to military service members, veterans, and their families. Similarly, FCA offers short-term respite grants, awarded through direct pay to the caregiver or through contracts with home care agencies. Moreover, the military's various "Wounded Warrior" programs, which focus on coordinating nonmedical care and assistance for wounded service members and their families, may aid service members or family members in arranging respite care, although they do not provide the care directly.

Still other organizations offer respite care, but in ways that may be of limited use to military caregivers. For example, some programs appear to be small in scope or focused on specific segments of the caregiving population such as individuals caring for senior citizens (for example, Home Instead Senior Care). Moreover, some programs offer respite care *incidentally* while providing other services to veterans and their families. For example, Hope for the Warriors offers a program that allows family members alongside service members in recovery to undergo therapy while respite care is provided. Similarly, WWP's Independence Program provides in-home physical therapy for severely injured veterans, and this can serve as respite for the caregiver while the veteran receives care. Some organizations provide emergency financial assistance that can be used to pay for respite care (see section titled "A Helping Hand").

### Structured Social Support

Social support can be a critical need of many military caregivers (Tanielian et al., 2013; NAC 2006) and comes in an array of forms. In this section, our focus is structured social support: organized in-person or online support that is likely to assist with caregiving-specific stresses or challenges. After adjustment for sociodemographic differences among the groups, significantly more post-9/11 caregivers indicated that they participated in structured social support groups in the past year than did pre-9/11 and civilian caregivers (24 percent vs. 5 and 8 percent, respectively). Civilian caregivers did not significantly differ from pre-9/11 caregivers in their participation in structured social support groups. However, among caregivers who did participate in structured social support groups in the past year, pre-9/11 caregivers rated them as significantly

## Structured Social Support: The Evidence

**Overview:** Structured support groups for caregivers of persons with dementia are effective, salient characteristics of more-effective groups have been identified; less is known about the effectiveness of other caregiver support groups.

**The Evidence:** A recent meta-analysis examined the effectiveness of social support groups for caregivers of people with dementia (Chien et al., 2011). Data combined across 30 studies indicate that there are observed effects of social support on caregivers' psychological well-being, depression symptoms, caregiver burden, and social outcomes, though the magnitude of effect is attenuated over time. Characteristics of the type of structured support (use of theoretical models and manuals, psychoeducational groups, length of group sessions, group sizes of six to ten members) and of care recipients (mild dementia) were associated with stronger effects. A review of 25 studies on support groups for family members of people with psychotic disorders (Chien et al., 2009) finds consistent evidence of effects on knowledge, burden, distress, and coping, though primarily immediately after the intervention ends or in the year following.

**Limitations:** Like respite and caregiver training, most of the extant research on caregiver structured social support has been conducted on caregivers of older care recipients with dementia. Studies of caregivers of people with mental illness are scant and of general poor quality; they tend to lack rigorous control groups, use inconsistent outcome measures, and do not examine long-term outcomes.

more helpful than did post-9/11 or civilian caregivers. Ratings by post-9/11 caregivers and civilian caregivers did not significantly differ.

Overall, numerous organizations offer structured social support to military caregivers; 53 of the 120 organizational entities identified in our environmental scan provide such support. This includes organizations such as American Veterans with Brain Injuries, which offers online peer support groups for family members or caregivers of veterans with brain injuries; USO, which hosts Caregiver Conferences at locations across the country; the VA Peer Support Mentoring Program, which matches new caregivers with more experienced caregivers and hosts caregiver and family support groups at VA medical centers; and WWP, which provides all-expense-paid one-day Family Support Retreats for military families at locations around the country.

Social support for caregivers varies greatly in its mode of delivery—that is, whether services are offered in person or online. Figure 3.5 illustrates the percentage of programs by mode of delivery. Of the organizational entities offering social support, just over half do so in person, while 26 percent offer services in person *and* online. In some instances, online services are in place for caregivers to obtain follow-up support after or in conjunction with in-person meetings; in other instances, organizations offer two entirely different social support services.

Organizations also differ greatly in their frequency, as shown in Figure 3.6. Some social groups gather weekly, while others gather annually and allow for ad hoc socializing in the interim period. For example, the Well Spouse Association offers a range

**Figure 3.5**
**Structured Social Support by Mode of Delivery (n = 39)**

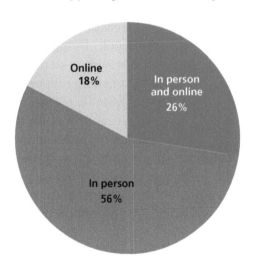

NOTE: Percentages reflect only the programs we interviewed that provided social support (n = 39). We were unable to ascertain reliable data on mode of delivery for programs that we did not interview.
RAND RR499-3.5

**Figure 3.6**
**Structured, In-Person Social Support by Frequency of**
**Delivery (n = 21)**

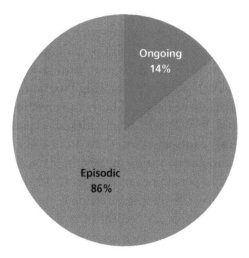

NOTE: Percentages reflect only the programs we interviewed
that provided in-person social support and not online social
support (n = 21). We were unable to ascertain reliable data
on mode of delivery for programs that we did not interview.
RAND *RR499-3.6*

of *ongoing* online, telephone, and in-person support. In contrast, organizations such as
the Explosive Ordnance Disposal (EOD) Warrior Foundation and Wounded Warriors
Family Support offer in-person caregiver retreats and events that are held *episodically*
(e.g., annually or occasionally throughout the year). Many organizations offering episodic social support services noted that caregivers often stay in touch informally after
retreats or events, either via email or Facebook. In total, more than three-fourths of
the programs interviewed in our scan that provide in-person structured social support
do so episodically; only three of 21 provide ongoing support. Despite the potential for
caregivers to form lasting relationships at episodic events, it is unclear whether this
social support is indeed likely to have a lasting impact on the daily lives of caregivers. Further, much of the episodic social support included in our environmental scan
requires caregivers (and sometimes care recipients) to travel away from their homes,
and at times long distances. Focus group research has suggested that caregivers may
face difficulty taking time away from their care recipient to attend such events (Tanielian et al., 2013). Thus, the practicality and effectiveness of this type of social support
is questionable.

More generally, it is not clear how well these various social support programs
reach their targeted populations, and evidence is lacking regarding the efficacy of these
programs. It is not evident whether characteristics such as mode of delivery have a
bearing on positive outcomes for caregivers. For example, it is unknown whether in-

person social support, as a whole, is more or less beneficial to military caregivers than online social support. Similarly, it is unknown whether active chats are more or less beneficial than passive chats or message boards, which are likely to be less intensive but used at the caregiver's leisure rather than at specific times.

### Structured Wellness Activities

Caregivers may benefit from a range of wellness activities, defined as organized services such as fitness classes, stress relief lessons, or outdoor physical activities that focus on improving mental or physical well-being. Twenty-one organizations identified in the environmental scan provide such activities, and among these organizations there exist 23 different wellness activities (as some organizations offered more than one type of service). Wellness activities, if efficacious, may help to allay the reductions in physical activity and healthy behaviors that caregivers often experience. Overall, 25 percent of caregivers indicated that, in the past year, they participated in structured wellness activities for themselves. Controlling for sociodemographic differences between groups, the proportion of caregivers participating in these activities did not significantly differ between pre-9/11, post-9/11, and civilian caregivers.

To provide a useful overview of these activities, we divided them based on two dimensions as shown in Table 3.7: (1) target population (i.e., caregiver focus vs. caregiver and service member/veteran focus) and (2) frequency (i.e., episodic vs. ongoing). Such a classification helps us to understand which are likely to help the caregiver individually vs. the caregiver and service member or veteran as a family unit. It also aids in understanding which services may be available on an ongoing or regular basis. In this subsection, we discuss the eight activities focused only on the caregivers themselves— that is, those services represented in the upper row of Table 3.7. In a subsequent subsection titled "Programs to Address Caregiver Family Well-Being," we discuss services focused on caregivers and veterans or service members.

Among these six programs, one is "ongoing," which provides services at multiple or regular intervals throughout the year. Specifically, Cause offers massage, Reiki, and reflexology services to family members (as well as veterans and service members sepa-

**Table 3.7**
**Structured Wellness Activities by Population of Focus and Frequency (n=18)**

| Population of Focus | Frequency of Service | | |
|---|---|---|---|
| | Episodic | Ongoing | Total |
| Caregiver | 4 | 1 | 5 |
| Caregiver *and* service member or veteran | 12 | 1 | 13 |
| Total | 16 | 2 | |

NOTE: This table includes only wellness activities offered by programs that were interviewed (n=18 activities offered by 16 organizations), since we were not able to determine information on frequency of service for programs that were not interviewed (n=5 activities offered by 5 organizations).

rately). However, the important fact here is that all Cause services are clustered around DoD or VA installations or health care treatment facilities, largely near Washington, D.C., and in Texas. Thus, we are aware of few ongoing wellness activities targeted specifically toward caregivers in other locations. That said, caregivers may engage in wellness services at local recreational centers or churches, but these organizations may not address the needs of caregivers specifically (and thus were not in the purview of our environmental scan).

As with *ongoing* wellness activities specifically for caregivers, five wellness activities are offered on an *episodic* basis. Most often, these activities occur during annual or occasional retreats or conferences for caregivers or family members. These include weekend retreats offered by the Well Spouse Association, day retreats offered by the Semper Fi Fund, the twice-annual conference hosted by USO, and three-day small group retreats offered by Courage Beyond, as well as activities offered by the USO Warrior and Family Care and Armed Services YMCA. The wellness activities at these events vary widely, but may include spa visits, journaling sessions, yoga, or other activities. The practicality and effectiveness of these wellness activities overall is not well known, since many of the assessments conducted by these organizations are informal or lack rigor. In general, increasing physical activity and healthy behaviors among caregivers has been found to be challenging, particularly among caregivers with high levels of burden (e.g., Mochari-Greenberger and Mosca, 2012; Rone-Adams, Stern, and Walker, 2004).

### Referral Services for Caregivers

Important to the issue of service availability is the issue of how caregivers identify services. Several resources are available to assist caregivers in locating the best services to meet their needs. Although the primary aim of our environmental scan was to identify "common caregiving services" such as respite and social support, we incidentally captured information about the breadth of available resource directories and referral services. One primary source of referral for military caregivers is the VA Caregiver Support Coordinators, who match caregivers with eligible services and provide information about caregiver resources. In addition, the National Resource Directory and DoD Office of Warrior Care Policy publish online and print versions of "Family and Caregiver Support" resources that are likely to be helpful to military caregivers. In addition, military referral hotlines such as Military OneSource, Army OneSource, and DSTRESS are possible referral sources for military caregivers.

A range of nonprofit and community organizations provide resource lists and referral services. These sources for referral vary substantially in their intensity and probable usefulness to military caregivers. For example, some offer in-person or telephone assistance along with a "warm hand-off" to appropriate service providers. Conversely, some simply offer a small list (via a website or printed materials) of known service-providing organizations. Other organizations offer referrals incidentally, as they provide services to caregivers and realize that caregivers have needs beyond what their own organization can offer. A full list of organizations that offer resource lists or referral services is included in Appendix E.

Overall, 11 percent of caregivers indicated that, in the past year, they used a referral service for finding programs to help their care recipient; an equal proportion reported using a referral service for finding programs to help with caregiving challenges. A much greater proportion (46 percent) of caregivers indicated that, in the past year, they used informal sources of information to help meet the challenges of caregiving. Controlling for sociodemographic differences among the groups, the proportion of caregivers using either a referral source or informal sources of information did not significantly differ between pre-9/11, post-9/11, and civilian caregivers.

## Family Relationships and Roles of Military Caregivers

The relationship that caregivers have with their care recipients, as well as the caregivers' and care recipients' marital status, are important aspects of the caregiving context. As noted in Chapter Two, the types of services and programs that caregivers can utilize often depend on their relationship with their care recipients. In addition, romantic relationships provide caregivers with a source of stability and social support that has been shown to help them deal with the stress of providing care (Pinquart and Sörensen, 2003a) and can help care recipients lead healthier lives (Cohen and Wills, 1985; Uchino, 2006).

As shown in Table 3.8, a higher percentage (37 percent) of post-9/11 caregivers are in a romantic relationship (i.e., married, partner, or significant other) with their care recipient than are pre-9/11 (20 percent) and civilian (16 percent) caregivers. Among *caregivers* not in a romantic relationship with the care recipient, roughly two-thirds were in a romantic relationship, with no differences between groups after controlling for sociodemographic differences between them.

Among *care recipients* not married to their caregivers, 55 percent of post-9/11 and 51 percent of pre-9/11 caregivers were in a romantic relationship, a difference that was not statistically significant. On the other hand, both were more likely to be in a romantic relationship than civilian care recipients, of whom 31 percent were currently in a relationship and 34 percent were widowed.

### Relationship Quality

Although relationships are important for the well-being of caregivers and care recipients, it is easy to imagine how providing care for a friend or loved one might place a strain on the relationship. Caregivers and care recipients may have to take on new roles that change the relationship dynamic—e.g., from partner to sole breadwinner, from friends to care provider and recipient (Archbold et al., 1990)—and the care recipi-

Table 3.8
Caregiver and Care Recipient Marital Status

| | Post-9/11 Military Caregivers | | Pre-9/11 Military Caregivers | | Civilian Caregivers | |
|---|---|---|---|---|---|---|
| | % | SE | % | SE | % | SE |
| Caregiver is care recipient's spouse, partner, or significant other | 37.3 | 5.0 | 19.6 | 2.4 | 15.7 | 1.2 |
| Caregiver is something other than care recipient's spouse, partner, or significant other | 62.7 | 5.0 | 80.4 | 2.4 | 84.3 | 1.2 |
| Caregiver marital status[a] | | | | | | |
| Married/living with partner | 71.2 | 6.1 | 65.9 | 2.9 | 60.9 | 1.8 |
| Widowed | 0.2 | 0.1 | 5.8 | 1.3 | 4.3 | 0.6 |
| Divorced | 5.3 | 1.4 | 11.9 | 1.9 | 11.8 | 1.1 |
| Separated | 7.3 | 4.1 | 1.3 | 0.5 | 3.5 | 0.7 |
| Never married | 16.0 | 5.6 | 15.1 | 2.2 | 19.5 | 1.6 |
| Care recipient marital status[a] | | | | | | |
| Married/living with partner | 54.7 | 5.2 | 51.1 | 2.8 | 30.6 | 1.7 |
| Widowed | 0.8 | 0.6 | 24.4 | 2.4 | 33.7 | 1.7 |
| Divorced | 4.8 | 1.2 | 15.1 | 2.0 | 13.7 | 1.3 |
| Separated | 4.4 | 3.1 | 0.7 | 0.3 | 2.3 | 0.7 |
| Never married | 35.3 | 5.1 | 8.6 | 1.7 | 19.7 | 1.5 |

a Among caregivers/care recipients who are not spouses, partners, or significant others.

ents' illness or injury itself may place stress on the relationship—e.g., post-deployment PTSD (Negrusa and Negrusa, 2012).

We compare the relationship quality of military and civilian caregivers and recipients who are romantically involved with that of non-caregivers in romantic relationships (i.e., with their spouse or partner). We also describe the quality of relationships between military and civilian caregivers and recipients who are not in romantic relationships (e.g., friends, child-parent relationships). In research with civilian non-caregivers, relationship quality has been shown to be a reliable predictor of divorce/separation among romantic partners (Karney and Bradbury, 1995) and spouses whose partners experience declining health are less satisfied with their marriages and more likely to consider divorce (Booth and Johnson, 1994). Previous research found that military caregivers reported that caregiving placed a strain on their relationship with the care recipient (NAC, 2010), but it is unclear from these findings whether the quality of relationships between military caregivers and their care recipient spouses/partners is actually different from the relationships of similar non-caregivers.

We examined relationship quality among all caregivers whose care recipient was their spouse, partner, or significant other, and compared caregiver-care recipient romantic relationship quality to that of non-caregivers in romantic relationships.

Relationship quality was measured with seven items that assess different aspects of the relationship, including how well the spouse/partner meets the respondent's needs, how much the relationship met the respondent's original expectations, and how satisfied the respondent is with the relationship in general (Relationship Assessment Scale [RAS]; Hendrick, Dicke, and Hendrick, 1998; Hendrick, 1988).

## Key Finding

The young age of post-9/11 caregivers caring for their spouse explains why they relate their relationship quality as worse than pre-9/11 caregivers, which combined increases the risk of future divorce in this group.

Our results suggest that non-caregivers in romantic relationships have greater relationship quality than do caregivers who have a romantic relationship with their care recipient. As shown in the first two columns of Table 3.9, tests of differences in mean relationship quality between groups revealed that non-caregivers reported significantly greater relationship quality than any of the caregiving groups. These significant differences in relationship quality hold even after adjusting for sociodemographic factors that may differ between caregiving groups (e.g., age, gender, income) and respondents' marital status (married vs. partners).

Within caregivers, the unadjusted average romantic relationship quality with their care-recipient spouse/partner was significantly lower among post-9/11 caregivers compared with pre-9/11 and civilian caregivers, who did not differ from one another. However, after adjusting for the sociodemographic differences between groups, the

**Table 3.9**
**The Effect of Caregiver Status on Relationship Quality with the Care Recipient, Unadjusted and Adjusted for Sociodemographic Characteristics**

| Caregiver Status[a] | Romantic Relationship Quality (n = 1,359) | | Nonromantic Relationship Quality (n = 2,054) | |
|---|---|---|---|---|
| | Unadjusted Mean[a] (SE) | Adjusted Mean[b] (SE) | Unadjusted Mean[c] (SE) | Adjusted Mean[d] (SE) |
| Post-9/11 military caregiver | 3.4(0.07) | 3.4(0.20) | 3.4(0.13) | 3.7(0.24) |
| Pre-9/11 military caregiver | 3.8(0.10) | 3.6(0.22) | 3.5(0.07) | 3.9(0.22) |
| Civilian caregiver | 3.7(0.07) | 3.6(0.21) | 3.4(0.04) | 3.9(0.21) |
| Non-caregiver | 4.0(0.04) | 3.9(0.21) | — | — |

[a] Significant differences at p < 0.05: Post-9/11 caregivers with pre-9/11 caregivers, civilian caregivers, and non-caregivers. Pre-9/11 caregiver with non-caregivers. Civilian caregiver with non-caregivers.

[b] Significant differences at p < 0.05: Non-caregivers with post-9/11, pre-9/11, and civilian caregivers.

[c] Significant differences at p < 0.05: None.

[d] Significant differernces at p < 0.05: None.

relationship quality of post-9/11 caregivers was no longer significantly different from pre-9/11 and civilian caregivers. As reported in Chapter Two, post-9/11 caregivers are younger on average than are pre-9/11 and civilian caregivers; also, older respondents reported greater romantic relationship quality than did younger respondents. Therefore, statistically controlling for age of respondent could have accounted for the unadjusted difference in romantic relationship quality between post-9/11 caregivers and the other caregiving groups.

Still, it is important to note that post-9/11 caregivers *are* younger and thus are likely to have been married for less time than pre-9/11 and civilian caregivers. We did not ask respondents how long they had been married; nonetheless, in cross-sectional surveys like ours, couples who have been married longer have happier relationships than those married less time.[8] Therefore, it is possible that controlling for age served as a proxy for length of relationship, perhaps obscuring a real difference between post-9/11 caregivers and the other caregiving groups. Indeed, when we removed age as a covariate from the regression model but retained the other sociodemographic covariates, post-9/11 caregivers had significantly lower romantic relationship quality than did pre-9/11 caregivers (adjusted means [SEs] of 3.6[0.18] and 3.9[0.17], respectively), but did not significantly differ from civilian caregivers (adjusted mean[SE] of 3.8[0.17]). Thus, the results suggest that post-9/11 caregivers who are romantic partners of their care recipients have lower relationship quality than pre-9/11 caregivers, and that this difference is accounted for by the fact that post-9/11 caregivers are younger. This implies that those post-9/11 caregivers in unhappy relationships may be at greater risk for future divorce (discussed in further detail in Chapter Four).

Nonetheless, there was a clear difference in romantic relationship quality between non-caregivers and each caregiving group. For example, 5 percent of non-caregivers reported that there were "very many" or "extremely many" problems in the relationship with their spouse or partner, while 10 percent of civilian caregivers, 10 percent of pre-9/11 caregivers, and 22 percent of post-9/11 caregivers reported similar levels of problems with their care recipient spouse/partner relationship.

We also measured relationship quality for caregivers who were in a nonromantic relationship with their care recipient (e.g., friends, parents) using a four-item measure capturing closeness, communication, similarity, and general relationship quality (i.e., how well the caregiver and care recipient "get along together") (Lawrence, Teenstedt, and Assmann, 1998). As shown in the last two columns of Table 3.9, relationship quality did not significantly differ between pre- and post-9/11 caregivers and civilian caregivers. Overall, caregivers who were in a nonromantic relationship with the care recipient reported a moderate level of relationship quality with their care recipient

---

[8]   Researchers have criticized these findings, noting that younger couples who were less happy with their relationships are likely to divorce, leaving only the happier, still-married couples to complete the survey (Karney and Bradbury, 1995). In fact, studies that have followed couples over time after their marriage have found that relationship quality decreases over time (Karney and Bradbury, 1995).

(unadjusted average score of 3.4 on a 5-point scale). For example, 68 percent of all non-spouse/partner caregivers reported that they were either very close or extremely close to their care recipient, and 29 percent indicated that they were slightly or moderately close. Thus, for caregivers who are in a nonromantic relationship with their care recipient, post- and pre-9/11 caregivers do not have worse relationship quality than civilian caregivers.

### Parenting

Another type of relationship that caregiving may affect is the one between the caregiver and his or her children. Research has demonstrated that stressors affecting a parent also affect their interactions with their children (Weinraub and Wolf, 1983). To the extent that providing care is stressful for the caregiver as described earlier, it is likely to negatively affect their parent-child relationships as well. In contrast, caregiving can also have positive influences on parents (also previously described), so it is likely that those positive influences will spread to positively affect their parent-child relationships. Note that these effects are independent of whether the child actually helps care for the care recipient, and whether the care recipient lives with the family.[9] That is, the parent's caregiving role can affect family life through time providing care, the stress of caregiving, financial expenditures, etc.—even when the care recipient lives outside the family's home and no other family member helps care for the care recipient.

In our survey, 39 percent of post-9/11 caregivers, 20 percent of pre-9/11 caregivers, and 27 percent of civilian caregivers reported having a child under the age of 18 who lived with them. To assess the relationship between caregiving and parenting, we asked these 672 caregivers to rate six questions concerning how caregiving has affected their relationship with their children (see Table 3.10). Three questions assessed the benefits of caregiving on child and family relations (e.g., "Caring for [the care recipient] has brought my children and me closer together as a family"), and three questions assessed negative effects of caregiving (e.g., "Caring for [the care recipient] has created a lot of tension in the household"). We calculated the average parenting impact score across all six questions.[10] As shown in Table 3.10, the unadjusted average score did not significantly differ among caregiving groups. Group differences on parenting impact scores remained nonsignificant after adjusting for differences in sociodemographic characteristics, as well as caregivers' symptoms of depression.

Figure 3.7 displays the percentage of caregivers who agreed or strongly agreed with each question, broken down by caregiving group. Between 44 and 53 percent

---

[9]  Some studies have estimated that there are 1.3–1.4 million children between 8 and 18 serving as caregivers (NAC and UHF, 2005); however, in our survey very few respondents reported that children under the age of 18 helped them with caregiving duties. This low number prevented us from quantifying the number of children serving as caregivers, describing the caregiving tasks they perform, or estimating potential consequences they face as a result of caregiving.

[10]  We reverse-coded the negative items so that higher scores meant less negative effects.

Table 3.10
The Effect of Caregiver Status on Parenting, Unadjusted and Adjusted for Sociodemographic Characteristics

| Caregiver Status | Parenting Impact (n = 653) | |
| --- | --- | --- |
| | Unadjusted Mean (SE)[a] | Adjusted Mean (SE)[b] |
| Post-9/11 military caregiver | 3.3(0.11) | 3.7(0.25) |
| Pre-9/11 military caregiver | 3.5(0.09) | 4.0(0.26) |
| Civilian caregiver | 3.5(0.06) | 3.8(0.25) |
| Non-caregiver | — | — |

[a] Significant differences at $p < 0.05$: Post-9/11 caregivers with pre-9/11 caregivers, civilian caregivers, and non-caregivers. Pre-9/11 caregiver with non-caregivers. Civilian caregiver with non-caregivers.

[b] Significant differences at $p < 0.05$: Non-caregivers with post-9/11, pre-9/11, and civilian caregivers.

of all caregivers agreed or strongly agreed with the questions assessing the benefits of caregiving on child and family relations. On the other hand, almost 44 percent of post-9/11 caregivers, compared with 21 and 29 percent of pre-9/11 and civilian caregivers, agreed or strongly agreed that caregiving was a burden on spending quality time with their children, and 46 percent of post-9/11 caregivers, compared with 17 and 22 percent of pre-9/11 and civilian caregivers, agreed or strongly agreed that caregiving created "a lot of tension in the household." About 27 percent of post-9/11 caregivers, compared with 5 and 8 percent of pre-9/11 and civilian caregivers, respectively, agreed or strongly agreed that caregiving has made them a worse parent. Thus, although military and civilian caregivers indicated that providing care benefited their child and family relations, a sizable minority of post-9/11 caregivers indicated that providing care was a burden on their family life.

## Programs to Address Caregiver Family Well-Being

A range of services are available to support the overall health and well-being of military caregivers *and their families*. Addressing the needs of military families has been recognized as a significant policy and programmatic priority (Institute of Medicine, 2013; Cozza, Holmes, and Van Ost, 2013). Caregiver family services, according to our classification framework, include structured wellness activities for families (n = 13), religious support networks (n = 4), and miscellaneous aid and assistance, which we label helping hand (n = 52). Caregivers may also benefit from a range of referral sources to assist them in identifying organizations that provide these family services. Later, we discuss this range of services to support the health and well-being of military caregivers and families.

### Structured Wellness Activities Targeted Toward Families

Caregivers and their families are likely to benefit from a range of structured wellness activities. Previously, we focused on structured wellness activities specifically for caregivers, and here we discuss those 13 activities targeted toward caregivers in conjunction

**Figure 3.7**
**Percent of Post-9/11, Pre-9/11, and Civilian Caregivers with Children Who Agreed or Strongly Agreed with Statements Assessing the Effect of Caregiving on Parenting and Family Relations (n = 657)**

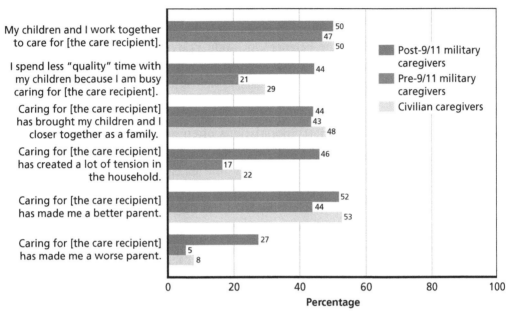

NOTE: Number of respondents in each group: n = 191 for post-9/11 caregivers, n = 109 for pre-9/11 caregivers, and n = 357 for civilian caregivers.
RAND RR499-3.7

with the care recipient. Only one of these, offered by Returning Heroes Home, is provided on an ongoing basis (but is only offered locally at Fort Sam Houston). The rest (and the majority) are offered on an episodic basis. These activities occur during annual or occasional retreats or conferences for caregivers in addition to service members or veterans. These services vary greatly in their offerings and are listed in full in Appendix E. However, they include such wellness activities as yoga, journaling sessions, hiking, boating, and fishing. Most of these events span one day or one weekend. Many of these activities are tailored toward wounded, ill, or injured service members or veterans as well as their caregivers or family members.

### Religious Support

Four organizations identified in the environmental scan specifically offer religious support, defined as religious- or spiritual-based guidance or counseling. This is not to say that military caregivers do not access religious support through other channels. Given that religion occupies a pivotal role in many military families (Bray et al., 2009; Bray et al., 2006), we suspect that military caregivers often seek support from local places of worship or community-based organizations—and, indeed, some research supports this assumption (Institute of Medicine, 2013). Almost 29 percent of caregivers in our study indicated that, in the past year, they used a religious or spiritual support network to help them meet the challenges of caregiving. Controlling for sociodemographic differences between groups, the proportion of caregivers using a religious or spiritual support network did not significantly differ between pre-9/11, post-9/11, and civilian caregivers.

Examples of organizations found to exist at the intersection of caregiver services and religious support include Marine Parents Operation Prayers and Letters, a project supporting Marines who have been injured, and Operation Heal Our Patriots, which provides counseling offered by chaplains at retreats, as well as baptism and marriage renewal.

### A "Helping Hand"

Injuries or illnesses among military populations often engender a range of complex caregiver and family needs (Cozza, Holmes, and Van Ost, 2013). Services targeting these caregivers' needs often do not fit clearly into categories such as health care or social support. Borrowing from prior research on military families (Miller et al., 2011), we used the term "a helping hand" to categorize and describe a range of miscellaneous aid such as loans, donations, legal guidance, housing support such as mortgage or rent payments, and transportation assistance. A total of 52 organizations (of the 120 identified in the environmental scan) provide some form of helping-hand assistance. Most of these organizations are nonprofit entities in addition to a handful of government organizations: the VA Caregiver Support Program, each military service's Wounded Warrior programs, and the Virginia WWP.

Helping-hand assistance targets a diverse set of expenses including basic living, travel, rent or mortgage, automobile and insurance, home maintenance, and legal services. Some organizations focus on specific types of assistance (e.g., travel expenses) while others provide for a broad range of needs. Some organizations target caregivers or families during the hospitalization period, although most have no such limitation. In most instances, eligibility for and receipt of financial assistance is contingent upon the service member or veteran providing proof of military service and in some instances the existence of an illness or injury. Evidence of financial need is often required as well. Many organizations offer assistance more than once, while a handful of organizations limit their assistance to one time only. A limited number of organizations offer financial assistance to service members or families routinely, shortly after a service member is injured. For example, the Air Force Aid Society issues a $500 grant upon medical evacuation, and the EOD Warrior Foundation issues an "initial grant package" that includes $3,000 in financial assistance.

Overall, 11 percent of caregivers indicated that, in the past year, they used a service that we would categorize as offering a "helping hand" to meet the challenges of caregiving.[11] Controlling for differences among the groups, the proportion of caregiv-

---

[11] Specifically, the question asked: In the past year, have you used a helping hand? For example, loans, donations, legal guidance, or housing assistance.

ers using a helping hand did not significantly differ between pre-9/11, post-9/11, and civilian caregivers.

### Referral Services for Caregivers and Families

As discussed earlier, caregivers must be able to identify the range of services available to use them. Resource lists and referral services that are likely to assist caregivers in finding services for themselves (discussed in the section titled "Programs to Address Caregiver Health and Well-Being") are likely to assist them in finding help for the entire family. Again, primary sources include the National Resource Directory (and particularly its Family and Caregiver Support section), the VA Caregiver Support Coordinators, and the Military OneSource, Army OneSource, and DSTRESS hotlines. In addition, numerous organizations offer resource lists and referral services, as listed in Appendix E.

## Employment and Financial Well-Being of Military Caregivers

As shown in Figure 3.8, post-9/11 military caregivers are different from their pre-9/11 military and civilian counterparts, in that 76 percent are in the labor force, relative to 55 percent of pre-9/11 caregivers, 60 percent of civilian caregivers, and 66 percent of non-caregivers. This difference is driven largely by the fact that post-9/11 military caregivers are more likely to be of working age: After accounting for age, there is no difference in the odds of being in the labor force across the four groups. Among all caregivers

**Figure 3.8**
**Employment Status of Caregivers and Non-Caregivers**

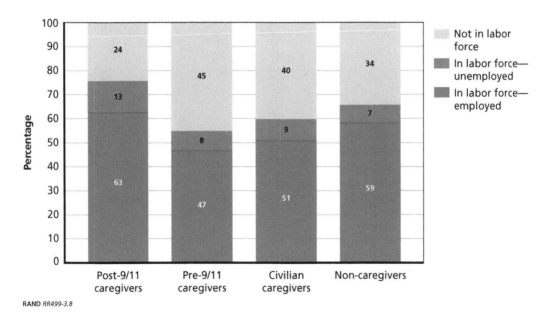

(post-9/11, pre-9/11, and civilian), approximately 10 percent (or 16 percent of those in the labor force) are unemployed. Of those in the labor force and employed, 75 percent of post-9/11 caregivers, 65 percent of pre-9/11 caregivers, 68 percent of civilian caregivers, and 77 percent of non-caregivers worked more than 35 hours per week at a job in the week prior to being surveyed, which equates roughly to having a full-time job.

The difference between post-9/11 and other caregiver groups is even more pronounced with respect to the employment status of the person for whom they are caring (Figure 3.9). Fifty-three percent of post-9/11 military care recipients are in the labor force (of whom 9 percent are unemployed) relative to approximately 10 percent of pre-9/11 military and civilian care recipients in the labor force. These differences persisted after controlling for age differences among the groups of care recipients, indicating that there are differences other than age between the post-9/11 care recipients and their pre-9/11 and civilian counterparts that contribute to differences in their odds of being in the labor force.

### Financial Strain

As discussed in Chapter Two, caregiving takes time and may affect the work schedule of caregivers who are employed. We asked all caregivers about whether they needed to make work adjustments as a result of caregiving, and the financial strain resulting from caregiving. We asked this of all respondents, not just those currently in the labor force, because we wanted to include measures about whether caregiving has caused caregivers to leave the labor force.

**Figure 3.9**
**Employment Status of Care Recipients**

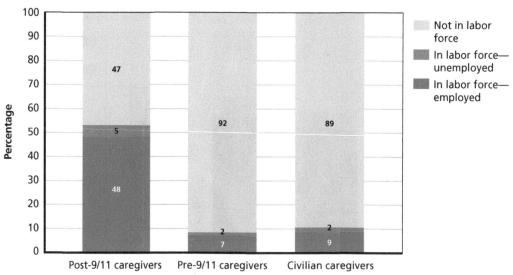

As shown in Figure 3.10, roughly two times as many post-9/11 military caregivers (47 percent) reported needing to make work adjustments as a result of caregiving as pre-9/11 caregivers (23 percent) and civilian caregivers (27 percent). Similarly, 62 percent of post-9/11 military caregivers reported that caregiving caused financial strain relative to roughly 30 and 40 percent of pre-9-11 caregivers and civilian caregivers, respectively.

The economic impact of caregiving is borne by caregivers both through the cost associated with providing care (e.g., health care costs, program costs) and through lost income and wages. We asked a series of six questions that focused on potential lost income and wages. These data are presented in Table 3.11. Half of all post-9/11 military caregivers and a quarter of pre-9/11 military and civilian caregivers reported taking time off from work or stopping work temporarily because of caregiving. Post-9/11 military caregivers endorsed five of the items at least twice as often as did pre-9/11 and civilian caregivers, including quitting work entirely, which was endorsed by just over a quarter of post-9/11 military caregivers and around 13 percent of their counterparts, and taking time off from school, which was endorsed by a quarter of post-9/11 military caregivers and only by 5 and 6 percent of pre-9/11 and civilian caregivers, respectively. The only item that was endorsed by similar proportions of caregivers across all groups was taking retirement earlier than expected, which was endorsed by 11 percent of post-9/11 caregivers, 8 percent of pre-9/11 caregivers, and 7 percent of civilian caregivers.

**Figure 3.10**
**Work and Financial Strain as a Result of Caregiving**

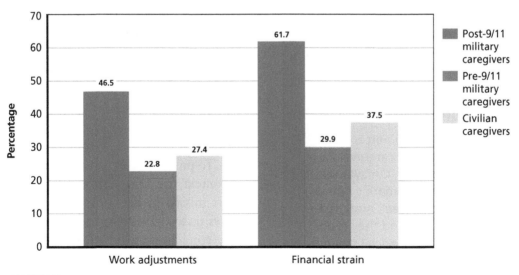

**Table 3.11**
**Caregiving-Induced Financial Strain**

| As a result of caregiving, did you ever... | Post-9/11 Caregivers | | Pre-9/11 Caregivers | | Civilian Caregivers | |
|---|---|---|---|---|---|---|
| | % | SE | % | SE | % | SE |
| Take unpaid time off from work or stop working temporarily? | 48.4 | 5.8 | 24.8 | 2.7 | 24.9 | 1.6 |
| Cut back the number of hours in your regular weekly job schedule? | 39.0 | 5.6 | 22.6 | 2.6 | 21.6 | 1.5 |
| Move to a job that pays less or provides fewer benefits, but that fits better with your caregiving schedule or responsibilities? | 16.3 | 4.0 | 8.4 | 1.9 | 8.5 | 1.1 |
| Quit working entirely? | 28.0 | 4.6 | 13.2 | 2.0 | 13.2 | 1.2 |
| Take retirement earlier than you would have otherwise? | 11.0 | 4.3 | 8.4 | 1.6 | 7.2 | 0.86 |
| Take time off from school or cut back on classes? | 25.6 | 5.1 | 4.8 | 1.1 | 6.1 | 0.96 |

**Work Absenteeism**

Absenteeism is measured as the amount of time employees are absent from work because of their own physical or mental health (Kessler et al., 2004). Absenteeism costs employers in terms of wages, but can also affect productivity when there are no substitute employees to compensate for an absent worker or when firms face a consequence associated with not meeting an expected deadline (Pauly et al., 2002).

Among respondents who reported being currently employed, we estimated how much work they missed in the past four weeks by subtracting the number of hours the respondent worked from the total number they reported was expected of them. Pre-9/11 military and non-caregivers reported negative mean hours worked per week. In other words, these caregivers reported working on average more time than their employer expects of them: pre-9/11 military caregivers worked a little under an extra 30 minutes per month (M = –0.4, SE = 3.4), whereas non-caregivers worked more than 90 minutes extra per month (M = –1.7, SE = 6.1). In contrast, civilian caregivers reported missing, on average, 9 hours, or approximately one day of work, in the past month (M = 9.0, SE = 3.5), while post-9/11 military caregivers reported missing, on average, close to 29 hours, or roughly 3.5 days, of work per month (M = 28.5, SE = 12.9).

To put the number of hours missed in context, we also compute a ratio of hours missed to hours expected, which allows us to draw comparisons between two employees who miss the same amount of total work hours, but who are expected to work different amounts

**Key Finding**

Approximately 76 percent of post-9/11 military caregivers are in the labor force. On average, they miss approximately one day from work per week more than non-caregivers, and they report twice as much financial strain from caregiving as pre-9/11 caregivers.

of time. For instance, an employee who misses 20 hours of work out of an expected 100 will have a work-hours-missed ratio of 20/100 = 0.20, or 20 percent. On the other hand, a second employee who misses 20 hours, but who is expected to work 160 hours in four weeks, only misses 12.5 percent (20/160) of his or her total work hour responsibilities. This measure indicates that pre-9/11 military caregivers work an extra 7 percent (M = 0.07, SE = 0.08) and non-caregivers work an extra 3 percent (M = 0.03, SE = 0.04) of what is expected of them. Post-9/11 military caregivers miss, on average, 9 percent of their expected work hours (M = 0.09, SE = 0.16); although they miss one day of work per month, the proportion of hours missed to hours expected is negligible among civilian caregivers.

### Programs to Address Income Loss

As described previously, caregivers may experience a loss of income, either due to lost wages as a result of caregiving or increased costs incurred in caring for someone. A small handful of services are available to address caregiver income loss. Most notably, two government programs, both relatively new, attempt to alleviate potential negative financial consequences associated with caregiving for post-9/11 care recipients and caregivers: DoD's SCAADL program and the VA Program of Comprehensive Assistance for Family Caregivers. These new programs support caregivers who assist their service members or veterans with ADLs. However, as summarized in Table 3.12, the programs differ from one another. One of the main differences is in eligibility criteria: SCAADL covers injuries and illnesses, but the VA Program of Comprehensive Assistance for Family Caregivers only covers injuries, including physical injury, TBI, psychological trauma, or other mental disorders (i.e., it excludes chronic conditions like cancer). The VA also requires that the caregiver has already provided at least six months of continuous assistance already; SCAADL does not impose this requirement.

Another key difference in eligibility is that the SCAADL criteria specify that the service member would require hospitalization, nursing home care, or other residential institutional care in the absence of such caregiver assistance. This language is not

**Table 3.12**
**Differences Between SCAADL and the VA Program of Comprehensive Assistance for Family Caregivers**

| SCAADL | VA's Program of Comprehensive Assistance for Family Caregivers |
|---|---|
| Covers injuries and illnesses | Covers only injuries |
| Without caregiver assistance, service member would be in a hospital, nursing home, or institution | Criteria do not specify that veteran would be in a hospital, nursing home, or institution without caregiver assistance |
| Stipend is paid to the service member | Stipend is paid to the caregiver |
| Stipend is considered taxable income | Stipend is not considered taxable income |
| Caregiver is not required to be a family member | Caregiver must be a family member or live with veteran |
| Training is available, but not required | Caregivers must complete required training |

included in VA's Program of Comprehensive Assistance for Family Caregivers eligibility criteria.

In addition to VA's Program of Comprehensive Assistance for Family Caregivers and SCAADL financial stipend offerings, another organization, Wounded Warrior Family Support, provides financial stipends for caregiving activities. It calculates wages and stipends to support child care or caregiving in different circumstances that are not covered under the VA programs. In some cases, the organization pays a family member a stipend for providing respite care. Making respite a paying job reduces the emotional factor, which can be an issue in many families. There are also a number of state programs that provide financial benefits to caregivers (see Appendix F).

Likely because of their eligibility for these programs, more post-9/11 military caregivers reported using a monthly stipend of payment from the VA in the past year than did pre-9/11 caregivers (17 percent vs. 4 percent, respectively).[12] However, and somewhat surprisingly, among those who received a monthly stipend or payment from the VA, pre-9/11 caregivers rated it as significantly more helpful than did post-9/11 caregivers.

In addition to programs that compensate for lost income, both federal and state policies aim to minimize the losses that caregivers may experience. Most notably, the FMLA entitles certain employees to take 12 workweeks during a 12-month period of unpaid, job-protected leave for specified reasons, including care for a spouse, son, daughter, or parent who has a serious medical condition. The 2010 NDAA expanded the FMLA provisions for military caregivers who are spouses, sons, daughters, or next of kin of the care recipient, offering 26 workweeks during a *single* 12-month period to care for a covered service member or veteran with a serious injury or illness.[13] In addition, depending on the state of residence, military caregivers may be eligible to receive state-funded payments for their role. Such opportunity is available in 19 states across the United States. (See Appendix F for more details.)

## Service and Resource Utilization Among Caregivers

Throughout this chapter, we have highlighted caregivers' use of specific programs and services; that information is summarized in Figure 3.11. Across services, 15 to 30 percent of post-9/11 caregivers have used such services in the past year: the lowest levels of use were for the stipend; the greatest levels of use were for religious support. Certain services (helping-hand services, structured social support, and structured education

---

[12] Respondents may interpret this question to indicate any source of payment from the VA, and is not necessarily directly tied to participation in the VA Program of Comprehensive Assistance for Family Caregivers.

[13] More information about the FMLA, including the definition of a "covered service member," is presented in Appendix F.

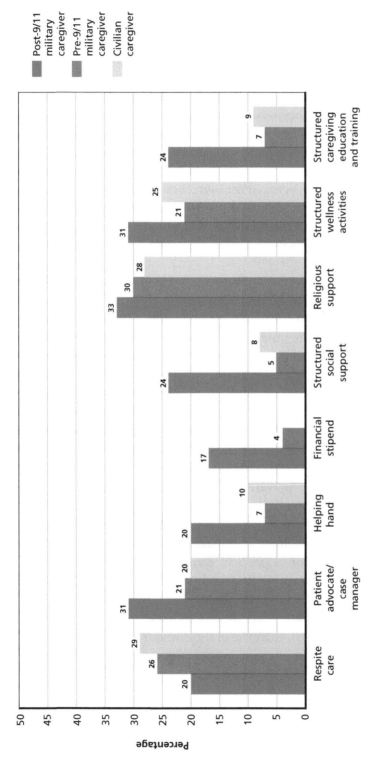

**Figure 3.11**
**Resource Utilization Among Caregivers**

RAND *RR499-3.11*

and training) were used by lower proportions of pre-9/11 and civilian caregivers than post-9/11 military caregivers, differences that held even after controlling for sociodemographic differences among the groups.

To align programs and services to meet caregivers' needs, it is critical to understand not only the types of services caregivers are currently using, but also the organizations they are accessing. Further, for those not accessing specific organizations, it is important to know whether they would have liked to use this resource and the reason for their preference; i.e., why they want or do not want to use it. Understanding these barriers and preferences, and how they vary across different groups of caregivers, can inform strategies for creating greater access to support among military caregivers.

As shown in Figure 3.12, across most sources of help, a higher proportion of post-9/11 caregivers used the source than did pre-9/11 caregivers, differences that remain significant even after adjusting for the different age and sociodemographic differences. The only exception was informal "use" of family and friends, used by approximately 90 percent of all caregivers.

### Sources of Help Specifically for Military Caregivers

More than half of all post-9/11 military caregivers and less than half of all pre-9/11 military caregivers report having used resources designed specifically for military caregivers. Seventy-three percent of post-9/11 caregivers indicated that they used the **VA** as a source of help with caregiving compared to 38 percent of pre-9/11 military caregivers. As described in Chapter Two, more post-9/11 military care recipients have a VA disability rating than pre-9/11 military care recipients; also as previously described, the VA Program of Comprehensive Assistance for Family Caregivers is only available to post-9/11 military caregivers. These differences may account for some of the discrepancy between post- and pre-9/11 military caregivers' use of the VA. Military caregivers were also asked about use of "**private or NGOs that specifically support military caregivers**:" 65 percent of post-9/11 and 18 percent of pre-9/11 caregivers reported using the services offered by these organizations. Finally, almost 55 percent of post-9/11 military caregivers reported having used **military-sponsored programs** for help with caregiving, whereas 22 percent of pre-9/11 caregivers reported using such programs. In all cases, differences between pre-9/11 and post-9/11 military caregivers remained significant after adjusting for sociodemographic differences between the two groups.

Though the varying resources are used at different rates, and pre-9/11 and post-9/11 military caregivers differ in their use of these resources, there is consistency in the reported reasons for nonuse. In all cases, roughly three-quarters of pre-9/11 and half of post-9/11 caregivers who did not use one of the three services indicated that they did not want to use the service. Among the relatively small proportion that wanted to use each resource but did not, the primary reason for nonuse was that they *were unaware of the resource or that it was difficult to find information about them*. Among post-9/11 nonusers who wanted to use each service, the proportion reporting that they did not use

Figure 3.12
Utilization of Organizations for Caregiver Support

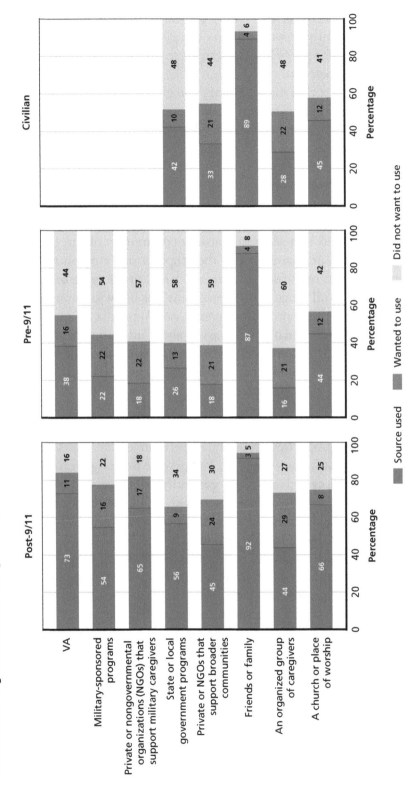

NOTE: Percentages may not add to 100 because of rounding and/or missing data.
RAND RR499-3.12

for this reason was 54 percent for the VA, 61 percent for private or nongovernmental organizations that specifically support military caregivers, and 72 percent for military-sponsored organizations (for pre-9/11 nonusers, corresponding proportions are 45 percent, 46 percent, and 46 percent).

These findings suggest that many military caregivers, particularly post-9/11 caregivers, use the VA for help with caregiving, and more than half use private or nongovernmental organizations and military-sponsored programs. In each category, most of those not using the given resource did not want to use that resource.

### Governmental and Nongovernmental Programs Supporting All Caregivers

In addition to sources of help that target just those caring for service members or veterans, military caregivers have access to state or local governmental programs and nongovernmental programs that serve the broader community of caregivers. Though we included certain such programs within the scope of our environmental scan (if explicitly serving caregivers or incidentally serving caregivers of aging or disabled populations), identifying the full range of such programs was not within our scope. However, we are cognizant that such programs do exist (see Appendix F) and that military caregivers may access them; as such, we also asked about utilization of these resources.

Civilian and post-9/11 military caregivers had comparable rates of use of these resources, which was around double the reported use by pre-9/11 military caregivers. Specifically, 56 percent of post-9/11 caregivers and 42 percent of civilian caregivers reported using **state or local government programs** (a difference that was not statistically significant); in contrast, 26 percent of pre-9/11 military caregivers reported using these resources. A small proportion (roughly 18 percent) of caregivers across groups had not used these programs but wanted to. For **private or nongovernmental organizations geared toward caregivers more generally**, 45 percent of post-9/11 and a third of civilian caregivers reported using such sources relative to 18 percent of pre-9/11 military caregivers (a difference that is statistically significant after adjustment for sociodemographic variables). In this instance, about a third of nonusers of these resources wanted to use them across all groups of caregivers—and again, the primary cited reason for nonuse among this group was being unaware of the organizations or reporting difficulty finding information about them (67 percent of post-9/11, 47 percent of pre-9/11 caregivers, and 51 percent of civilian caregivers).

Based on these findings, we observe that government and nongovernment programs are common sources of support for caregivers, especially post-9/11 caregivers. However, in each category, use is less than optimal and caregivers reported difficulty in finding information about them. This suggests the need for increasing awareness of available programs among caregivers.

## Formal and Informal Social Network Sources of Help

As previously described, social support can be a critical need of many military caregivers (Tanielian et al., 2013; NAC, 2006), and generally, social support has been shown to lead to positive outcomes among family caregivers (e.g., Lofvenmark et al., 2013; Hanks et al., 2012; Wilks and Croom, 2008). Just under half of the services identified in our environmental scan provide structured social support, organized in-person or online support that is likely to assist with caregiving-specific stresses or challenges. In addition, caregivers frequently rely on informal social networks (e.g., friends, family) for help with caregiving.

A significantly higher percentage of post-9/11 caregivers (44 percent) **used organized caregiver groups** than did civilian caregivers (28 percent); and a higher proportion of civilian caregivers used this resource than did pre-9/11 military caregivers (16 percent). All of these differences remain statistically significant after controlling for sociodemographic differences. Of those who had not used organized caregiver groups, roughly 52 percent of post-9/11 caregivers, 25 percent of pre-9/11 caregivers, and 30 percent of civilian caregivers wanted to use them for help with caregiving; again, the most cited reason for not using this source was that caregivers were unaware of the organizations or it was difficult to find information about them (81 percent of post-9/11 caregivers, 55 percent of pre-9/11 caregivers, and 57 percent of civilian caregivers among nonusers wanting to use).

We also asked specifically about relying on a support network from a **church or place of worship** for help with caregiving. More post-9/11 caregivers (66 percent) relied on church-based support than pre-9/11 and civilian caregivers (44 percent and 45 percent, respectively). Roughly 20 percent of nonusers across groups wanted to use a church or place of worship as a source for help with caregiving; the vast majority of caregivers who did not use a church or place of worship for help with caregiving also did not want to (about 80 percent across groups).

Across sources of help, more caregivers relied on **friends and family** for help than on any other source. Across caregiving groups, 89 percent of caregivers reported that they used friends and family to help with caregiving in the past year and there were no differences among groups once accounting for sociodemographic differences.

Based on these findings, we observe that caregivers rely upon multiple social networks: Friends and family were the most prevalent source, followed by churches or places of worship, and, finally, organized caregiver support groups. Given the reliance on these networks for social support among caregivers, ensuring the stability of these networks over the long term may require attention.

## Summary

As hypothesized, post-9/11, pre-9/11, and civilian caregivers reported lower levels of physical and mental health than non-caregivers, differences that could not be explained by differences in sociodemographic characteristics. In particular, post-9/11 caregivers evidenced the greatest magnitude of difference with non-caregivers, in ways that indicated they were especially vulnerable to unfavorable health outcomes. Among all caregivers, key aspects of caregiving that contributed to depression included the number of the care recipient's medical conditions, time spent caregiving, and helping the care recipient cope with behavioral problems. Perhaps more concerning is that within this vulnerable group, between 18 percent (of pre-9/11 military caregivers) and 33 percent (of post-9/11 military caregivers) lack health care coverage. Few programs offer non-standard physical health care, though a notable few provide resources to assist caregivers with their own health care expenses. More, but still relatively few, nonstandard resources are available that provide mental health care. More common is structured social support, such as ongoing online networks of caregivers or episodic conferences and retreats for caregivers, and structured wellness activities. A handful of organizations offer respite care.

The impacts of caregiving on families and workplaces are more pronounced among post-9/11 military caregivers, largely because of their age. Of all caregivers caring for a spouse, post-9/11 military caregivers report the lowest levels of relationship quality with the care recipient. This difference is largely accounted for by the younger age of post-9/11 military caregivers, but it still places these newer romantic partnerships at greater risk of separation or divorce. Episodic structured wellness activities are available for caregivers that may support families, and there are a handful of religious and other helping-hand services that can assist with various aspects of family life. Almost three-quarters of post-9/11 military caregivers are in the labor force, which makes the fact that they, on average, report 3.5 more days of missed work per month than non-caregivers of concern to employers. The lost wages from work, in addition to costs incurred associated with providing medical care, result in financial strain for these caregivers, and relatively few programs offer stipends to help offset these losses.

Finally, caregivers (particularly post-9/11 caregivers) use both government and nongovernment sources of support. However, aside from programs for military caregivers specifically, use is less than optimal and caregivers reported difficulty in finding information about them. This suggests the need for increasing awareness of available programs.

# CHAPTER FOUR

# Evolving Needs: Sustaining Caregiver and Care Recipient Well-Being Now and in the Future

Caregiving has been traditionally construed as an issue relevant to the aging and elderly population. This has largely been driven by challenges faced by middle-aged caregivers tending to the needs of their aged parents. The focus on caregivers for the aging makes sense: A third of pre-9/11 and civilian caregivers are children of the person they are caring for, and over half are caring for someone over age 65. More recently, caregiver research and support programs have included consideration of parents and siblings of persons with special needs across the lifespan (NAC and AARP, 2009). As a result, many policies and programs have been developed to provide information, social support, and benefits for caregivers serving the aged and chronically disabled.

Post-9/11 military caregivers are fundamentally different from civilian and pre-9/11 caregivers in important ways: One-third are spouses, 25 percent are parents, and all are caring for someone under age 65. Two-thirds of post-9/11 care recipients have a mental health or substance use disorder, which may increase risk for premature death from unnatural causes, cardiovascular disease, and engagement in health-compromising behaviors, such as smoking and sexual risk-taking as well as substance use (Wahlbeck et al., 2011; Harris and Barraclough, 1997; Wulsin, Vaillant, and Wells, 1999; Rugulies, 2002; Lasser et al., 2000; Holmes, Foa, and Sammel, 2005; Kessler et al., 1996). In other words, post-9/11 care recipients are young and many will live well into the future; the types of conditions that they are living with have implications for their needs for caregiving assistance, as well as the long-term well-being of the caregivers who care for them. This means that military caregivers, the programs that serve them and their care recipients, and society at large needs not only to address the current needs of this population, but should begin planning for their future needs as well.

It is reasonable to expect that over time, the needs of military caregivers will change. This change will come about as the needs of their care recipient change—their veteran's conditions may improve through treatment, recovery, and rehabilitation; or perhaps worsen as a result of future illness (which may or may not be service-related) or injury. As a result, the caregiving tasks needed may also shift in nature or in quantity. At the same time, the caregiver's situation may also change and affect the caregiving dynamic. With the passage of time, experience gained through training, or support derived from resource utilization, an individual caregivers' capacity and that of their network may evolve in positive, negative, or mixed ways. On the one hand, a caregiver network may be enhanced through training, support, and supportive environments; the caregiver network could also become depleted as they become burdened from the negative consequences of caregiving (such as detriments to health and well-being). Any decrements to the caregiver network could in turn negatively affect the care recipients' well-being and even create a risk of increased reliance on other sources for support.

As we discussed in Chapter One, care recipients and caregivers sit at the center of a larger social context (see Figure 4.1). There has been a great deal of research with respect to understanding the roles, burdens, consequences, and value of caregiving in the United States; almost all of this work has been primarily focused on civilian care-givers for the elderly population. While many of the burdens and consequences are borne at the individual and family level, others are borne by society more broadly.

Researchers have estimated the costs of caregiving in terms of increased health risks and lost productivity, and the value of caregiving in terms of defrayed costs to the health care system. It stands to reason that if the costs are to be minimized and the value optimized, we need to consider the implications for the long-term well-being of the caregiver and care recipient. We discuss these prior findings and implications for understanding the short- and long-term benefits and costs of military caregiving.

To ensure that caregiver and care recipient well-being are preserved to the great-est extent possible, we use our findings to highlight how policies and programs should be thinking about the future of support for military caregivers within this larger social environment. We examine areas of potential strength and vulnerability and consider how program availability changes over time might affect the landscape of support for

**Figure 4.1**
**The Social Ecology of Military Caregiving**
**in the United States**

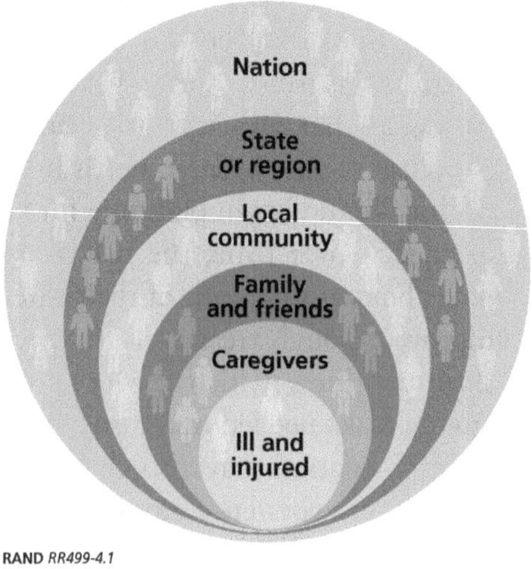

military caregivers. These analyses could be used to inform planning for sustainable and dynamic solutions to minimize the burden of caregiving.

While we have already documented characteristics of the population, areas of need, and utilization of services at a single point in time, we will highlight four other areas relevant for ensuring the long-term well-being of military caregivers and the people they serve. First, we discuss very general projections of when and where we might see a decrease or increase in the needs of military caregivers, focusing specifically on aging caregivers who are caring for their sons and daughters, or young men and women caring for their spouse and whose relationships are vulnerable to divorce. These analyses can help to highlight potential areas and sources of potential vulnerability in caregiving continuity. To inform options for ensuring continuity in caregiving, we discuss what individual future planning may entail from the caregivers' perspective, drawing primarily from the literature of parents caring for aging disabled children in need of caregiving support. Then, we briefly describe the longevity of organizations serving caregivers and the implications this has for their sustainability. Finally, we draw upon the prior literature that estimates the value and costs of family caregiving in the United States to examine how the contributions made, and the consequences experienced, by military caregivers may affect U.S. society more broadly.

## Aging Parents and Fragile Marriages

Like all relationships, that between caregiver and care recipient is constantly in flux. The changing dynamic of the care recipient's health, the caregiver's health, and the relationship between the two is likely to influence the care that is provided. In the most extreme cases, caregivers are no longer able or willing to perform caregiving tasks, and the care recipient will need to find a substitute. This substitute may be another caregiver or institutional support; without a substitute, care recipients are possibly at risk of adverse outcomes, including deteriorating health, crime and violence, homelessness, or premature death.

We illustrate this with an example. To begin, 25 percent of post-9/11 military caregivers are parents to the care recipient, roughly equaling 269,940 caregivers nationally. In comparison, 10 percent of civilian caregivers are parents to their care recipient, or 1.7 million caregivers. We make an assumption that when the parent who is providing care turns 75 years of age, the care recipient will need to find alternative care. This very basic projection model does not account for care recipients who will get better or will die, nor does it account for those caregivers who can provide care well after 75 (or who are unable to provide care at some point before they turn 75). However, the assumptions are reasonable for the illustrative purpose here.

The proportion of parent caregivers who turn 75 and for whom care recipients will need to find alternative models of care is presented in Figure 4.2. As might be expected, civilian caregivers currently providing care to an adult child (represented by the green line) span a wide age range and, as such, there is a linear trend in the relationship between time and needing alternative care. On the other hand, we see little need for alternative care arrangements for post-9/11 care recipients until around 2023. However, the proportion increases more dramatically beginning at that point: 15 years from now (2028), 30 percent of post-9/11 caregivers who are parents (roughly 80,000) may need to find alternative care for their child. Thus, we see that by 2028, tens of thousands of veteran care recipients may have their care continuity jeopardized. If replacement caregivers are not identified from within their support networks, or from professional, paid sources, these individuals may become increasingly reliant upon government or social welfare programs for caregiving assistance.

Just as parents grow older, romantic relationships of caregivers caring for spouses are also subject to change. Providing care to a spouse who has a physical and/or psychological disability is difficult, and places a strain on the relationship and on family life. As noted earlier, caregivers experience lower relationship quality with their care-recipient spouse/partner than do non-caregivers with their spouse/partner, and research demonstrates that low relationship quality is associated with separation and divorce. A couple's probability of divorce is difficult to predict and depends on many factors (Amato, 2010), but it is clear that a couple's risk of divorce partly depends on their age: Younger couples are more likely to eventually divorce than older ones (Brown, Lin, and Payne, 2012). We know of no data that specifically assess the divorce rate of caregiver–

**Figure 4.2**
**Projected Proportion of Post-9/11 Military and Civilian Caregivers Who Are Parents Over the Age of 75, 2013–2048**

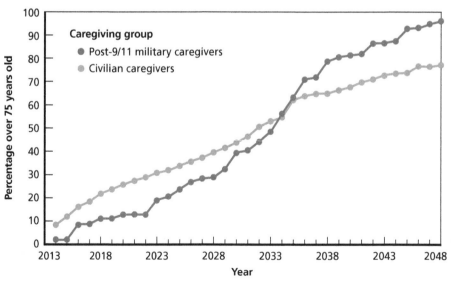

care recipient couples, and it is possible that caregivers are more or less likely to divorce than the general population. Still, the population divorce rate stratified by age group is the best metric available for estimating the probability of divorce for caregiver–care recipient couples. Using estimates of divorce rates by Brown, Lin, and Payne (2012), we estimated that 30 percent of spouse/partner caregivers across military and civilian caregivers alike are likely to separate from or divorce their care recipient spouses. Since, as noted earlier, post-9/11 caregivers are more likely to be in a romantic relationship with their care recipients, 9 percent of all post-9/11 caregivers, 7 percent of all pre-9/11 caregivers, and 5 percent of all civilian caregivers are at risk for losing their primary caregiver through divorce or separation.

## Future Planning for Caregivers

The changing demographic of caregivers and the dynamic relationship between caregivers and care recipients signals the need for long-term planning. This need is likely more pronounced for post-9/11 military care recipients who are younger and for whom future planning is likely to be more important than for pre-9/11 and civilian care recipients.

As opposed to caregivers who care for their aging and elderly parents, future planning is a more pronounced and long-standing concern for parent caregivers of children with intellectual disabilities who may very well outlive them (Coppus, 2013). However, such planning is not necessarily common or routine (Bowey and McGlaughlin, 2007; Carr, 2005; Krauss et al., 1996). The title of one article from 2010 on caregivers of people with a disability reveals: "It terrifies me, the thought of the future" (Mansell and Wilson, 2010). For this community, poor planning can result in emotional trauma and inappropriate placement (Taggart et al., 2012; Heller, Caldwell, and Factor, 2005; Thompson and Wright, 2001), cause unplanned burden on siblings or other extended family (Taggart et al., 2012), and also impose costs to providers (Bigby and Ozanne, 2004).

It is unclear the extent to which military caregivers and their care recipients have planned, or needed to plan, for the future; in our survey, time constraints limited our own ability to ask about future planning. Nonetheless, we recognize that such planning—including primarily financial, legal, residential, and vocational/educational matters—may become critically important for post-9/11 military caregivers over time, particularly for those relying upon parents and aging spouses. The caregiving burden may fall to their own children, extended family, or perhaps to society more broadly. To inform considerations for future planning, we turn to the extant research on aging parents caring for their children with developmental or intellectual disabilities. We highlight, to the extent that they are relevant to military caregivers, barriers that these aging adult caregivers have encountered with respect to future planning, and innovations that have been developed to support such planning.

Lack of knowledge about services available for aging care recipients, or being ill-informed about the processes for accessing such services, may hinder some caregivers from planning ahead for their loved one. For example, caregivers may not know about residential placement options or may not realize there are limited slots (and associated waiting lists) associated with placement in preferred facilities (Taggart et al., 2012). More likely, however, is the emotive experience of considering the future. As described by Taggart and colleagues (2012), future planning requires that caregivers consider their own mortality or that they may eventually be unable to provide the caregiving support that their loved one requires. Caregivers also may harbor anxieties about alternative residential arrangements and thus not make such arrangements until absolutely necessary.

Though there is variability in the extent to which caregivers plan for the future, innovations in this area promote future planning for this group in ways that have, in a few cases, shown to be effective. For example, one peer-based intervention included both caregivers and care recipient in future planning discussions—relative to nonparticipating families, those that did participate made more concrete steps in planning for the future, and caregiving burden was also reduced (Heller and Caldwell, 2006).

Very few of the military caregiver–specific programs we identified offered specific long-term planning assistance to military caregivers. Beyond the usual advice for planning legal issues for the care recipient (powers of attorney, living wills, estates and trusts), there is little guidance for military caregivers to help address long-term needs for themselves. Caregiving networks for parents of disabled children often encourage their constituents to plan for specific transitions that their care recipient will inevitably face, and to make arrangements for housing or replacement caregiving in the event they are no longer able to provide this support. Planning for the caregiver's own future can provide security for the care recipient's future as well, particularly if the caregiver becomes incapacitated in some manner (for example, due to compromised health or death).

## Sustainability for Programs Serving Caregivers

While it is reasonable to expect that government-sponsored programs will endure as a result of legislation enacting them as permanent programs (as well as federal and state budgeting processes that ensure their financial stability), it is possible that the tightening of budgets could decrease capacity and thus access to these programs. The majority of government programs for military caregivers identified in our scan are also relatively new. Since all government-sponsored initiatives are subject to federal and state budgetary concerns, the newer organizations supporting caregivers, in particular, may be subject to changes in appropriations, particularly if they do not prove to be effective.

Of greater concern among veteran policy analysts, however, is the sustainability of programs that are nongovernmental (Williamson, 2009; Harrell and Berglass, 2012). Whether it is due to their reliance on soft sources of financial support; the maturity of their infrastructure for oversight, capacity, and accountability; or data on their effectiveness, understanding the long-term sustainability of these programs is critical for ensuring a landscape of support programs that can endure. For example, programs that are ineffective, have low capacity to meet demand, or exist within organizations that may face tightening budgets or lowered philanthropic support may be vulnerable to closure or redirection.

To understand the potential risk for these issues among the military caregiver support programs we identified, we examined the distribution of programs according to maturity (as measured by years of operation) and tax status (as a measure of their potential reliance on soft, philanthropic support). As shown in Figure 4.3, approximately half of the not-for-profit and private, for-profit programs serving military caregivers have been in existence for less than ten years, with a quarter (21 not-for-profits and 2 private, for-profit programs) in existence for less than five years. Though not necessarily a direct marker of sustainability (i.e., some new programs will thrive, and programs in existence for more than ten years may close), these new programs may be particularly vulnerable to the issues of waning public interest, lowered philanthropic support, or capacity concerns in fiscally constrained times.

**Figure 4.3**
**Years of Operation by Organizational Tax Status (n = 114)**

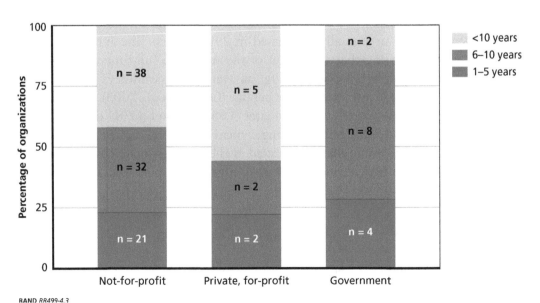

## Potential Benefits and Costs to Society

Caregiving contributions can confer direct benefits to the care recipient (in terms of increasing well-being and faster recovery/reintegration) as well as defrayed costs to society with respect to the unpaid contributions from their care (by enabling disabled individuals to live outside of institutions). Feinberg et al. (2011) estimated the value of family caregiving for adults over the age of 18 years to be $450 billion in 2009 by assigning an economic value to an hour of family caregiving ($11.16) and applying that to an estimate of 42.1 million caregivers performing, on average, 18 hours of caregiving per week (multiplied by 52 weeks per year).[1] Applying their methodology to our own values (though retaining their value of $11.16 as the economic value of one hour of family care), we estimate the yearly value of post-9/11 military caregivers to be $3 billion, pre-9/11 military caregivers to be $10.6 billion, and civilian caregivers to be $41 billion.[2]

While these benefits provide a rough estimate of caregivers' unpaid contributions, they fail to adjust for the increased costs that caregivers also confer on society. As we noted in Chapter Three, caregivers incur costs at the individual level in terms of increased risk for health deterioration, depression, and decreased well-being. They experience changes in their relationships with others in their families and within their communities, which also translate into costs. In addition, largely as a consequence of the impact on their ability to engage in the workforce as well as increases in personal and family costs for services, they suffer increased financial burden, income loss, and increased barriers to sources of support and services (such as health insurance). These impacts affect not only the individual but also other members of the family, employers, and society more broadly.

Using data collected through a national Gallup survey of working American caregivers, Witters (2011) calculated the costs of family caregiving in terms of lost productivity to be $25.2 billion annually (estimated in 2011 dollars). The author arrived at this number by estimating that 17 percent of the American full-time workforce is a caregiver and that caregivers report missing, on average, 6.6 workdays per year; they assumed a cost of $200 in lost productivity per day (Goetzel et al., 2003). Applying this algorithm to our own data yields costs estimates of $5.9 billion (in 2011 dollars) among post-9/11 caregivers and $23.2 billion among civilian caregivers; because pre-9/11 caregivers work, on average, more than is expected of them, we estimate cost-savings (i.e., time spent working for which they are not paid) for this group of around $1 billion.

---

[1]   The economic value of one hour of family care is based on a weighted average of the state's minimum wage, the median hourly wage of a home health aide, and the private pay hourly rate to hire a home health aide.

[2]   Our estimate is significantly lower than Feinberg et al. (2011) because our data indicate fewer caregivers (likely due to our more exclusive definition of caregiver; see Appendix C) and our data also suggest fewer average hours of caregiving per week (four to five hours per week versus 18 hours per week).

While significant, these costs may underestimate the actual costs to society because they use an average of lost time across all caregivers. Caregivers are unique, and individual attributes may confer substantially more or less costs, such as caregivers' professions or their health or well-being. For example, as shown in Chapter Three, we estimate that between roughly 20 and 40 percent of caregivers may have depression; studies not specific to caregivers suggest that rates of absenteeism and presenteeism (how efficiently and well a worker performs on the job) are higher among individuals who have depression compared with those who do not (Lerner et al., 2004; Kessler et al., 2003). Symptoms of depression—such as the loss of interest and pleasure in normal activities, slowed thinking, decreased concentration, and sleep problems—may have direct impacts on an employee's performance at work and may partially explain the higher costs evident among individuals with depression and, in turn, among caregivers (Goetzel et al., 2003; Wang et al., 2007; Lerner and Henke, 2008).

While we rely upon these earlier studies to provide rough estimates of the economic benefits and costs of caregiving on society as an illustrative example of the social ecological framework of our study, it also informs how one views the costs of war on society. Given that military caregivers assume their roles largely as a consequence of the disabilities incurred or aggravated by members of the armed forces during their time of service, the costs they confer on society have been considered part of the long-term care costs associated with caring for veterans. However, given their increased risk for negative consequences that had not been documented before, earlier calculations may have underestimated the total costs of war (Bilmes, 2013).

Efforts to address and mitigate the negative consequences and increased costs of caregiving can potentially increase the value that military caregiving confers on society. Future studies that gather more detailed information and data about the effectiveness of various caregiver support interventions—and their impact on the costs of lost productivity (at both the individual and societal level)—might inform the business case for increasing support for this vulnerable population.

## Summary

We expect that caregiving burdens will change over time, and that the needs of caregivers will similarly evolve. For care recipients relying upon parents for caregiving support, within just 15 years, their caregivers could no longer be able to serve in this capacity. This suggests that tens of thousands of post-9/11 veterans may need alternate sources of caregiving in the near future, and if other family members cannot render this support, these veterans may become increasingly reliant upon governmental sources of formal caregiving. While our estimates are not as precise, we also posit that an additional 10 percent of post-9/11 veterans is at risk for losing a caregiver through divorce. Caregivers and care recipients need to plan for the future realistically, including considering alternative residential arrangements and engaging members of an extended care network in future plans when possible.

We also examined the maturity of current military caregiver programs to understand whether there are risks to sustainability. Many of the services geared toward military caregivers are new; the novelty of these programs make them particularly vulnerable to the issues of waning public interest, lowered philanthropic support, and capacity concerns.

Finally, using literature from the civilian caregiving setting as well as from studies on the effects of mental health problems on society, we discuss the potential costs to society associated with the issues and challenges faced by military caregivers. We apply these methods to our own data to derive fairly crude estimates. Some have tallied the costs of war to include the downstream costs associated with caring for the veterans. These efforts may have underestimated the total costs of war because they excluded the full costs associated with the caregiving burdens faced by military caregivers and their own downstream consequences.

# CHAPTER FIVE

# Closing Gaps: Conclusions and Recommendations

## Conclusions

Recognizing the sacrifices and contributions of our armed forces remains a national priority. Since its earliest years, the United States has had specific policies and programs designed to care for our wounded warriors (Rostker, 2013). Since its founding, the Veterans Administration, and now the Department of Veterans Affairs, has provided medical care, rehabilitation, and disability benefits to facilitate the reentry of our most wounded veterans. Over the years, these programs have been expanded to facilitate disabled veterans achieving optimal functioning and to facilitate reentry into the workforce for all veterans as they separate from military service.

The subset of veterans who suffer a disabling wound, illness, or injury—particularly if service-connected—have received an unprecedented amount of public attention and benefited from increased investments in the care and transition systems designed to support them. Alongside these veterans exists a cadre of informal military caregivers who aid in their treatment, recovery, and reintegration. Prior to this study, little was known about the needs of these caregivers, or the types and sources of care that they require.

This report describes the results of the first empirically driven study of the magnitude of military caregiving in the United States. Based upon a rigorous, probabilistic survey of U.S. households, we estimate that there are currently 5,499,253 military caregivers supporting current or former members of the U.S. Armed Forces, representing 24.3 percent of the overall current adult caregiving population in the United States today. We found several notable differences between non-caregivers and caregivers (for example, caregivers have elevated rates of depression); within caregivers between military and civilian caregivers (for example, civilian caregivers assist with more ADLs and IADLs); and within military caregivers between those caring for individuals who served before and after September 11, 2001 (for example, post-9/11 military caregivers report generally greater use of caregiving support services).

We also identified a host of policies, programs, and resources that support caregivers. For example, there are federal policies that offer caregivers access to services, benefits, and employment protections. Many of these policies exist for caregivers broadly, although some are restricted based upon the age of the care recipient (most often for care recipients that are over the age of 60) or the caregiver's relationship to the care recipient. Most federal policies enact programs that are implemented through the states, and in some cases individual states may offer additional policies and program opportunities. While these federal and state policies and programs afford benefits for military caregivers who also meet their criteria, recently there have been two specific federal initiatives to ensure coverage for caregivers of current and former military personnel regardless of age. These initiatives, however, are in their infancy and specifically target veterans of the post-9/11 era.

Instead of focusing on the array of "resources" available through directories, blogs, and informational websites, we set out to find organizations that provide **direct or intensive interaction** through the provision of specific services to military caregivers. These criteria excluded blogs, directories, and general information sources. While these resources may be of value and importance to facilitating information sharing among caregivers, we wanted to document the extent to which available services were aimed at the needs reported by military caregivers. In our scan of these services, we identified 120 organizations that provide direct or intensive services to military caregivers, 88 of which focused on the military population specifically. We found variation in terms of depth and breadth of services provided across the seven categories of interest, including common caregiver services (respite, patient advocacy and care management, helping hand, financial support, structured social support, religious support, structured wellness activities, and structured education or training) and provision of clinical care (health and mental health care). However, the focus of these programs tended to be on the wounded veteran or military families more broadly; of the 88 programs focused on the military, 71 served caregivers incidentally.

While our study has many and considerable strengths, it is not without limitations. As we outlined in our introduction, we rely upon self-reporting from care recipients and caregivers. While we used well-validated measures to assess health and functioning, individuals may under- or overreport their symptoms. In addition, we surveyed only individuals living outside of formal institutions. Thus, we underrepresent caregivers for care recipients living in nursing homes or other rehabilitation facilities. For our scan, we relied upon publicly available information and snowball sample techniques to identify potential programs. This approach may miss programs and organizations that are small and operate at a local or county level. Our assessments offer insight into caregivers and their needs at a single point in time. As we discussed in Chapter Four, we expect that the needs of both care recipients and caregivers will change over time and with interventions. Similarly, our scan identified programs during a defined time period. Finally, we had limited access to information about costs for programs and budgets within organizations. It was beyond our scope to assess the individual programs' quality and cost-effectiveness, or to assess the known and unknown opportunity costs associated with different programs and services.

While these caveats are important, the unique nature of our approach and the strengths of our ability to compare across populations and programs enable us to make several conclusions about military caregivers and the resources available to support them. Our main findings follow.

## 1. Relative to Non-Caregivers, Caregivers Have Consistently Worse Health Outcomes and More Strained Family Relationships

A wealth of past research highlights poorer outcomes among caregivers than non-caregivers in the domains of physical and mental health, relationship quality, and work and financial strain; our results confirm this past research. While these findings are not novel, such replication is important for many reasons. First, replicating the study in a nationally representative sample of military caregivers reveals a magnitude of association that is less biased than one that would be produced by a convenience-based sample. Specifically, past research indicates that studies of convenience samples tend to produce inflated estimates of the differences between caregivers and non-caregivers (Pinquart and Sörensen, 2003b). The current findings demonstrate that the magnitude of differences between caregivers and non-caregivers is noteworthy and not simply the result of sampling bias. For example, nearly 40 percent of post-9/11 caregivers met criteria for probable depression, a rate twice as high as that observed among pre-9/11 and civilian caregivers, and four times higher than that observed among non-caregivers. Second, we used well-validated measures of health and relationship quality, which lends credence to our findings. For example, rather than assessing depression by asking respondents whether they had had depression since becoming a caregiver (e.g., NAC, 2010), we assessed depression with a measure that has been validated against gold-standard diagnostic interviews of depression. Third, our sample represents a range of types of relationships of caregivers to their care recipients, rather than focusing only on spouses or family members. Thus, our findings have broader generalizability to the caregiver population. Fourth, we compared caregivers and non-caregivers while adjusting for a wide array of sociodemographic characteristics that could confound the effect of caregiver status on outcomes; differences remained after these adjustments, increasing the likelihood that there is something about being a caregiver that contributes to these outcomes.

## 2. Military Caregivers Caring for Service Members and Veterans Who Served After September 11, 2001, Differ Systematically from Caregivers for Those Who Served in Prior Eras, as Well as from Civilian Caregivers

With some minor exceptions, it is clear across multiple domains that post-9/11 caregivers differ from pre-9/11 caregivers and civilian caregivers, groups that generally look comparable to one another. Post-9/11 military caregivers differ from other caregivers:

- *Individually.* Compared with other caregivers, post-9/11 military caregivers are younger, more likely to be spouses of the care recipient and more likely to have served in the military themselves; three-quarters are in the labor force (versus 60 percent of other caregivers).

- *In the person they are caring for.* Post-9/11 care recipients are younger and more likely to be nonwhite, and more than 50 percent are in the labor force (versus 10 percent of other care recipients). Similarly, they are more likely than other care recipients to have a mental health or substance use problem, though post-9/11 care recipients have slightly greater functioning ability than other care recipients.

- *In the care that they provide.* Civilian and pre-9/11 caregivers are more likely to help with at least one ADL and at least one IADL than post-9/11 military caregivers. However, this is largely driven by the needs of the care recipient: When assistance with a task is needed, most post-9/11 military caregivers provide such assistance.

- *In their health.* In both their physical and mental health, post-9/11 military caregivers have worse outcomes than other caregivers; for mental health, this difference can largely be attributed to differences driven by both characteristics of post-9/11 military caregivers (younger age) and aspects of the caregiving context (total number of the care recipient's medical conditions, time spent caregiving, and helping the care recipient cope with behavioral problems). Moreover, post-9/11 military caregivers were less likely to have health care coverage and a usual source of medical care than other caregivers.

- *In the support that they receive.* Fifty-three percent of post-9/11 military caregivers report having nobody in a caregiving network who helps support them. Paradoxically, or perhaps precisely because of their lack of a network, post-9/11 caregivers are more likely than other caregivers to use mental health resources and to use such resources more frequently. Similarly, they use helping-hand services, structured social support, and structured education and training on caregiving more frequently as well. They also are more likely to receive financial stipend support, which may be driven by the fact that the main provider of such support for military caregivers (the VA Program of Comprehensive Assistance for Family Caregivers) is restricted to caregivers serving post-9/11 veterans.

- *In the impact caregiving has on their families.* Post-9/11 military caregivers caring for a spouse have worse relationship quality than other caregivers, a finding likely due to youth and shorter marriages.

- *In their work and professional careers.* Not only are they more likely to be employed, but post-9/11 military caregivers report greater financial strain—and miss, on average, 3.5 days of work per month; in contrast, civilian caregivers miss one day of work per month on average, while pre-9/11 military caregivers tend to work more hours than is expected of them.

Noting differences across all of these domains is important for tailoring programs to meet the needs of this group of caregivers. Importantly, organizations with a history of helping caregivers, like the American Red Cross or FCA, may need to adapt products geared toward caregivers of the elderly to be more in line with a population of younger caregivers caring in different ways for individuals with different, and often multiple, conditions. Moreover, products may need to be adapted or developed to cater to a population caring for employed care recipients (for example, training on working with employers to accommodate disabilities in the workplace, see Osilla and Van Busum, 2012) or with spouses on how to promote intimacy with disabled care recipients or those with mental health conditions like PTSD.

In addition to suggesting the need to better serve post-9/11 military caregivers, findings of elevated rates of depression, lower relationship quality, and higher rates of absenteeism among post-9/11 caregivers carries with them important implications that call for early interventions before more serious or additional adverse events result. Caregivers with depression are at increased risk of developing several medical conditions, such as type II diabetes (Eaton et al., 1996; Knol et al., 2006; Mezuk et al, 2008), Parkinson's (Shen et al., 2013), and coronary heart disease (Wilsum and Singal, 2003); among parents, depression increases their children's risk for adverse emotional and behavioral outcomes (Goodman et al., 2011; Ramchandani et al., 2005). It is also well documented that depression has a "contagious" property within interpersonal relationships (Joiner and Katz, 1999), meaning that a caregiver with depression increases the risk for, and sustains depressive symptoms in, their care recipients or other family members. Poor relationship quality with a spouse, partner, or significant other is associated with a host of negative short-term outcomes including poorer physical health (Kiecolt-Glaser et al., 1987; Wickrama et al., 1997), negative parent-child relations (Erel and Burman, 1995), and poor child adjustment (Grych and Fincham, 1990); in the long-term, it increases the risk of divorce (Karney and Bradbury, 1995). The costs of absenteeism may not only be lost wages and financial strain for the employee, but also could include employer suffering if there are no substitute employees to compensate for an absent worker or when firms face a consequence associated with not meeting an expected deadline (Pauly et al., 2002).

### 3. Though They Serve Military Caregivers, Most Programs for This Group Serve Them Incidentally—The Focus Is Typically on the Ill, Injured, or Wounded Service Member or His or Her Family

Most of the programs serving military caregivers tend to serve them incidentally. Either these programs have as their primary focus the wounded, ill, or injured service member and make available programming for their (primarily family) caregivers, or they serve military families and within that group have services for the subset that is serving as a caregiver. Programs that serve caregivers incidentally tend to offer structured wellness activities, patient advocates or case managers, and helping-hand services; those that serve caregivers specifically tend to offer stipends to offset income loss, structured education and training on caregiving, and structured social support for caregivers.

Embedding services specific to caregivers in organizations that serve these individuals incidentally is not necessarily a bad idea. In many instances these are long-standing organizations that are likely to continue to exist well into the future, when military caregiving needs might increase (see Conclusion 5). However, these organizations should consider who their target population is and how they want to market services to them. If these organizations want to serve all caregivers, marketing to and providing services for extended family and nonfamily members is important. If the focus is to remain exclusively on the wounded, ill, or injured (and, by extending service offerings to family members, serve caregivers incidentally) or on family caregivers exclusively, there will be a notable lack of resources for extended family and nonfamily caregivers, a group that makes up roughly one-third of caregivers across all post-9/11 and pre-9/11 caregivers.

### 4. Noticeably Lacking in the Array of Services Offered to Military Caregivers Are Both Standard and Nonstandard Health Care Coverage and Programs to Offset the Income Loss Associated with Caregiving

In Chapter One, we described four goals that organizations may have as their objective in offering services to military caregivers. We return to that framework here to identify whether there is a known need for these services, and if the available services offered within each are addressing that need.

- *Services aiding caregivers to provide better care* (patient advocacy or case management and structured education or training). More than 34 percent of post-9/11 caregivers report being extremely challenged by medical uncertainty of the care recipient's condition; half that proportion of pre-9/11 and civilian caregivers report such challenges. Trainings for caregivers that have been evaluated have shown positive results, but the extent to which the training for military caregivers follow evidence-based protocols is unclear. Further, no current training we found was being evaluated in a rigorous way to examine short- or long-term outcomes beyond caregiver satisfaction with the training. We also found that post-9/11 caregivers reported significantly higher challenges in obtaining necessary medical and other services for their care recipients as compared with other caregivers. While many programs identified in our scan offered patient advocacy and case management support, only about one-fifth of all caregivers were using this type of support program. Despite reporting being more challenged in this area, post-9/11 caregivers did not report higher utilization of these services than did other caregivers. Among those who did use this type of external support, post-9/11 military caregivers rated them as significantly more helpful than other caregivers did. Thus, even though they were no more likely to use them, post-9/11 caregivers reported a higher benefit of these programs in meeting one of their challenges.

- *Services addressing caregiver health and well-being (respite care, health and mental health care, structured social support, and structured wellness activities targeting caregivers solely).* As described under Conclusions 1 and 2, caregivers have consistently worse health outcomes than non-caregivers—and among caregivers, post-9/11 military caregivers' outcomes are consistently worse than those of other groups. Access to health care and routine health care check-ups are preventive measures that help ensure that medical conditions are identified early in their course, which, in turn, improves the effectiveness of prescribed treatments. However, close to half of all post-9/11 military caregivers do not have such access, and only four programs are available to specifically help caregivers in this area (there are three times this number that offer some form of mental health care). Also in limited quantity is respite care, offered by eight organizations, though notably fewer post-9/11 military caregivers (18 percent) have used respite care than civilian caregivers (30 percent). In contrast, more programs promote caregiver wellness via structured wellness activities (e.g., fitness classes, stress relief lessons, or outdoor physical activities) for them and their families; the effectiveness of these approaches on caregiver health and well-being is unknown.
- *Services addressing caregiver family well-being (structured wellness activities targeting care recipients and their family caregivers or family members of caregivers, a religious support network, and a helping hand).* In addition to higher rates of mental and physical health outcomes, romantic relationships between caregivers and spouses are of lower quality than between non-caregiving partnerships. To address this need, religious programming and structured wellness activities are often geared toward families. The effectiveness of such programs at improving relationship quality, however, remains disputed. In cases of more severe relationship distress, evidence-based relationship therapy has been shown to be effective in improving relationship quality (e.g., Christensen and Heavey, 1999), and therapies that integrate couple-based interventions with treatment for emotional disorders such as depression can improve relationship functioning and lessen individual psychological symptoms (e.g., Lebow et al., 2012). However, these interventions have not been validated with caregiver and care recipient couples, who may face different relationship stressors than non-caregiver couples.
- *Services addressing income loss (financial stipend).* Finally, there are limited stipends available, primarily for post-9/11 caregivers or those who care for the elderly, to help offset income loss that results from caregiving. This important service helps address the financial challenges that caregivers report having and that may result from, among post-9/11 military caregivers, a largely employed group of caregivers who miss, on average, 3.5 days of work per month relative to non-caregivers. However, among those who received a monthly stipend or payment from the VA, pre-9/11 caregivers rated it as significantly more helpful than did post-9/11 caregivers.

## 5. The Need for Military Caregivers Is Not Going Away, and This Demand May Actually Increase Over Time, and Have an Economic Impact on Society

Traditionally, both advocacy and research on caregivers has concentrated on persons caring for their elderly relatives or, more recently, their adult children with special needs. For the former of these groups, AARP projects that the caregiving support ratio (or number of potential family members aged 45–65 relative to the number of persons over age 80), which currently hovers at 7-to-1, will drop to 3-to-1 by 2050 (Redfoot, Feinberg, and Houser, 2013), given demographic trends in the United States. Similarly, we project depletion in military caregivers, particularly for post-9/11 military caregivers, caused by a reliance on parents caring for their adult children, and on young caregivers caring for their spouses whose marriages are at increased risk for divorce.

While the value of caregiving may be high for the care recipient and helpful for defraying medical care and institutionalization costs, the burden of caregiving exacts a more significant toll on the economy and society as a consequence of the impact in the employment setting as well as excess health care costs to tend to caregivers' own increased health needs. Using literature from the civilian caregiving setting as well as from studies on the effects of mental health problems on society, we estimate the costs of lost productivity are $5.9 billion (in 2011 dollars) among post-9/11 caregivers and $23.2 billion among pre-9/11 caregivers.

## 6. While Notable Federal Policies Have Been Expanded or Created to Cater to Post-9/11 Military Caregivers, State-Run and State-Level Policies Focus Caregiving Resources on Those Providing Care to the Elderly

There has been a recent influx of policies and programs geared specifically to caregivers serving veterans or service members who served after September 11, 2001. Notable among these are the VA Program of Comprehensive Assistance for Family Caregivers, created by the Veterans' Caregiver and Omnibus Health Benefits Act of 2010 and the SCAADL, authorized by the fiscal year 2010 NDAA. While noteworthy, the majority of policies, programs, resources, and research on caregivers have focused on *family* caregivers caring for an elderly relative. For example, $150 million is allocated to states annually to support family caregiving under the Family Caregiving Support Program, but the amount allocated is determined by the proportion of the state population over the age of 70. Additionally, those eligible to receive services from the program are adults caring for elderly family members or family members with Alzheimer's and associated conditions, or grandparents serving as caregivers to children under 18 or adults with a disability (see Appendix F).

Medicaid is also a large funder of caregiving support services via its Home and Community-Based Services (HCBS) waiver-funded programs, which defines a family caregiver as "an adult family member, or another individual, who is an informal provider of in-home and community care to an older individual." Although these services are also geared by legislation to serve caregivers of the elderly, 40 states have provided supplemental funding to cover those caring for individuals who are 18 or 21 and older (see Appendix F).[1]

## Recommendations

Ensuring the long-term well-being of military caregivers will require concerted and coordinated efforts to fill the gaps we have identified. Based on our research, we make 11 recommendations that are organized around four specific strategic objectives: (1) empower caregivers; (2) create caregiver-friendly environments; (3) fill gaps in programs and services to meet needs; and (4) plan for the future. These recommendations are meant to provide suggestions for meeting caregivers' needs and filling gaps in programs and services. As relevant, we refer to external literature for additional support for these recommendations. It was beyond the scope of our analyses to assess the costs associated with implementing these recommendations, and we purposely did not target specific responsible parties or approaches. Implementing these recommendations will likely require action from multiple stakeholders, including but not limited to policymakers at the federal, state, and local levels, employers, health care providers, religious leaders, members of the nonprofit community, and veterans, service members, and caregivers themselves. We encourage these stakeholders to collaborate with each other, consider alternatives, and to the extent feasible, rely upon the level of evidence of effectiveness to choose options with the highest potential value and greatest chance of filling the gaps we identified during our study. In most cases, there will be several options and opportunities for implementing these recommendations that include creating new activities as well as working within existing activities and/or organizations.

### Objective 1: Empower Caregivers

Caregivers provide value not only to their care recipient but also to the broader community and nation. As they tend to the needs of our nation's veterans, they facilitate recovery, rehabilitation, and reintegration. Over time, they render assistance and support to enable their loved ones to live full and productive lives. Facilitating this process requires that caregivers are informed, trained, and supported to be maximally effective. If caregivers are ineffective or unavailable, disabled veterans may become increasingly reliant upon government institutions and social welfare programs. Increased caregiver stress may also result in caregiver neglect or abuse of the care recipient (Paveza et al., 1992). We have shown that caregiving can have negative consequences on caregivers, their families, employers, and society. Thus, ensuring caregivers are empowered to capably serve in their roles as caregiver in addition to whatever other social role they occupy (e.g., parent,

---

[1]  The ten states that restrict HCBS funding to care recipients 60 or over are: Kansas, Minnesota, Iowa, Missouri, Arkansas, Louisiana, Massachusetts, New York, Rhode Island, and South Dakota.

employee) can confer benefits to care recipients, their families, and society. Efforts are needed that will help empower military caregivers and should include those that build their skills and confidences in caregiving, mitigate potential adverse consequences of caregiving, and inform the public of the value of caregivers:

1. **Provide high-quality, dynamic education and training to help military caregivers understand their short- and long-term role, teach them necessary skills, and foster growth and confidence in their capabilities.** Training caregivers can be an effective way to both enhance the care and well-being of the wounded, ill, or injured, and also reduce caregiver burden. While more recent initiatives like the VA Program of Comprehensive Assistance for Family Caregivers have made the receipt of training a prerequisite for eligibility, such trainings usually occur early when caregivers first assume a caregiving role or begin to use a caregiving program. Caregivers' needs for training and education may vary over time; to meet this variability, programs may offer episodic trainings at conferences or "continuing education" like that provided by the VA.[2] To be effective, training must address the full spectrum of information and skills that caregivers need; this includes training on caring for and living with persons with depression, PTSD, and other behavioral health conditions. To appeal to caregivers, training must occur in a way that is efficient, especially for the younger generation of post-9/11 military caregivers with job and family responsibilities. In our earlier work, many caregivers noted this as a potential area of concern (Tanielian et al., 2013).

   Innovations in training caregivers and meeting their needs can and should move beyond approaches that apply different training modalities, like being offered both in person or online. For example, one relatively new innovation seeks to build caregivers' confidence, address income loss, and benefit society at the same time. This program, called Path Toward Economic Resilience and developed by a team of researchers at Northwestern University, helps caregivers find jobs that use their acquired caregiving skills (Simon et al., 2013). This program may specifically appeal to military caregivers, though future research is needed to evaluate the program's appeal with this population as well as its effectiveness.

   Research also plays a role in helping identify trainings of high quality. As described in Chapter Two, there is scant research on training caregivers to care for persons with mental health conditions, which is particularly relevant for post-9/11 caregivers. Training with a set curricula that is standardized can be evaluated and, if effective, could be replicated in other settings. Furthermore, if these evaluations are made publicly available, they could be listed on the FCA's Innovations Clearinghouse on Family Caregiving website, which lists evidence-based, emerg-

---

[2] VA Caregiver Coordinators use informal feedback opportunities to gather information from caregivers about their needs for additional training. The VA Caregiver Coordinators then share this information with the central office to inform the content, timing, and delivery mechanism for future training seminars.

ing, and model trainings for caregivers, though most items currently listed are for caregivers of the elderly, persons with dementia, or those with cancer. Having trainings evaluated and listed on websites such as these encourage other organizations that want to offer caregiving training to offer services that are evidence-based. This helps ensure that the training caregivers receive is of the highest quality. As such, caregiver training programs should be accompanied by evaluation efforts that serve to assess the impact of the trainings, both in terms of perceived value to the caregiver and in terms of providing knowledge and skills for performing caregiving tasks.

2. **Encourage and support caregivers in obtaining health care coverage and utilizing existing structured social support; such actions will help to address and mitigate any consequences of caregiving.** Given the increased risk of health-related problems for military caregivers, specific interventions that aim to prevent, recognize, and treat the adverse consequences of caregiving may be required. In addition to efforts that seek to lessen hours spent caregiving (discussed in Recommendation 7), ensuring that caregivers have health care coverage is critical for their health and well-being, and as many as 40 percent of post-9/11 military caregivers do not have such coverage. Also alarming is that 20 percent of pre-9/11 and civilian caregivers do not have such coverage. Currently, families of those veterans who were medically retired from service should have coverage via TRICARE; those enrolled in the VA Program of Comprehensive Assistance for Family Caregivers who are not otherwise insured are provided coverage via the Civilian Health and Medical Program of the Department of Veterans Affairs. Otherwise, military caregivers are left to access health care coverage through the same mechanisms as civilians: through their employers, through the newly established Health Benefit Exchanges, through Medicaid (for households under 133 percent of the FPL, which includes roughly 20 percent of military caregivers), or through Medicare for those over 65.

Not only do caregivers need health insurance benefits, they also require peer-based social support to address feelings of isolation by increasing connectedness within the population. This is particularly critical among post-9/11 military caregivers, of whom 53 percent report having no other caregiver in their caregiving support network. There are 53 services currently offering peer support, both regularly and episodically, and both in person and online. However, only 21 percent of post-9/11 military caregivers, and many fewer pre-9/11 military caregivers, access this support. This number is even lower among friends and neighbors who serve as caregivers. Promoting these services is important, as is evaluating their effectiveness at reducing caregiver burden, sharing information, enhancing caregiving skills, and building supportive networks.

3. **Increase public awareness of the role, value, and consequences of military caregiving.** Public awareness or education is needed to ensure that military care-

givers' concerns are heard, needs are addressed, and value recognized. Public awareness also creates the type of support critical for ensuring continued support for our nation's wounded, ill, and injured veterans and service members, as well as their caregivers; it also creates support for demanding accountability and support from the private, independent sector. In our earlier research, we found that military caregivers often do not label themselves as caregivers. Programs in our scan also noted that identifying military caregivers can be a challenge. The term caregiver itself may be confusing, as it could be used to refer to formal health care providers, child care workers, or nursing home attendants; some thought it was synonymous with family. Once explained in terms of the roles and tasks that caregivers perform, many additional individuals might recognize that caregiving is more common and that they are, or have been, caregivers themselves. In turn, this may create a public that is more supportive of the individuals in these roles. Efforts that specifically highlight and acknowledge the number and role of military caregivers can help address any misperceptions as well.

Specific awareness efforts, such as targeted outreach and education, may be needed in two environments in which caregivers often face challenges: health care settings and the workplace (see Recommendations 4 and 5).

### Objective 2: Create Caregiver-Friendly Environments

Military caregivers will, over the course of their lives, come into contact with a variety of institutions, organizations, and settings. For those organizations and programs that serve military populations, and those that serve the mentally ill and disabled, increased efforts to educate staff about the role and needs of military caregivers could help build more respectful and trusting interactions. This may include financial, judicial, and educational settings among others. However, particularly important are workplaces and health care settings.

More than half of military caregivers were engaged in the workforce, with two-thirds of post-9/11 military caregivers working full or part time. While caregivers are expected to perform on the job in their employment setting, they also serve a critical role in facilitating the care and treatment of their care recipient. While close to half of post-9/11 military caregivers do not have health care coverage, they nonetheless interact regularly with their care recipient's health care providers.

4. **Promote work environments supportive of caregivers.** Increased rates of absenteeism and the costs of lost income, wages, and lower productivity are of significant concern to both caregivers and employers. In 2007, the U.S. Equal Employment Opportunities Commission (EEOC) issued guidance to clarify the circumstances under which discrimination against workers with caregiving responsibilities might violate federal employment discrimination laws. The EEOC provided several examples of best practices for employers that go beyond fed-

eral discrimination requirements and that would remove barriers for caregivers in the workplace (EEOC, 2007); later the AARP Public Policy Institute (2011) recommended six employer practices to ensure family caregivers were protected from employment discrimination that closely aligned with those practices recommended by the EEOC. These practices are summarized in Table 5.1, though more information on each is available on the EEOC website (2007).

In addition to those activities already described, workplace-based services to mitigate stress can be an effective strategy for caring for caregivers (Witters, 2011). Currently, the VA Program of Comprehensive Assistance for Family Caregivers provides consulting services through its Caregiving Hotline, and facility-level assistance is available through their Caregiver Coordinators. Employers of military caregivers might connect with these services, but also seek to augment the VA offerings, especially for caregivers who are either not affiliated with the program or prefer to use non-VA sources of support. One way to do so is to offer employee assistance programs—employer-sponsored programs that provide assessment, counseling support, and referrals for additional resources to company employees and the members of their households. Studies have shown that these programs reduce absenteeism and enhance work productivity by 43 percent (Attridge, 2001; Attridge, 2002); 76 percent of large companies representing over 14 million employees provide an employee assistance program as part of the standard benefit package (Hartwell et al., 1996). Although we did not ask about provision of these services, a 2011 Gallup poll of working caregivers suggested that just over half worked for an employer that did not offer such a program (Witters, 2011).

In its assessment of the costs of caregiving on the U.S. economy, Gallup noted that while no single caregiver workplace program can make a major impact in the reduction of absenteeism, the collective effects of caregiver benefits (e.g., networks of support groups, employee assistance programs for emotional distress, access to health counselors) can have a high return on investment (Witters, 2011). In their survey, they assessed caregiver benefits available to employed caregivers in the workplace and the associated reduction in days missed per year, and reported that caregivers who worked in settings that offered an employee assistance program to address emotional distress reported 1.1 fewer days missed per year on average.

Thus, not only can employers make employee assistance resources available to employees, but companies that run employee assistance programs might benefit from connecting with and learning about the caregiving support services offered by the VA and other organizations. While it is beyond the scope of this report to assess the specific cost-effectiveness of employee assistance programs for military caregivers, the decreases in lost productivity may provide a strong business case for employers.

**Table 5.1**
**EEOC Employer Best Practices for Workers with Caregiving Responsibilities**

Be aware of, and train managers about, the legal obligations that may affect decisions about treatment of workers with caregiving responsibilities.*

Develop, disseminate, and enforce a strong EEO policy that clearly addresses the types of conduct that might constitute unlawful discrimination against caregivers.*

Ensure that managers at all levels are aware of, and comply with, the organization's work-life policies.

Respond to complaints of caregiver discrimination efficiently and effectively.

Protect against retaliation.

When recruiting, hiring, or promoting:
- Focus on the applicant's qualifications.
- Review employment policies and practices.
- Develop specific, job-related qualification standards.
- Ensure that job openings, acting positions, and promotions are communicated to all eligible employees regardless of caregiving responsibilities.
- Implement recruitment practices that target individuals with caregiving responsibilities who are looking to enter or return to the workplace.*
- Identify and remove barriers to reentry for individuals who have taken leaves of absence from the workforce due to caregiving responsibilities or other personal reasons.
- Ensure that employment decisions are well documented and transparent (to the extent feasible).

Terms, conditions, and privileges of employment:
- Monitor compensation practices and performance appraisal systems for patterns of potential discrimination against caregivers.
- Review workplace policies that limit employee flexibility.*
- Encourage employees to request flexible work arrangements.*
- If overtime is required, make it as family-friendly as possible.
- Reassign job duties that employees are unable to perform because of caregiving responsibilities.
- Provide reasonable personal or sick leave to allow employees to engage in caregiving.
- Post employee schedules as early as possible.*
- Promote an inclusive workplace culture.
- Develop the potential of employees, supervisors, and executives without regard to caregiving or other personal responsibilities.
- Provide support, resource, and/or referral services that offer caregiver-related information to employees.*

* Those practices that align closely with the best practices recommended by the AARP Public Policy Institute (2011).

5. **Health care environments catering to military and veteran recipients should make efforts to acknowledge caregivers as part of the health care team.** Military caregivers assume responsibilities to help maintain and manage the health of their care recipient: 50 percent report administering physical or medical therapies or treatment, but they also manage pain and emotional stability, and help promote healthy behaviors. Performing these tasks effectively requires that they interact regularly with health care providers: physicians, nurses, and case managers. In our earlier work, we heard directly from caregivers that some health care providers and environments were not as understanding or accommodating of their engagement and involvement in the care recipients receive.

Some settings may need specific caregiver documentation to allow the caregiver to participate in treatment sessions. In other settings, there is recognition of the role of caregivers and specific efforts to engage them. In several VA facilities, there are interventions geared specifically toward caregivers and policies that serve to raise awareness among health care providers of caregivers' roles. In addition to formal programs and policies in actual health care settings, efforts could be taken to train groups of health care providers to take more detailed patient histories that include assessing whether patients have a caregiver, to engage caregivers in the health care planning, and to follow up with caregivers to promote treatment adherence. Communication skills training has been developed specifically for health care professionals to minimize the stress experienced by patients, families, and caregivers, and such training appears to be effective in the short term (Moore et al., 2013). While specific curricula could be developed, opportunities to change the culture in health care could occur at professional meetings, continuing medical education events, and through the professional literature. While there are several opportunities for providers to learn more about caregivers online and in peer-reviewed journals, providers might also benefit from tailored information and fact sheets pushed to them through professional societies, professional training, or through leadership initiatives in health care settings.

### Objective 3: Fill Gaps in Programs and Services to Meet Needs

We identified more than 100 programs that aim to serve military caregivers; however, most serve caregivers incidentally because they are members of the care recipient's family. These programs tend to be geared toward the care recipient and his or her family is invited to participate, or they are geared toward military and/or veteran families, of whom caregivers are a subset. Similarly, many activities supporting caregivers (e.g., structured wellness activities, trainings) take time and are just one more activity to perform on a given day. Support to lessen the time caregivers spend providing care, which is directly linked to depression in this group, is sparser.

6. **Ensure caregivers are supported based on the tasks and duties they perform.** In general, eligibility for most caregiver support programs is determined by one of two factors: age of the care recipient (focusing on recipients over age 60) or relationship to the caregiver. The former criteria exclude most of those caring for post-9/11 service members and veterans; the latter omits extended family and friends, who collectively account for nearly 30 percent of all military caregivers. Further, some programs apply additional criteria, such as a VA disability rating or honorable discharge status, which further restricts the availability of resources.

To the extent feasible, programs should be eligible to all caregivers who might benefit from them. Some organizations determine eligibility on a case-by-case basis. If not feasible, criteria should be established or revised to specifically include caregivers that are extended family and friends. Organizations that serve wounded, ill, or injured service members and veterans and who serve caregivers to the extent that they are family members, or those that serve military and veteran families and serve caregivers to the extent that they are a subset, will need to consider if and how to include extended and nonfamily caregivers in their target audience. If organizations do not expand eligibility, this population of caregivers may go under- or unserved. Further, this population may grow over time, as they may be the ones called upon to replace caregivers who are no longer able to fulfill their caregiving role or who leave romantic relationships with the care recipient. Regardless of who is eligible for programs, assurances must be in place to detect, prevent, and respond to instances of caregiver neglect or abuse (Nerenberg, 2002).

From a policy perspective, many states have already augmented federal initiatives to expand offerings to serve care recipients under age 60 as well as to broaden caregiver eligibility to include extended and nonfamily members (see Appendix F). Post-9/11 military caregivers may be better served across all states and localities if the National Family Caregiver Program would be expanded to include services for those under 65 and if federal HCBS legislation authorized services for nonelderly individuals.

7. **Respite care should be made more widely available to military caregivers, and alternative respite strategies should be considered.** Few caregivers report having accessed respite care, and only a handful of organizations offer such care. To the extent that adverse outcomes associated with caregiving (e.g., depression) are influenced by the time they spend caregiving, finding temporary relief from caregiving seems critical. For those with busy schedules—like post-9/11 caregivers, juggling competing roles of caregiver, employee, and parent—other programs like structured education and training, wellness activities, or social support groups may be helpful but also add complexity to already hectic routines.

Respite for military caregivers should be considered carefully, and existing programs for patients with cancer, the frail/elderly, care recipients with dementia, or the physically disabled may need adaptation to better serve military care recipients. This is particularly important for care recipients with mental health issues, like PTSD. The challenges of caring for someone with behavioral issues are suggested by the finding that even after accounting for time spent caregiving, assisting the care recipient in coping with stressful situations and avoiding triggers of anxiety or antisocial behavior was a significant predictor of depression. Thus, respite may be even more critical for these caregivers, but finding other caregivers who are willing and/or equipped to deal with care recipients who have these types of issues may be a challenge. For these individuals, home health aides or volunteers unknown to the care recipient may be inappropriate and even detrimental. However, alternative and more suitable respite arrangements are possible. For example, Fisher House offers "Hero Miles," which provides roundtrip airline tickets to family members and close friends to visit ill, injured, or wounded service members who are undergoing treatment at an authorized medical center. Incentivizing family and friends to provide respite to the primary caregiver may be one way to give primary caregivers a break from caregiving that accommodates the complex conditions of some military care recipients.

In 2006, the Lifespan Respite Care Act was signed into law (P.L. 109-442), which authorizes Congress to spend approximately $288 million between fiscal years 2007 and 2011 to help family caregivers access affordable and high-quality respite care. Since 2009, $2.5 million has been allocated annually to the program, which provides respite grants to states (see Appendix F). Fully funding the program could expand respite services for military caregivers, and is a national policy priority for advocacy groups like the FCA.

### Objective 4: Plan for the Future

As we noted in earlier chapters, military caregivers are a diverse group. For post-9/11 military caregivers, they are young and may be in their roles for decades to come. Similarly, over half of the programs we identified to support military caregivers are also young. Ensuring the long-term well-being of caregivers and the agencies that aim to support them may each require efforts to plan strategically for the future, not only to serve the dynamic and evolving needs of current military caregivers, but to anticipate and meet the needs of future military caregivers in a changing political and fiscal environment. Planning for the future will require that efforts to support caregivers address the following:

8.   **Encourage caregivers to create financial and legal plans to ensure caregiving continuity and succession for care recipients.** Organizations that serve military caregivers could fill a gap by creating and sharing guidance about long-term financial and legal planning. Financial and legal planning programs are available for some caregivers, but these often are geared toward those caring for the elderly or persons with dementia and Alzheimer's, and thus focus on such issues as retirement and estate planning. Planning for post-9/11 care recipients will be necessarily different. These plans need to ensure the financial stability of caregivers and their families, and may include strategies to make up for lost wages and retirement and pension benefits. But they also need to consider the financial stability of their care recipient, who may need resources to purchase caregiver support if their current caregiver is rendered no longer able to do so. The legal plans will need to prepare for the appropriate powers of attorney and executors for any estates or trusts, but may also require that new guardians and caregivers be appointed in the event that the current primary caregivers are no longer available.

9.   **Enable sustainability of programs by integrating and coordinating services across sectors and organizations through formal partnership arrangements.** Just as caregivers and their needs are diverse, so are the organizations that serve them. Organizations vary with respect to the eligibility of the people they serve,

the services they offer, and the mechanisms through which they deliver programs. Prior writings on the support of veterans and their families have called attention to the proliferation of serving organizations and programs (Berglass, 2010; Weinick et al., 2010). While this proliferation may speak to the increasing attention and desire to serve veterans and their families, and while it provides options for veterans and their families who are seeking support, it also potentially creates confusion in navigating a crowded and changing landscape. We must ask: How many programs are needed? What is the right capacity? How can synergies be achieved?

The current number of organizations raises two pertinent issues. First, if not coordinated, the landscape of services available to military caregivers becomes a "maze" of organizations, services, and resources in which caregivers can easily become overwhelmed (Tanielian et al., 2013). One solution to help address the navigation challenges has been the implementation of resource directories—such as the National Resource Directory website (undated) and others that have been created by other organizations at the state and local level or according to particular areas of focus (e.g., respite care). However, veterans and their families are still left to sift through the choices to find the most appropriate services for which they may be eligible. Despite the creation of the caregiver page within the National Resource Directory, caregivers still are likely to be overwhelmed when searching for help. Another challenge is created when there are multiple, competing, and uncoordinated directories of services for caregivers.

Second, the sustainability of the programs and organizations serving military caregivers will be affected by the degree to which they rely upon "soft" money, the maturity of their infrastructure, and the effectiveness of their programs (Williamson, 2009). While attention and commitment for supporting veterans and their families is currently high, decreased public attention to this population as deployments to Afghanistan and Iraq continue to diminish have caused many to speculate that there will be a concurrent decrease in the level of private and philanthropic support for the many nongovernment programs that make up the current landscape of support for veterans, their families, and specifically their caregivers (Carter, 2013; McDonough, 2013).

One way to address both issues is to create formal partnerships across organizations. Such partnerships have been advocated by policy analysts concerned about the sustainability of services geared toward military personnel, veterans, and their families (Carter, 2013). However, effective partnerships will require more than a handshake or links on each other's websites. It will require exploring opportunities for true coordination, including the creation of coalitions, and for organizations to consider the benefits of integration in service delivery.

While the VA plays a critical central role in supporting military caregivers, a significant proportion of caregivers have been relying upon nongovernmental programs for support, which comprise 80 percent of the services currently available to military caregivers. While many of these organizations have developed significant brand recognition and are the beneficiaries of large media campaigns and fundraising efforts, others (especially those smaller in scale) may not benefit from the brand recognition, publicity afforded by high-profile veterans and celebrities, and/or fundraising prowess. Beyond securing stable funding sources to finance these organizations and their programs, efficiencies could be achieved through the integration of some of these efforts into fewer, cost-effective programs. If integration is not feasible, both large and small organizations can endure through partnerships with government-sponsored programs or (other) larger organizations in an effort to provide complementary or supplementary services. Such consolidation could also potentially reduce the "maze" that caregivers perceive when sorting through the landscape of programs and services available to them.

Coordination may be facilitated by a centralized body that connects caregivers, support organizations, policy officials, professionals, and researchers. By gathering the input of these stakeholders, a well-financed and governed body could provide the necessary leadership to improve policies, programs, and services for military caregivers through research, outreach and education, professional development, and dissemination of best practices. Such an organization could serve to connect government and nongovernmental organizations, facilitate integration and coordination of services, and set forth strategic research and education plans for improving services and policies that support military caregivers. An example of such a model may be a National Center of Excellence, which serves to bridge sectors and facilitate improvements in particular areas of service or research.

10. **Foster health/well-being through access to high-quality services. Not only is there a need for sustainable programs, but high-quality support services will be necessary to protect caregiver effectiveness and mitigate the negative consequences of caregiving.** The Institute of Medicine (2001) has defined high-quality medical care as care that is effective, safe, patient-centered, timely, efficient, and equitable. This definition can be used to apply to support programs as well. At present, however, little is known about the quality (or effectiveness) of available military caregiver programs. Our scan focused on documenting the availability of programs across service areas; it should not be used to infer that all of these programs offer evidence-based, effective services. In fact, some may be offering services with little or no evidence to support their effectiveness or quality. Ensuring quality programs are in the service landscape is important because research has shown that the provision of high-quality care can improve outcomes.

Understanding the quality of services requires specific efforts to measure and assess the structure, process, and outcomes associated with these services. Unfortunately, conducting in-depth evaluations of all of the identified programs in our scan was beyond our scope. But we also did not hear of caregiver support programs conducting rigorous evaluations or studies to document their effectiveness, or that they had implemented continuous quality improvement initiatives. Currently, the FCA and RCI maintain databases on evidence-based programs, and the FCA resource includes information about model programs and emerging practices. In addition, the VA is funding several research projects to assess the effectiveness of caregiver services and interventions. Organizations that implement military caregiver programs could benefit from using these resources to inform their own service delivery, but over the long term, demonstrating their value may require that they also evaluate the extent to which their services are improving outcomes for their participants.

11. **nvest in research to document the evolving need for caregiving assistance among veterans (as they age) and the long-term impact of caregiving on the caregivers.** The current study provides a point-in-time understanding of the needs and burdens of military caregiving. While we can provide a glimpse into the future of military caregiving by looking at the characteristics of post-9/11 caregivers and the factors that might affect their caregiving demands, we can only make projections. Similarly, while the needs of pre-9/11 veterans may be akin to what post-9/11 veterans will eventually need, there are significant differences in the makeup and expectations of the pre-9/11 and post-9/11 generations—and as a result, the crystal ball may not be as clear as needed. In the future, rigorous, cross-sectional research, like ours, can shed light on the needs of caregivers and how those needs compare to the ones presented here.

Research is needed in the short term in three areas. First, longitudinal research should be initiated now that follows a cohort of military caregivers over time to reveal how caregiving demands, networks, and burdens change as a result of changes in care recipients' needs. Very little longitudinal research has been conducted with caregivers, and virtually none with military caregivers, leaving a sizable gap in the scientific literature that limits our understanding of the dynamic nature of caregiving. Second, as post-9/11 veterans and their caregivers grow older, their needs and reliance upon VA and non-VA programs may also evolve. Projecting future demands on the VA system and on non-VA entities will be important for ensuring sufficient capacity and resources. Finally, as highlighted in Recommendations 1 and 10, evaluations of effective caregiving support programs are needed to ensure that resources are both efficiently and wisely allocated and to promulgate programs that are evidence-based.

These 11 recommendations are aimed at securing the future for current military caregivers—if acted upon, they will serve to improve policies, programs, and services for future caregivers as well. As mentioned above, there are multiple stakeholders who will help improve support for military caregivers, and a coordinated response among them is likely to be most efficient. Of particular importance are the federal and state policymakers responsible for creating and implementing policies, programs, and services for supporting military caregivers. At the federal level, at least four departments (DoD, HHS, DoL, and VA) have direct oversight of policies catering to this population. Increasing information-sharing and coordination of services across these entities can promote great effectiveness. States also play an important role, most often in implementing the programs outlined by federal policies. As such, governors may wish to appoint councils or working committees within their own states to ensure maximum coordination and effectiveness in an effort to meet caregivers' needs.

## Final Thoughts

Honoring our veterans and facilitating their well-being remains a national priority. Numerous initiatives and oversight bodies exist to ensure that the access and quality of benefits and services afforded to our veterans continue to improve so that as a nation we can fulfill a promise to those who have served. A large cadre of military caregivers serve in the shadow of these veterans, playing an essential role in facilitating the recovery, rehabilitation, and reintegration of the wounded, ill, and injured. But, as we have highlighted throughout this report, caregiving duties often come with consequences. Military caregivers have higher rates of depression than non-caregivers, are more likely to lack a regular source of health care than non-caregivers, and those caring for spouses have relationships of lower quality than non-caregivers. Their caregiving responsibilities also alter—in both positive and negative ways—the dynamics within their families, including how they are able to care for their children. There are also impacts on larger society, as caregiving responsibilities affect productivity. To the extent that caregivers' well-being is compromised, they may become unable to fulfill their caregiving role, leaving the responsibilities to be borne by other parts of society. Thus, ensuring the short- and long-term well-being and functioning of caregivers is paramount to fulfilling a promise to veterans. Based on our findings with respect to the consequences of caregiving and the gaps in the array of policies and programs to support military caregivers, we have outlined a series of recommendations. If implemented, these recommendations can serve to fill gaps in the availability and quality of policies, services, and programs to support military caregivers.

# Survey Methods

## Overview of Study Aims and Design

RAND's survey of military caregivers had two primary objectives: (1) to enumerate adult military caregivers in the United States, and (2) to assess the needs and well-being of military caregivers. Our definition of *military caregivers* includes anyone who provides unpaid care and assistance for, or manages the care of, a current or former member of the U.S. military, National Guard, or reserves who has an illness, injury, or condition for which they require outside support.

To achieve the first objective, we fielded an online screener that assessed military caregiver status (according to our definition) to a probability-based, nationally representative sample of adults in the U.S. general population. We estimated the percentage and number of adult military caregivers who met this definition of a military caregiver based on respondents who directly reported being military caregivers and respondents who reported that they were wounded, ill, or injured, and receiving unpaid caregiving assistance (see Appendix C for more detail on the statistical procedure for enumerating military caregivers).

To achieve the second objective, we fielded an online survey about military caregivers' needs and well-being to two groups of respondents identified by their responses to the online screener: (1) wounded, ill, or injured service members and veterans who reported receiving unpaid caregiving assistance, and (2) adult military caregivers. Given the survey's focus on the needs of military caregivers, those service members and veterans who reported receiving unpaid caregiving assistance were asked to provide basic demographic information about their primary caregiver and the types and amounts of caregiving assistance that they received. Military caregivers were asked about the types and amounts of caregiving assistance that they provided to their care recipient and about their utilization of caregiving resources, their needs, and their well-being.

To facilitate interpretation of survey findings on military caregivers' needs and well-being, we also administered online surveys to unpaid adult caregivers of disabled civilians over the age of 18 (i.e., adults) *without* a history of military service (i.e., civilian caregivers), and adults who were not current caregivers of any disabled adults or children (i.e., non-caregivers). These groups served as control groups to which military caregivers were compared on the needs and facets of well-being assessed in the surveys. We sought to compare military caregivers with civilian caregivers on demographic characteristics and utilization of caregiving resources to assess how effectively the broader array of caregiving resources caters to military caregivers. We compare military caregivers with non-caregivers on needs and well-being in the areas of psychosocial functioning, mental health, and physical health. Because we anticipated that the age and sex distributions of the military caregiver sample would consist predominantly of older adults and females, we pursued a matched sampling strategy in which the age and sex distributions of the non-caregiver sample were matched to those of the military caregiver sample.

Survey instruments for each population were designed to assess the same outcomes and domains where relevant to permit comparisons across populations. All survey instruments were translated into Spanish to permit recruitment of individuals whose primary language is Spanish.[1]

## Sampling Procedures

Because the aims of this study are to make population-level statements about the number of military caregivers in the general U.S. population and the needs and well-being of the U.S. military caregiver population, we sought to recruit the majority of study participants from a probability-based online panel that is designed to be nationally representative of households in the U.S. general population across a broad range of demographic characteristics; i.e., GfK's KnowledgePanel (KP). For all populations except for military caregivers, the entire sample was recruited from KP.

Based on the available research on military caregivers, we expected a very low prevalence of military caregivers in the U.S. general population. Therefore, to design a sampling plan that would result in sufficient sample sizes (i.e., n = 1,000 military caregivers) to yield reliable parameter estimates and acceptable standard errors, and would permit comparisons of different subgroups of interest, we conducted a preliminary check in June 2013 to estimate the number of military caregivers that we would likely recruit from KP. Our preliminary check entailed administering a brief screener to a random sample of 1,000 members of KP, which had 44,734 households enrolled at that time, to determine how many panelists met our definition of a military caregiver. We also assessed how many panelists met our definition of a wounded veteran or service member with an unpaid caregiver.

This preliminary check indicated a very low prevalence of military caregivers (2.4 percent) and wounded veterans or service members with unpaid caregivers

---

[1]   A forward-translation of the English survey instrument to Spanish was done by a third-party vendor that specializes in translation, Cetra Language Solutions. A translator in RAND's Survey Research Group reviewed and edited the Spanish-translated survey to arrive at a final version.

(1.4 percent) in the panel. Given the typical response rate of 60–65 percent for KP surveys, we projected final sample sizes of roughly 640 military caregivers in KP,[2] and 380 wounded veterans or service members with an unpaid caregiver.[3] Thus, we anticipated that we would be unable to reach our targeted sample size of 1,000 military caregivers by recruiting from KP alone. Further, we sought specifically to increase the number of caregivers caring for someone who served after September 11, 2001. We therefore supplemented the sample of military caregivers recruited from KP with a convenience sample of approximately 200 caregivers of OEF/OIF/OND service members and veterans recruited from WWP, a nonprofit veterans' service organization dedicated to addressing the needs of wounded OEF/OIF/OND veterans that has a registry of caregivers for this population. A sample size of 200 permits comparisons between OEF/OIF/OND caregivers and caregivers of veterans of other eras of military service. We will describe sampling and procedures in greater detail for both of these sampling frames; in Appendix B, we describe our weighting procedures for combining the samples.

## KnowledgePanel

KP is a probability-based online panel that is designed to represent the U.S. general population of noninstitutionalized adults on a wide array of sociodemographic characteristics according to population benchmarks from the Current Population Survey (U.S. Census Bureau and Bureau of Labor Statistics, undated). Households enrolled in KP at the time of this study were randomly sampled from one of three sampling frames: (1) the U.S. residential landline telephone universe, from which random digit dialing was used to recruit KP members starting in 1999, (2) an address-based sampling frame constructed from the U.S. Postal Service's Delivery Sequence File that includes cell-phone only households and covers 97 percent of households in the United States, from which KP members were recruited starting in 2009, or (3) a random-dialing sampling frame that specifically targets residential landlines in census blocks with high concentrations of Spanish-speaking Hispanic residents to recruit them into a supplemental panel called KnowledgePanel Latino (GfK, 2013). The address-based sampling frame has replaced the original random-dialing sampling frame comprising the U.S. residential landline telephone universe. At the time of the current study, the majority (62 percent) of KP members had been recruited through the address-based sampling frame.

Households without Internet access are given a netbook computer and free Internet service so they can participate in online surveys. Household sampling occurs through-

---

[2]  The estimate of the number of military caregivers in KnowledgePanel who could be recruited to participate in the survey was calculated as follows: 2.4-percent prevalence x 60-percent response rate x 44,734 households in KnowledgePanel = 644.

[3]  The estimate of the number of disabled veterans and service members with unpaid caregivers in Knowledge-Panel who could be recruited to participate in the survey was calculated as follows: 1.4-percent prevalence x 60-percent response rate x 44,734 households in KnowledgePanel = 376.

out the year and is done without replacement. Households randomly sampled from the address-based sampling frame are invited to enroll in KP by mailings in both English and Spanish; households that do not respond to the mailings are invited by telephone when a telephone number for the household is available. To enroll in KP, a member of the invited household must respond to the invitation and provide basic demographic information by mail, phone, or online. When this study was conducted in the fall of 2013, there were 41,163 KP households with an English or Spanish speaker over the age of 18 who was an "active panelist," i.e., a panelist who had completed at least one KP survey in the previous three months. The great majority of the panelists were English speakers (95 percent; n = 39,140).

### Screener

In the fall of 2013, we contacted all 41,163 KP households. Many households contained more than one panelist, but only one respondent per household was sampled to maintain independence of observations. KP sent one randomly selected adult in each household an email invitation to complete the online screener for assessment of their eligibility to participate in the study, which meant determining whether the respondent met eligibility criteria for one of the four target populations (military care recipients, military caregivers, civilian caregivers, and non-caregivers), or none of them in the case of respondents who were hired caregivers or unpaid caregivers of disabled children. Of the 41,163 panelists invited to complete the screener, 28,164 completed the screener for a screener response rate of 68 percent, which is consistent with the response rates typically observed for KnowledgePanel surveys.

### Survey

Of the 28,164 respondents who completed the screener, 27,705 (98 percent) met definitional criteria for one of the four target populations. The majority of the 459 respondents who were not classified in one of the four target populations were caregivers of disabled children, not adults (Figure A.1).

Because of definitional overlap among some of the target populations, such that a respondent could fall into more than one population (e.g., a respondent could be both a military care recipient and a caregiver), screener respondents who met the definition of more than one group were sorted into one of the four groups to ensure mutually exclusive samples of survey respondents according to the following hierarchy: (1) military care recipients, (2) military caregivers, (3) civilian caregivers, and (4) non-caregivers. This hierarchy was ordered from lowest to highest expected prevalence of the first four groups in the general U.S. population based on the preliminary check of KP described previously and a national survey of unpaid caregivers in the United States conducted by the NAC in 2009.[4]

---

[4]   A national survey of unpaid caregivers conducted by the NAC in 2009 indicated that 26.8 percent of adults in the United States had provided unpaid caregiving assistance to an adult in the past year, and, of the adult care-

**Figure A.1**
**Reason for Not Meeting Definitional Criteria for One of the Four Target**
**Populations (n = 459)**

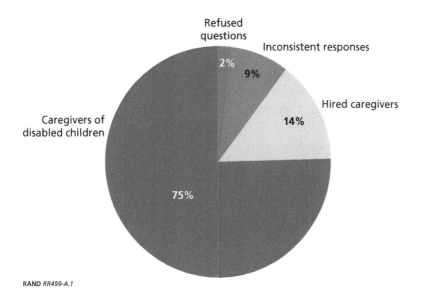

RAND *RR499-A.1*

All screener respondents who qualified as military care recipients or military care-givers were invited to participate in the survey. Based on the prevalence of civilian care-givers in the United States reported in the NAC study, we expected that the number of civilian caregivers who could be recruited from KP would be well over the targeted sample size of 1,000 survey respondents. Therefore, we initially invited only one ran-domly selected panelist out of every five panelists who screened into the civilian care-giver group to complete the survey. However, the percentage of panelists who screened in as civilian caregivers in the first few days after the launch of the screener suggested a lower prevalence of civilian caregivers than expected. The civilian caregiver survey was then opened up to all civilian caregivers in the panel who met the eligibility criteria.

We also expected that the number of non-caregivers who could be recruited from KP would be well over the targeted sample size of 1,000 survey respondents. There-fore, we initially randomly selected one panelist out of every 20 panelists who screened into the non-caregiver group to complete the survey. However, because we sought to match the non-caregiver sample to the military caregiver sample on age and sex, we adjusted the sampling of eligible non-caregivers for the survey based on the age and sex

givers who completed the survey, 82 percent were providing care for someone who had not been in the military. Multiplying 26.8 percent by 82 percent yields an estimated prevalence of 22 percent of adults in the general U.S. population who are unpaid civilian caregivers. According to the same survey, 28.5 percent of adults in the United States had provided unpaid caregiving assistance to a disabled adult or child in the past year, resulting in an esti-mated prevalence of non-caregivers of 71.5 percent.

distributions observed in the military caregiver sample after the launch of the screener. Because the military caregiver sample was slightly skewed to include more women than men, we oversampled female non-caregivers to match the proportion of females in the military caregiver sample. Among the 24,616 screener respondents who qualified as non-caregivers, one out of every 15 female non-caregivers and one out of every 25 male non-caregivers were randomly selected and invited to complete the survey; a total of 1,183 non-caregivers were invited to complete the survey. The age distribution of the non-caregiver sample aligned closely with that of the military caregiver sample without any sampling adjustments. Figure A.2 visually summarizes the sampling procedures for KP.

Eligible survey respondents were invited to participate in the survey immediately following completion of the screener. The invitation described the purpose of the study, the estimated time to complete the survey (20 minutes for the military care recipient and non-caregiver surveys, 25 minutes for the civilian caregiver survey, and 30 minutes for the military caregiver survey), the amount of points that the respondent would receive for completing the survey,[5] the voluntary nature of participation, and contact information for RAND's Human Subjects Protection Committee and GfK.

Of the 4,272 screener completers who were eligible for and invited to complete the survey, the vast majority (n = 3,852; 90 percent) completed the survey. Of the 3,852 survey completers, 37 (1 percent) completed the survey in Spanish. Table A.1 displays the number of screener respondents for each target population who were eligible for the survey, the number of panelists who completed the survey, and the conditional survey response rates.

### Wounded Warrior Project

The Wounded Warrior Project® is a nonprofit organization founded in 2003 to honor and empower service members and veterans who incurred physical or mental injuries, illnesses, or wounds, co-incident to their military service on or after September 11, 2001. WWP maintains a database of names and contact information of 4,258 individuals who have registered with WWP and self-identified as caregivers of wounded, ill, or injured OEF/OIF/OND service members or veterans. The database also includes information on the nature of the caregiver's relationship to their care recipient (i.e., spouse/other, sibling, or parent of the care recipient). We aimed to recruit at least 200 OEF/OIF/OND caregivers from WWP with sufficient representation of caregivers in each of the three strata of relationship types to permit comparisons of these three groups on outcomes assessed in the survey. Accordingly, we sampled all WWP caregivers with a valid email address in the database who were siblings (n = 43) or parents (n = 352) of their care recipient and

---

[5]  As an incentive for completing surveys, KP members receive points that can be exchanged for money, prizes, or products. One thousand points is roughly equivalent to $1. In exchange for completing the military care recipient, non-caregiver, or civilian caregiver survey, a total of 5,000 points was offered. In exchange for completing the military caregiver survey, a total of 10,000 points was offered.

**Figure A.2**
**Illustration of the Procedure for Sampling from KnowledgePanel**

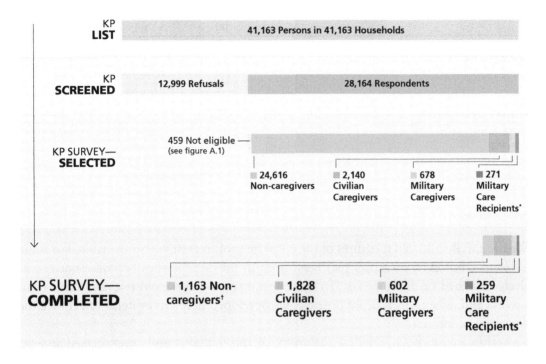

KP **LIST**    41,163 Persons in 41,163 Households

KP **SCREENED**    12,999 Refusals    28,164 Respondents

KP SURVEY— **SELECTED**    459 Not eligible — (see figure A.1)

24,616 Non-caregivers    2,140 Civilian Caregivers    678 Military Caregivers    271 Military Care Recipients*

KP SURVEY— **COMPLETED**    1,163 Non-caregivers[†]    1,828 Civilian Caregivers    602 Military Caregivers    259 Military Care Recipients*

*Includes wounded veterans and service members
[†]1 out of 15 females selcted; 1 out of 25 males selected. Selection of adult non-caregivers is stratified by gender and age in order to ensure similar composition as the pool of military caregivers.

RAND RR499-A.2

randomly sampled 1,641 (44 percent) of the 3,750 WWP caregivers who were spouses or had some other type of relationship to their care recipient.[6]

A WWP representative sent email invitations to a total of 2,036 individuals, and 20 percent (n = 399) of these individuals completed the screener. As expected, a very high proportion of screened individuals met our definition of a military caregiver and were eligible for the military caregiver survey (80 percent; n = 321). A $15 incentive was offered for survey participation. Of the eligible military caregivers, 284 (88 percent) completed the survey.

---

[6]  Other types of relationships between the caregiver and the care recipient include other family members and nonrelatives not already captured in any of the other categories, e.g., children, friends, and neighbors of the care recipient.

**Table A.1**
**Survey Response Rates for Target Populations Within KnowledgePanel**

|  | Eligible Survey Respondents (n) | Survey Completers (n) | Conditional Response Rate (%) |
|---|---|---|---|
| Wounded veterans or service members with an unpaid caregiver | 271 | 259 | 96 |
| Adult military caregivers | 678 | 602 | 89 |
| Civilian caregivers | 2,140 | 1,828 | 85 |
| Adult non-caregivers[a] | 1,183 | 1,163 | 98 |

NOTE: Response rates were computed as the number of survey completers divided by the number of panelists who were eligible for the survey based on their responses to the screener.

[a] Eligible non-caregiver survey respondents are those who met our definition of a non-caregiver based on their screener responses and were then randomly selected to complete the survey.

## Measures

We used well-validated measures of the constructs of interest where available. For some outcomes, however, measures had been used in previous studies but were not extensively validated or did not exist. In these instances, we borrowed relevant items from surveys and, when this was not possible, we developed new survey items to capture the construct of interest.

This section begins with a summary of the domains and constructs that were measured in each of the four populations in Table A.2. Next, we describe how they were scored for this analysis.

### Care Recipient Well-Being
#### *Patient Health Status*

We measured patient health status using the 12-item WHODAS-2, which assesses six domains of health and disability: cognition, mobility, self-care, getting along with others, daily life activities, and participation in community activities. Studies have shown that the WHODAS-2 is a valid and reliable measure of disability status (Garin et al., 2010). Difficulty was rated on a scale from 0 ("none") to 4 ("extreme" or "cannot do"). Military care recipients completed the self-assessment form of the scale, and caregivers rated the health of their care recipient using the equivalent proxy form of the scale. Research has shown that, internationally, 40 percent of adults score a 0 on this measure, indicating that they have no limitations due to their health (Üstün et al., 2010). More than 52 percent of the population scores a 2 or less.

#### *Current Medical Conditions*

Military care recipients and caregivers were provided with a list of 18 medical conditions and asked to indicate whether they/their care recipient had been diagnosed as having each condition. For each condition the patient had received a diagnosis,

**Table A.2**
**Measure Domains Completed by Each Population**

| Domain | Population | | | |
| --- | --- | --- | --- | --- |
| | Military Caregivers | Civilian Caregivers | Non-caregivers | Military Care Recipients |
| **Care recipient well-being** | | | | |
| Care recipient health status | X | X | — | X |
| Current medical conditions | X | X | — | X |
| Disability status and VA disability rating | X | — | — | X |
| **Care recipient demographic information** | | | | |
| General demographic information | X | X | — | X |
| Military history | X | — | — | X |
| **Caregiving tasks, time, network, and support** | | | | |
| Assistance with activities of daily living and caregiving history | X | X | — | X |
| Caregiving network | X | X | — | X |
| Task-related social support | X | X | — | — |
| Emotional social support | X | X | X | — |
| **Caregiving challenges, needs, and resources** | | | | |
| Challenges | X | X | — | — |
| Resources used to help meet challenges | X | X | — | — |
| Access to organizations providing resources | X | X | — | — |
| Barriers and bridges to using resources | X | X | — | — |

**Table A.2, cont.**

| Domain | Population | | | |
| --- | --- | --- | --- | --- |
| | Military Caregivers | Civilian Caregivers | Non-caregivers | Military Care Recipients |
| Caregiver/control respondent well-being | | | | |
| Depression | X | X | X | — |
| Anxiety | X | X | X | — |
| General health | X | X | X | — |
| Healthcare access and utilization | X | X | X | — |
| The experience of caregiving | | | | |
| Caregiver strain | X | X | — | — |
| Benefits of caregiving | X | X | — | — |
| Relationship quality | | | | |
| Spouse/partner relationship quality | X | X | X | — |
| Other relationship with care recipient | X | X | — | — |
| Caregiver financial and employment strain | | | | |
| Financial strain | X | X | X | — |
| Impact of caregiving on career | X | X | — | — |
| Absenteeism | X | X | X | — |
| Children and parenting | | | | |
| Impact of caregiving on family life | X | X | — | — |
| Caregiver/control demographic information | X | X | X | — |

NOTE: An "X" indicates that the construct was assessed in the corresponding sample, and a "—" indicates that the construct was not measured in the corresponding sample.

a follow-up question asked whether the condition "was related to or directly caused by [their] military service." The list of conditions was adapted from the NAC veteran caregiver survey (2010) and included the most common medical conditions among veterans—e.g., tinnitus; hearing loss; PTSD; back pain; limitation of motion of the knee; hypertension or high blood pressure; traumatic arthritis (VA, 2011a)—as well as other common medical conditions—e.g., cancer, dementia. We also provided room for respondents to write in other conditions or diagnoses. These write-in responses were examined by a registered nurse and, where possible, recoded into one of the original condition categories.

### Disability Status and VA Disability Rating

Using items taken from the American Community Survey (U.S. Census Bureau, 2013), military care recipients and military caregivers were asked to report whether the veteran had a VA service-connected disability rating, and if yes, whether that rating was 0 percent, 10–20 percent, 30–40 percent, 50–60 percent, or 70 percent or higher. Disability ratings are made according to VA criteria (VA, undated), and higher ratings indicate greater disability levels and higher disability compensation payments. Respondents who indicated that the care recipient did not have a VA disability rating were asked a series of follow-up questions to assess why. Specifically, caregivers of veterans or service members without a disability rating or the veteran or service member him/herself were asked if the veteran had ever applied for a service-connected disability rating, and if yes, whether that application was denied or still under review. If the veteran or service member had not applied for a service-connected disability rating, respondents were asked whether the veteran was planning to apply for a disability rating in the future.

### Care Recipient Demographic Information

We assessed a variety of demographic and descriptive information about care recipients, including their length of service, era of service, age, race/ethnicity, gender, income level, among other things. This information was gathered using standard measures widely used in survey research. Veteran/service member respondents reported this information on themselves, and caregivers reported this information for their care recipient. See Table A.3 for a list of care recipient demographic variables.

### Caregiving Tasks, Time, Network, and Support
#### Assistance with ADLs and Caregiving History

We assessed care recipients' functional status using 16 items adapted from the NAC veteran caregiver survey (2010). These items measured the care recipient's need for help in performing ADLs (e.g., getting dressed, getting in and out of beds and chairs) and IADLs (e.g., grocery shopping, housework). All respondents indicated whether the care recipient needed help with each activity ("yes" or "no"), and if help was needed, caregivers reported how often they helped the care recipient with the task ("never," "sometimes," or "often"), while care recipients indicated how often their main caregiver helped with each needed task. Next, respondents reported how much time they/their main caregiver spent in a typical week helping the patient "in all of the ways just indicated." Responses were made on a scale from "less than one hour," "1 to 4 hours," "5 to 8 hours," "9 to 20 hours" and multiples of 10 hours through "more than 80 hours." In addition, respondents indicated the number of years they had been providing care to the care recipient (or how long their main caregiver had been providing care to them).

### Caregiving Network

We assessed the network of caregivers that helped take care of the care recipient by asking respondents to report the total number of people who provided unpaid care for or managed the care of the care recipient. If respondents reported one or more additional caregivers, they were asked to report each caregiver's age, whether the caregiver lived with the care recipient and/or the respondent, the caregiver's relationship to the care recipient and to the primary caregiver, and the number of hours in a typical week

**Table A.3**
**Care Recipient Demographic Variables**

General demographic information

Relationship of care recipient to caregiver, 14 categories (e.g., friend/neighbor, spouse)

Age (open-ended)

Sex (male or female)

Ethnicity, seven Hispanic/Latino categories (e.g., Puerto Rican, Mexican)

Race, 13 categories (e.g., White, Black or African American, Chinese)

Employment status, seven categories (e.g., working, self-employed; not working, disabled)

Romantic relationship status, six categories (e.g., married, widowed, divorced)

Number of household residents (open-ended)

Household income in past year (open-ended)

Current residence in a medical center, nursing home, or some other care facility (yes/no)

Co-residence of care recipient and caregiver (yes/no)

Military history

Era of service, 12 categories (e.g., September 2001 or later, August 1990 to August 2001 [including Persian Gulf War])

War zone deployment (yes/no, and during which era of service)

Branch(es) of service, 11 categories (e.g., Army active component, Army Guard)

Years of military service (open-ended)

Current military status, five categories (e.g., Retired from the military, Discharged with severance or military disability payments)

Military disability status, three categories: Permanent Disability Retirement List, Temporary Disability Retirement List, Neither of these

Years since most recent military separation (open-ended)

that the caregiver spent helping the care recipient (scale from "less than one hour" to "more than 80 hours"). In order to reduce the burden on respondents with large caregiving networks, this information was requested for a maximum of five caregivers. Respondents were also asked about the number of paid, hired professional case/care managers or social workers who helped coordinate care and whether they believed the care recipient/they themselves had "the right number, too few, or too many people providing care, paid or unpaid."

### Task-Related and Emotional Social Support

Caregivers completed two items assessing the amount of task-related support available to them for help taking care of their patient. The first item asked, "If you ever felt you needed help with a caregiving task, how easy or difficult would it be for you to get that help?" The second item, taken from the NAC military caregiving survey (2010), asked, "If you ever felt you needed to take a break from your caregiving, how easy or difficult would it be for you to get someone else to take on your caregiving responsibilities?" Both items were rated on a four-point scale from "very difficult" to "very easy," with a fifth option of indicating that the question was "not applicable, I don't need help with caregiving tasks" for the first question and "not applicable, [care recipient's name] can be alone without a caregiver" for the second question. Emotional social support was assessed with a single item with a yes/no response: "If you needed someone to listen to your problems if you were feeling low, are there enough people you can count on, not enough people, or is there no one you can count on?"

## Caregiving Challenges, Needs, and Resources

In order to assess caregivers' challenges, needs, and the resources they use to help meet those needs, we adopted the needs assessment framework developed by Miller et al. (2011). Their measurement tool was designed to assess problems that service members and their families experienced across many domains, the types of help respondents needed to address their problems, what types of resources respondents accessed to obtain help (e.g., VA programs, local government programs), and the barriers they faced in obtaining help from those resources. We adapted this measurement framework to apply to the problems, needs, and resources used by both military and nonmilitary caregivers. Thus, caregivers were asked a series of questions assessing the daily life challenges they face, their resource needs, the programs or entities they use to help address those needs, and how well those programs/entities have helped meet their needs.

### Challenges

Caregivers were asked to indicate the extent to which they had experienced various challenges in the past year. The specific challenges were adapted from the NAC military caregiving survey (2010), Miller et al.'s (2011) list of military family challenges, and challenges reported by military caregivers in *Cornerstones of Support* (Tanielian et al., 2013). The list of challenges included in the survey is as follows:

- uncertainty about the medical aspects of [care recipient]'s illness or condition
- obtaining medical care or other assistance for [care recipient]'s illness or condition
- obtaining services to help you as a caregiver
- your own physical health, mental health, or well-being
- your finances
- finding neighbors, friends, or family members to help you with caregiving tasks
- finding someone to provide emotional support for you when you need it
- balancing caregiving with work responsibilities
- balancing caregiving with family and household responsibilities
- balancing caregiving with leisure activities
- other types of challenges with caregiving.

In the survey, "[care recipient]" appeared as the first name or nickname of the care recipient, as reported by the caregiver. For each challenge, respondents indicated how much this type of problem challenged them in the past year using a four-point scale: "extremely challenged," "somewhat challenged," "a little challenged," or "not at all challenged."

### Resources Used to Help Meet Challenges

In the next section of questions, caregivers were asked to indicate "which of the following resources you used in the past year (if any) to help meet these challenges, and how helpful the resource was in dealing with these challenges." The specific resources were taken from the current study's environmental scan of military caregiver programs, the NAC military caregiver survey (2011), and Miller et al.'s (2011) list of military family resources. The resources included in the survey were:

- respite care/someone who provided care to [care recipient] while you did other things
- a referral service for finding programs to help [care recipient] (For example, a call-in help number for <*military*>[7] caregivers like yourself.)
- a referral service for finding programs to help you with your caregiving challenges
- health care resources for yourself (For example, doctor appointments, visits to health care facilities.)
- psychological counseling from a trained health care professional for yourself (For example, from a psychologist, psychiatrist, or social worker.)
- structured wellness activities for yourself (For example, classes or group activities on exercise, yoga/meditation, healthy eating.)
- structured social support groups such as online and in-person support groups for caregivers

---

[7] Alternative wording for military caregivers or items only shown to military caregivers.

- an advocate or case manager: someone to try to get or coordinate help for [care recipient]
- a religious or spiritual support network
- a monthly stipend or payment from the VA in exchange for the care you provide[8]
- a helping hand (For example, loans, donations, legal guidance, or housing assistance. Please do not include assistance or help that you reported in response to the previous question.)
- structured education or training (For example, in-person classes, one-on-one training, online modules, or printed workbooks to inform you about caregiving.)
- informal sources of information (For example, magazine articles, websites such as WebMD, and informational pamphlets.)
- some other resource.

In the survey, "[care recipient]" appeared as the first name or nickname of the care recipient, as reported by the caregiver. For each resource, respondents indicated whether they used the resource in the past year, and if so, how helpful the resource was on a three-point scale: "very helpful," "somewhat helpful," or "not at all helpful."

### Access to Organizations Providing Resources

In order to assess the organizations and entities that caregivers accessed to help meet their resource needs, we provided respondents with a list of organizations or people they may have used to help with the challenges of caregiving. The list of programs/ entities is presented here, and was derived from the current study's environmental scan of military caregiver programs, and the organizations/entities reported by military caregivers in *Cornerstones of Support* (Tanielian et al., 2013).

- VA[9]
- military-sponsored programs[10]
- state or local government programs: for example, a county-run health care center
- private or nongovernmental organizations that specifically support veterans, service members, or their families: for example, a veterans' service organization such as the American Legion or WWP[11]
- private or nongovernmental organizations that support *<broader communities, above and beyond veterans, service members, or their families[12]/individuals or their families>*: for example, a local charitable organization or private health care center

---

[8] Alternative wording for military caregivers or items only shown to military caregivers.

[9] Alternative wording for military caregivers or items only shown to military caregivers.

[10] Alternative wording for military caregivers or items only shown to military caregivers.

[11] Alternative wording for military caregivers or items only shown to military caregivers.

[12] Alternative wording for military caregivers or items only shown to military caregivers.

- friends or family
- an organized group of <*military*>[13] caregivers
- a church or place of worship
- some other place (please specify)

Only military caregivers were asked about military-specific programs (e.g., VA). For each program or entity, caregivers indicated how helpful the program had been with dealing with the challenges of caregiving ("very helpful," "somewhat helpful," "not at all helpful) or if they had not used the program for help with caregiving.

### Barriers and Bridges to Using Resources

Miller et al.'s (2011) needs assessment framework includes a component assessing the barriers (and potential bridges) to accessing programs/entities for help with caregiving challenges. We assessed these barriers and bridges in three steps.

The first step involved listing each program/entity that the respondent indicated he or she did not use for help with caregiving in the previous section (if any). For each program/entity not used, respondents indicated whether they would have preferred to use the program/entity for help with caregiving challenges, or would have preferred not to use the program/entity for help with caregiving challenges. For example, a caregiver may have not used the VA for help with caregiving challenges, but he or she would have preferred to use this entity if they had access to it. Conversely, a caregiver may not have used a church or place of worship for help with caregiving and preferred not to use it.

Respondents' reasons for their preferences were assessed in the second and third steps. After reporting their preferences for program/entity use, respondents were given the list of programs/entities they indicated they would have preferred to use. For each program/entity, respondents were asked to select all of the reasons they had not used the preferred program/entity. The potential reasons were taken from Miller et al. (2011), and included: "unaware of them/difficult to find information about them," "might hurt my or [care recipient's name]'s reputation to use them," "wait list/response time too long," "inconvenient location/difficult to access," "unfriendly or unwelcoming," "have used them for other needs," "[care recipient] is not eligible for their services," and "other (please specify)." For example, a caregiver may have preferred to use the VA for help with caregiving but did not because the care recipient was ineligible for services.

Lastly, caregivers were given the list of programs/entities that they previously indicated they would prefer not to use for help with caregiving. For each program/entity, respondents were asked to select all of the reasons they preferred not to use the program/entity. The potential reasons were the same as those given in Step 2. For example, a caregiver may have not used the VA for help with caregiving, and he or she

---

[13] Alternative wording for military caregivers or items only shown to military caregivers.

preferred not to use the VA because the wait list or response time at their local VA is too long, and/or because it is in an inconvenient location.

## Caregiver and Control Respondents' Well-Being
### Depression

We assessed caregivers' and non-caregivers' depression via self-report using the eight-item version of the PHQ-8, a clinically validated measure of depressive symptoms based on the DMS-IV criteria for depressive disorders (Kroenke, Spitzer, and Williams, 2001; Kroenke et al., 2009). Respondents rated how often in the past two weeks they had been bothered by eight symptoms of depression (e.g., "having little interest or pleasure in doing things"). Ratings were made on a 4-point scale from 0 = "not at all" to 3 = "nearly every day," and scores were summed to create an index of depressive symptoms ranging from 0 to 24. Past research demonstrated that a PHQ-8 score of greater than or equal to 10 indicates probable moderate to severe depression (Kroenke et al., 2009). This cutpoint has been shown to have excellent specificity (.92) and sensitivity (.99) in the detection of clinical diagnoses (Kroenke, Spitzer, and Williams, 2001).

### Anxiety

We assessed caregivers' and non-caregivers' self-reported anxiety using the four-item anxiety subscale of the Mental Health Inventory–18 (Sherbourne et al., 1992). Items assessed how often in the past month respondents had experienced each anxiety symptom (e.g., "been anxious or worried") using a six-point scale from "none of the time" to "all of the time." Scores on individual items were transformed from their original six-point scale to a scale that ranged from 0 to 100 and then averaged to create an index of anxiety symptoms. Higher scores indicate higher levels of anxiety.

### General Health

We assessed caregivers' and non-caregivers' general health status using one item taken from the SF-36 (Hays, Sherbourne, and Mazel, 1993): "In general, would you say your health is: excellent, very good, good, fair, or poor?" In addition, four questions from the SF-36 assessed whether respondents had any role limitations due to their physical health in the month prior to the survey (e.g., whether they "were limited in the kind of work or other activities" because of their physical health). Both of these scales were scored according to the RAND scoring method (Hays, Sherbourne, and Mazel, 1993) such that possible scores ranged from 0 to 100. Higher scores indicate better general health and fewer role limitations due to physical health.

### Health Care Access and Utilization

We assessed caregivers' and control respondents' health care access and utilization using a set of questions taken from the National Health Interview Study (U.S. Centers for Disease Control and Prevention, 2013). Health insurance coverage was assessed by asking respondents whether they had "any kind of health care coverage, including health insurance, prepaid plans such as health maintenance organizations, or government plans such as Medicare or Indian Health Services." Respondents then indicated whether they had a usual source of health care for when they are sick or need health advice. If respondents indicated they did not have a usual source of health care, a follow-up question asked respondents to indicate why (e.g., "don't need a doctor/haven't had any problems," "don't like/trust/believe in doctors," "don't know where to go"). Respondents also indicated how many times in the past year they had visited a hospital emergency room or an urgent care facility for any health reason, when they last visited a doctor for a routine checkup (within the past year, two years, five years, or more than five years ago), and whether they had seen or talked to a mental health professional in the past year. If they had seen a mental health professional, a follow-up question assessed the number of visits they had made in the past year.

### The Experience of Caregiving

Military and civilian caregivers completed two scales assessing their positive and negative experiences with providing care.

#### *Caregiver Strain*

We assessed caregivers' negative experiences with caregiving using the Caregiver Strain Index, which is a validated measure of caregiving stress and strain (Robinson, 1983). Caregivers reported whether they had experienced 12 different types of strain associated with caregiving (e.g., "it is a physical strain," "some behavior is upsetting," "there have been family adjustments"). Responses were coded 1 for "yes" and 0 for "no" and summed to create the index ranging from 0 to 12.

#### *Benefits of Caregiving*

In addition to stress and strain, caregiving can provide opportunities for personal growth (Pearlin et al., 1990). We measured this benefit of caregiving with four items used in previous studies of caregivers' experiences (Pearlin et al., 1990; Skaff and Pearlin, 1992). These items assessed how much caregivers perceived that they had grown as a result of the caregiving experience (e.g., "become more aware of your inner strengths," "grown as a person"). Items were rated on a four-point scale from "not at all" to "very much," and responses were averaged to form an indicator of personal growth.

### Relationship Quality

We assessed the quality of the relationship between caregivers and care recipients using two different measures. The specific measure that respondents completed depended upon a caregiver's relationship to the care recipient.

Caregivers who indicated that the patient was their spouse or partner, as well as non-caregivers who reported they were married or living with a partner, completed a seven-item measure of intimate relationship quality (Hendrick, Dicke, and Hendrick, 1998; Hendrick, 1988). The RAS is a valid and reliable scale assessing relationship satisfaction and intimacy (Hendrick, Dicke, and Hendrick, 1998). Items assess different aspects of the relationship, including how well the spouse/partner meets the respondent's needs, how much the relationship met the respondent's original expectations, and how satisfied the respondent is with the relationship in general. Items were rated on five-point scales (e.g., "not at all" to "extremely") and were averaged to form a measure of spousal/partner relationship quality.

Caregivers who indicated that they had some other relationship with the care recipient completed a general four-item measure of caregiver relationship quality oriented toward nonintimate relationships (Lawrence, Tennstedt, and Assmann, 1998). These four items assess relationship closeness, communication, similarity, and general relationship quality (i.e., how well the caregiver and care recipient "get along together"). Items were rated on five-point scales (e.g., "not at all" to "extremely") and averaged to form a measure of nonromantic relationship quality.

## Caregiver Financial and Employment Strain
### Financial Strain

Caregivers and non-caregiver control respondents reported their level of financial strain using two items taken from the Economic Strain Scale (Pearlin et al., 1981). Specifically, respondents were asked to rate how much difficulty their household had paying bills in the past six months ("no difficulty at all," "a little difficulty," "some difficulty," or "a great deal of difficulty"), and whether "your household has enough money to afford the kind of housing, food and clothing you feel you should have?" ("definitely not enough," "not quite enough," "mostly enough," or "definitely enough"). These two items were averaged to form an indicator of household financial strain.

### Impact of Caregiving on Career

We assessed the lifetime impact of caregiving on respondents' career or education decisions using six items taken from the NAC caregiver survey. These items assessed whether the caregiver had ever had to sacrifice their job (e.g., "take unpaid time off from work or stop working temporarily"), career (e.g., "take retirement earlier than you would have otherwise"), or schooling ("take time off from school or cut back on classes") as the result of caregiving.

### Absenteeism

Absenteeism is the amount of time employers are absent from work because of their own physical or mental health (Kessler et al., 2004). Respondents answered questions modeled after the World Health Organization's Health and Productivity Questionnaire (Kessler et al., 2004; Kessler et al., 2003). Respondents indicate how many hours they are expected to work over the course of seven days as well as how many days in the past month they had missed an entire workday because of problems with their own physical or mental health (i.e., not the care recipient's health), missed part of a workday because of problems with their physical or mental health, missed an entire workday for some other reason (including vacation), missed part of a workday for some other reason, or went in early/got home late/worked on a day off. Respondents also report how many hours altogether they worked in the past four weeks. Absenteeism is measured in two ways. First, we computed the total number of hours missed in the past four weeks by subtracting the number of hours the respondent worked from the total number expected of them (multiplied by four). To draw comparisons between two employees who miss the same amount of total work hours, but who are expected to work different amounts of time, we also computed a ratio of hours missed to hours expected.

## Children and Parenting
### Impact of Caregiving on Family Life
Caregivers with one or more children under the age of 18 completed a six-item measure assessing how caregiving has affected their family life. Caregivers were asked to report how much they agreed with each of the following statements using a five-point scale (from "strongly disagree" to "strongly agree"):

1.  My children and I work together to care for [care recipient]
2.  I spend less "quality" time with my children because I am busy caring for [care recipient]
3.  Caring for [care recipient] has brought my children and me closer together as a family
4.  Caring for [care recipient] has created a lot of tension in the household
5.  Caring for [care recipient] has made me a better parent
6.  Caring for [care recipient] has made me a worse parent.

Items 1, 3, and 5 were reverse coded, and a Cronbach's alpha score for the items was calculated. The alpha score was .68, indicating that the scale demonstrated acceptable reliability. Thus, items were averaged to form an indicator of parenting strain.

## Caregiver and Control Demographic Information
We assessed a variety of demographic and descriptive information about caregiver and control respondents, including their age, race/ethnicity, gender, income level, and military history. This information was gathered using standard measures widely used in survey research. See Table A.4 for a list of care recipient demographic variables collected for caregiver and control respondents.

**Table A.4**
**Caregiver and Non-Caregiver Control Demographic Variables**

| Demographic Information |
| --- |
| Age |
| Sex |
| Ethnicity |
| Race |
| Highest level of education attained |
| Employment status |
| Romantic relationship status |
| Home ownership |
| Household Internet access |
| Number of household residents |
| Household income in past year |
| Home address ZIP code |
| Primary language (Spanish vs. English) |
| Primary caregiver status* |
| Number of children |
| Number of children who are also the care recipient's children |
| Number of children under 18 |
| Any children with special needs |
| Caregiver Military History |
| Whether caregiver had ever served in military reserves or National Guard or was active duty in the U.S. Armed Forces |
| Era of service |
| War zone deployment |
| Branch(es) of service |
| Years of military service |
| Current military status |
| Military disability status |
| Years since most recent military separation |

* Question only asked for caregivers.

# Survey Analysis

## Overview of the Survey Analysis

The primary purpose of the survey analysis was to describe the broader population of U.S. military caregivers in terms of their sociodemographic characteristics, needs, and well-being; caregiving assistance provided to veterans and service members; and utilization of caregiving resources (e.g., programs and services for caregivers). To place these findings in context, military caregivers were compared with two control samples recruited from KnowledgePanel: civilian caregivers and adults who are not caregivers. The civilian caregiver sample served as the standard of comparison primarily for sociodemographic characteristics, caregiving assistance provided, and caregiving resources utilized. The control non-caregiver sample, which was matched to the military caregiver sample on sex, served as the standard of comparison primarily for military caregivers' needs and well-being. Thus, descriptive statistics on these dimensions are reported for each of these groups when applicable. We describe our sampling weights, data verification procedures, and analytic approach for comparing outcomes across our survey populations.

## Sampling Weights

The purpose of weighting is to generalize the study findings to the broader population(s) of interest. We produced three sets of weights: screener weights, post-stratification weights, and blending weights. Screener weights correspond to respondents that completed a screener, while the remaining weights correspond to respondents to the full survey. These weighting processes were performed using the statistical raking algorithm known as iterative proportional fitting (IPF). See Särndal (2007) for a description of relevant techniques. IPF is a procedure for adjusting a two-dimensional table of data cells so that the cell values add up to selected totals (or benchmark values) for both the columns and rows of the table. After running IPF, the weights were trimmed to prevent outlying values.

## Screener Weights

The screener weights, applied to the KP screener data, allowed us to obtain national estimates of prevalence. The screener weights help generalize results from the KP sample of screened respondents (n = 28,164) to the U.S. population of noninstitutionalized adults. These weights were created in two rounds of IPF. The first round adjusts the weighted full KP sample to match the sociodemographic characteristics of the U.S. population using benchmarks from the Current Population Survey (U.S. Census Bureau and Bureau of Labor Statistics, undated), the American Community Survey (ACS) (U.S. Census Bureau, 2013) for distributions of the military experience, and from the Pew Hispanic survey for language proficiency. To account for nonresponse, an additional round of IPF was performed where screener respondents were weighted to benchmarks derived from the entire KP panel for all of the characteristics presented in Table B.1. Once created, the screener weights were trimmed at the 2.5th and 98.5th percentile of the weights' distribution.

Screener weights are applied in the analysis to enumerate military caregivers in the United States, described in greater detail in Appendix C.

## Post-Stratification Weights

The next step was to compute a set of post-stratification weights corresponding to each of the four groups: military care recipients, military caregivers, civilian caregivers, and non-caregivers. Due to the lack of availability of population-representative comprehensive data for these groups, we used the screener-weighted KP samples to create benchmark distributions for each of the four groups. Using these benchmark distributions, post-stratification weights were applied to the KP sample to adjust the screener weights for selection and nonresponse in between the screen and full survey phases.

To derive appropriate post-stratification weights, the adjustments are done separately by group. At each step, the pool of KP survey respondents is "benchmarked" to the weighted distribution obtained from screener respondents using IPF. Given that all KP screener respondents in the first two groups (military care recipients and military caregivers) were asked to complete the full survey, this step may not seem necessary. However, it was needed to account for nonresponse that occurred between taking the screener and completing the survey. The nonresponse rate at this step was 4 percent for the veteran group, 11 percent for the military caregiver group, and 15 percent for the civilian caregiver group. For the fourth (or, non-caregiver) group, a small proportion of the KP screener respondents were asked to complete the full survey (due to the high prevalence of this group), and reweighting by IPF was necessary for this group to account for any self-selection biases. The post-stratification weights were trimmed at the 2.5th and 98.5th percentile of its distribution.

Post-stratification weights were used to calculate point and interval estimates of means and frequencies for outcomes assessed in the survey (e.g., probable MDD) for the military care recipient, military caregiver, civilian caregiver and non-caregiver

**Table B.1**
**Variables Used for Screener Weights**

| Sociodemographic Variables |
| --- |
| Sex |
| Age (18–29, 30–44, 45–59, and 60+) |
| Interactions (i.e., multivariate effects) between sex and age |
| Census region (Northeast, Midwest, South, West) |
| Residence in metropolitan area |
| Interactions between census region and metropolitan area |
| Race/Hispanic ethnicity (White/Non-Hispanic, Black/Non-Hispanic, Other/Non-Hispanic, 2+ Races/Non-Hispanic, Hispanic) |
| Education (Less than high school, high school or equivalent, some college, bachelor's, more than bachelor's) |
| Household income |
| Primary language by census region (Non-Hispanic, Hispanic English Proficient, Hispanic Bilingual, Hispanic Spanish Proficient) |
| **Military Service Variables** |
| Military service status |
| Time/era of service |
| Disability related to service |
| Disability score |

groups. Calculation of these types of estimates for military caregivers required blending of data sources (as we will describe).

## Blending Weights

Our analyses of military caregivers and the people they care for incorporated three sources of information:

1. Military caregiver respondents from KP who provide information on their own characteristics and that of their care recipient
2. Military care recipient respondents from KP who provide information on their own characteristics and that of their primary unpaid caregiver
3. Military caregiver respondents from WWP who provide information on their own characteristics and that of their care recipient.

Data from each of these sources cannot be equally weighted because the second two sources are not nationally representative. Specifically, military care recipient respondents will exclude care recipients who are unable to participate in an online survey for health reasons, and will also exclude those who are institutionalized; WWP respondents are a convenience-based sample that, when compared with KP post-9/11 military caregivers, care for veterans and service members who are younger and have more severe injuries. To account for such discrepancies, blending weights were created to enable joint analyses of data from these three sources.

The first step in the creation of blending weights was to derive benchmark values of variables to which the blended data will be calibrated. Reliable benchmark values on caregivers easily could have been derived using data from only caregiver respondents within the KP. However, it was determined that these values could be supplemented though the incorporation of reports from KP veteran care recipients, which ensures larger sample sizes of certain groups (such as caregivers of post-9/11 veterans) and thereby allows calculation of improved benchmarks for pre-9/11 and post-9/11 groups. To use data from both caregivers and care recipients while adjusting for small discrepancies between respondents, we developed a set of benchmarking weights. These weights were calculated for the combined sample by running IPF while using benchmark values for the variables listed in Table B.2 using only KP caregiver respondents. We note that military care recipient reports on caregivers come only from noninstitutionalized military care recipients and regard only their primary caregiver; thus, only caregivers of noninstitutionalized veterans who reported being the primary caregiver from the KP were used in this calibration process. For the remaining KP military caregiver respondents, their respective post-stratification weight was used as their benchmarking weight.

Four sets of **blending weights** were then calculated to enable the combination of information from the various data sources on military caregiver characteristics.

The first two sets of blending weights were used to combine data from the caregiver respondents from KP and WWP for post-9/11 caregivers and pre-9/11 caregivers. This set of weights was calculated by isolating post-9/11 caregivers among the KP and WWP, then applying IPF to calibrate to benchmark values for the variables listed in Tables B.2 and B.3. The benchmark values were estimated using the benchmarking weights (applied to post-9/11 KP caregiver and veteran respondents). The second set of blending weights was calculated in a similar fashion to the first set, though for pre-9/11 caregiver respondents from the KP and WWP panels. These first two sets of blending weights for post-9/11 and pre-9/11 respondents were applied within analyses

**Table B.2**
**Variables Used for Blending of KP Sources (Veteran and Caregiver Reports) on Caregiver Characteristics**

| |
|---|
| Care recipient and caregiver live together |
| Caregiver has no one in caregiving network |
| Care recipient has TBI |
| Care recipient has a neurological condition |
| Time spent caregiving |
| Care recipient has a VA disability rating of 70 percent or above |
| Care recipient's functioning (WHODAS) |

**Table B.3**
**Variables Used for Blending of KP and WWP Military Caregivers**

Sociodemographic Variables

Sex

Age (18–29, 30–44, 45–59, and 60+)

Interactions (i.e., multivariate effects) between sex and age

Household income

Military Service and Related Medical Conditions

Deployed to a war zone

Disability related to service

Disability score (10–20 percent, 30–40 percent, 50–60 percent)

Service-related medical conditions (physical impairment, hearing/vision impairment, mental health
   and substance abuse, chronic conditions)

Early-Technology Adopter Characteristics

Tendency to try new products before other people do

Tendency to try new brands out of preference for variety and/or boredom with old products

Tendency to look for what is new when shopping

Desire to be the first among family and friends to try something new

Desire to tell others about new brands or technology

that involved caregiver characteristics produced from caregiver reports alone, on which veterans provided no information (e.g., depression levels of caregivers).

The third and fourth sets of blending weights enabled us to combine data from all three sources of information (KP caregiver respondents, KP care recipient respondents, WWP caregiver respondents) relating to caregiver characteristics. The third set was calculated by applying IPF among post-9/11 caregivers from the KP and WWP reports from caregivers and the KP reports from veteran care recipients; the fourth set of weights is calculated similarly among pre-9/11 caregivers and care recipients. The same benchmark values used to generate all four sets of blending weights. The third and fourth sets of blending weights were applied within all analyses that involved caregiver characteristics for which we also had a veteran report.

The calculation of blending weights included calibration to benchmark values for "early technology adopter" characteristics (Table B.3), in addition to characteristics reported in Table B.1, because previous research has shown that early adopter characteristics often differentiate Internet opt-in (convenience) samples from probability-based samples such as the KP. DiSongra et al. (2011) elaborate on the need for and process of calibrating samples via early-adopter characteristics. The blending weights were trimmed at the 1st and 99th percentiles.

After weighting and prior to data analysis, we ran diagnostic checks to see if the weighted versions (with blended weights) of outcome measures of interest were jointly congenial when calculated across the multiple sources. For example, we reran several of the regression models presented in Chapter Three that blend data from the KP and WWP. This diagnostic test involves the inclusion of a binary predictor variable within each regression model to indicate whether the respondent belonged to the WWP sample. When the blending weights were not used, this binary variable frequently was statistically significant, indicating an influence of the WWP panel above and beyond that of the other predictors/characteristics included in the models. However, when the pre- and post-9/11 weights (e.g., the 1st and 2nd sets of blended weights) were used, this binary variable became nonsignificant, indicating no observed extraneous association with the (WWP) panel.

We concluded that all data from the KP and WWP were appropriately blended, conditional upon the use of the appropriate sets of blending weights. Thereby, data from these samples were used in conjunction when comparing post-9/11, pre-9/11, and civilian caregivers.

## Analysis of Data Quality

Survey data were initially examined to ensure that all responses were within their range of plausible values. We also conducted data-quality checks to identify cases with implausible response patterns that suggested lack of attention to the survey.

### Item Nonresponse

We examined the amount of missing data on each survey item, where missing data by item is calculated as the portion of eligible individuals that responded (i.e., did not refuse) for each item.

Missing data on items was low; that is, for nearly all items, fewer than 5 percent of respondents had missing data. Therefore, univariate analyses were done using complete case adjustments. For regression models, however, complete case analysis is less preferable because certain units may have most (but not all) predictor variables observed. Despite the low prevalence of missing data across the items used in regressions, imputations were generated for demographic covariates such as those listed in Table B.1. We note that missing data for demographic variables were only an issue for respondents from WWP. We also note that the only variable with a noteworthy rate of missing data was household income, for which about 11 percent of the units from WWP failed to respond. Imputations were generated via the package *mice* in *R*, which uses a multivariate imputation model. We generated a single imputation—as opposed to multiple imputations in the vein of Rubin (1987)—due to the low rates of missing data.

Depression and anxiety levels were calculated by aggregating across eight and four survey items, respectively. Rates of missing data were low (between 1 and 2 percent) for each of these items. For units that responded to more than half but not all of the relevant items for depression (about 4 percent of all units fall into this category), a case-wise mean imputation scheme was used. Specifically, an imputation for the missing depression items within these cases was taken as the mean of the depression items for which the respective unit did respond. Units that responded to less than half of the items related to depression were dropped from analyses involving depression (this accounted for 1.0 percent of all units). A similar process was used for the items related to anxiety (resulting in imputations for 1.7 percent of all cases and deletion of 0.8 percent of all cases for anxiety-related analyses).

Out of 1,145 total military caregivers and veteran self-reports in the KP and WWP samples, 116 respondents (10 percent) failed to report whether the veteran care recipient served before or after September 11, 2001. This binary indicator provides a critical stratification within our sample. Using information related to the veteran's age, years since separation from the military, and sample, we logically imputed this binary indicator (any military service after September 11, 2001) in 111 of these 116 observations.

Furthermore, 53 observations out of 259 survey respondents who provided era-of-service information were flagged as having responses to other variables inconsistent with their era of service. For instance, several respondents reported separating from the military within the last five years, but also reported not serving in the post–September 11, 2001, time period. For all such illogical observations, conservative data cleaning rules were developed to do one of the following:

- verify the reported era of service
- assign a new logical value through other reported variables
- solely drop the observation from any pre- or post-analysis
- drop from all analyses.

Decision rules were based upon an case-by-case analysis of each observation's veteran age, years since separation from military service, years of military service in total, deployment time periods, and caregiver age and relationship to veteran. Of the 53 values flagged for inconsistent responses, 26 observations were verified (not cleaned), 16 were cleaned, five were dropped solely from pre- or post-analyses, and six were dropped from all analyses.

More information about both imputation and data cleaning can be seen in Table B.4.

## Data Analysis

Data analysis consisted primarily of estimation of population-level characteristics and outcomes for the following groups of survey completers:

- veterans and service members receiving care
- caregivers for pre-9/11 veterans and service members

Table B.4
Description of Imputation and Data Cleaning for Era of Services

| | Military Care Recipients | Military Caregivers | Total |
|---|---|---|---|
| Unknown Era of Service | 3 | 113 | 116 |
| Total Dropped from Measurement | 0 | 5 | 5 |
| Total Imputed | 3 | 108 | 111 |
| Post-9/11 | 2 | 31 | 33 |
| Pre-9/11 | 1 | 77 | 78 |
| Known Era of Service | 256 | 773 | 1,029 |
| Consistent | 236 | 740 | 976 |
| Potentially Inconsistent | 20 | 33 | 53 |
| Verified | 3 | 23 | 26 |
| Cleaned | 9 | 7 | 16 |
| Dropped Pre/Post | 3 | 2 | 5 |
| Dropped from Measurement | 5 | 1 | 6 |
| **Total Observations** | **259** | **886** | **1,145** |

- caregivers for post-9/11 veterans and service members
- caregivers for civilians
- all others (i.e., non-caregivers)

Also, we performed hypothesis tests to discern whether the characteristics and outcomes were statistically significant across these groups. Primarily, these tests included comparison of variable means or categorical frequencies across two or more subsamples corresponding to the groups listed. Further, where appropriate, the sampling weights described in the previous section were applied throughout the estimation and testing of characteristics and outcomes.

For continuous variables, weighted means and standard errors (and the resulting interval estimate of the weighted mean) were computed for each sample with SAS PROC SURVEYMEANS in SAS version 9.3. Variances of weighted quantities were calculated using Taylor series approximations. For categorical variables, weighted percentages were computed for each sample with SAS PROC SURVEYFREQ.

Tests for significant differences between each group of caregivers (post-9/11 caregivers, pre-9/11 caregivers, civilian caregivers) and non-caregivers were presented in Chapters Two and Three for several personal and health-related outcomes. Military caregivers from KP and WWP were included in these analyses to ensure adequate sample size for comparisons involving post-9/11 and pre-9/11 military caregivers. These tests were conducted with post-stratification weights in SAS PROC SURVEYREG and SAS PROC SURVEYLOGISTIC for continuous and categorical outcomes, respectively. Each outcome was regressed on caregiver status, which was represented by a set of three dummy-coded binary indicators for each of the caregiver groups, with non-caregivers serving as the reference category (or, when only among caregivers, with civilian caregivers serving as the reference category). The significance of the caregiver status effect was assessed with joint tests of significance of the dummy-coded indicators.

Multivariate regression models were also estimated to compare the three caregiver groups to non-caregivers (or military caregivers to civilian caregivers) on outcomes with adjustment for several potentially confounding sociodemographic characteristics. For the outcomes examined in Chapter Three, a core set of sociodemographic covariates was included in adjusted multivariate regression models unless otherwise indicated. These covariates included the respondent's history of military service, sex, age, race/ethnicity, marital status, household size, household income, and residence in a major metropolitan area.[1]

---

[1]   Age, household size, and household income were continuous variables in the adjusted regression models. All other covariates in these models were binary indicators, with race/ethnicity represented by a set of four dummy-coded indicators corresponding to Hispanic, black non-Hispanic, other non-Hispanic, and multiracial non-Hispanic with white non-Hispanic as the reference category.

# Enumeration of Military Caregivers

One of the major aims of this study was to enumerate the total number of military caregivers in the United States. We used data from the screener administered to KP enrollees in the enumeration. There are multiple ways we can enumerate the number of caregivers (since, in addition to reports by military caregivers, we have reports of caregiving rosters by proxy sources). The two estimates of the total number of military caregivers can be combined to produce a final, superior estimate.

The first estimate was found by summing the screener weights for all KP screener respondents who reported being a military caregiver. This estimate indicates 5,499,253 military caregivers nationally (SE: 322,141).

A second estimate was calculated by, first, isolating the pool of veterans or service members receiving care within the KP screener respondents. Next, for each such respondent, we multiplied his or her corresponding screener weight by the number of caregivers that he or she reported having. The resulting products were aggregated over the respective pool of respondents, which yields a second estimate of the total number of military caregivers in the United States. This method provides a value of 3,229,626 caregivers (SE: 281,221).

These two estimates could be combined to produce a final estimate; however, these estimates are notably different. For instance, each estimate is well outside the confidence bounds of the other. We deem the first estimate to be more trustworthy because the second estimate is based off of proxy reports of caregiving rosters. For instance, interviews with veterans who receive unpaid care indicated that, on average, they have 1.66 caregivers each. However, military caregivers reported that there were 2.43 total caregivers in their caregiving network, on average. Further, by dividing the enumerated value of the total number of caregivers by the enumerated value of the total number of veterans receiving unpaid care, we estimate 2.72 veterans per caregiver. This provides evidence that the veterans are underreporting the number of caregivers they have. Therefore, as our reported value of the total number of military caregivers nationwide, we use the value of 5,499,253.

We also estimate the number of military care recipients, military care recipients who are also caregivers, and civilian caregivers. In these instances, we sum the screener weights for all KP screener respondents in each category. The resulting estimates are

1,900,498 (SE: 198,754) for military care recipients, 294,640 (SE: 87,002) veterans or service members who both rely on caregiving support and are also caregivers to other adults, and 16,865,682 (SE: 446,333) civilian caregivers. Combining the number of military caregivers, veterans or service members who both rely on caregiving support but are also caregivers to other adults, and civilian caregivers yields a total of 22.6 million caregivers of adults.

All quantities pertinent to the enumeration of caregivers and military care recipients (including weighted totals and their associated variances) were calculated using PROC SURVEYMEANS in SAS.

## Comparison with Other Prevalence Estimates

We are unaware of any other study to have enumerated the number of military caregivers, but our estimate of the total number of all caregivers (22.6 million) is similar in magnitude to other estimates of caregivers—specifically, NAC and AARP in 1997 reported 22.4 million households, and Arno et al. (1999) estimate 27.6 million. It is noticeably lower than the estimate of 65.7 million caregivers provided by NAC and AARP (2009) and the estimate provided by Fox and Brenner (2012) that indicated 30 percent of U.S. adults are caregivers. We identify three possible reasons for this discrepancy. First, the NAC and AARP estimate asks about the number of caregivers in the household; they identify 36.5 million households with at least one caregiver present. In our sample, we only allow one caregiver per household. Second, 14 percent of the NAC and AARP estimate are caregivers to children under 18; our eligibility criteria requires that the individual be a caregiver to an adult. Third, 30 percent of the NAC and AARP estimate includes persons who have served as caregivers in the past year but are not currently serving in this role; our criteria require the person be a current caregiver. If we apply these two restrictions consecutively to the NAC and AARP estimate of households with a caregiver, we estimate 21.9 million current households with an individual currently caring for an adult care recipient.

Although this new estimate conforms well to the one we produce, the NAC and AARP definition of caregiving, along with that produced by Fox and Brenner, may also be more inclusive. The screener NAC and AARP use is as follows:

> **In the last 12 months,** has anyone in your household provided unpaid care to a relative or friend 18 years or older to help them take care of themselves? Unpaid care may include help with personal needs or household chores. It might be managing a person's finances, arranging for outside services, or *visiting regularly to see how they are doing.* This person need not live with you.

Fox and Brenner (2012) use a similar definition, including regular visitation to see how the care recipient is doing.

In comparison, we applied stricter criteria:

Do you provide unpaid care and assistance for, or manage the care of, someone who is at least 18 years old and has an illness, injury or condition for which they require outside support? *This may include help with tasks such as personal care, bathing, dressing, feeding, giving medicines or treatments, help with memory tasks for someone with brain injury, help coping with symptoms of Posttraumatic Stress Disorder (PTSD), transportation to doctors' appointments, or arranging for services, etc.* You do not need to live with the person. Care and assistance are considered unpaid if you provide them without receiving financial compensation in exchange for doing so.

## Comparison with the American Community Survey

Another potential method for estimating the number of veterans requiring caregiving assistance (and thus their caregivers) would be to use data from the ACS, an ongoing statistical survey conducted by the U.S. Census Bureau, sent to approximately 250,000 addresses monthly (or 3 million per year) with 2 million interviews completed annually. The ACS surveys a representative sample of persons living in housing units and group quarters in the United States. Data are collected primarily by mail, with follow-ups by telephone and personal visit. While there are no questions in the ACS questionnaire that directly ask whether a service member or veteran is a recipient of paid or unpaid caregiving, there are questions regarding veteran status that have been used by some to approximate the number of military caregivers.

We used the ACS 2011 Public Use Microdata Sample file as a source to determine the potential number of veterans residing in the United States who require caregiving assistance for purposes of comparison with our estimate based upon the national probability survey of households described in Appendix A. Using responses to the ACS questionnaire's question, "Has this person ever served on active duty in the U.S. armed forces, military reserves, or National Guard?" we identified 22.4 million persons as having ever served on active duty among the U.S. noninstitutionalized population. This is the same data source used by the VA to reflect the number of veterans residing in the United States. Using responses to a question about era of service: "When did this person serve on active duty in the U.S. armed forces?" we estimate that 15.6 percent (3.5 million service members and veterans) served after 9/11, with the remainder serving prior to 9/11.

Of the estimated 22.4 million service members, 15.6 percent had a service-related disability rating; 23 percent of those had a disability rating of 70 percent or greater. There are four items that asked about cognitive difficulty, ambulatory difficulty, self-care difficulty, and independent living difficulty for the respondent. Anyone who indicated having these difficulties and had ever served in active duty met our definition of a service member or veteran potentially requiring caregiving. We found that 7.2 percent indicated having cognitive difficulty; 14.3 percent indicated having ambulatory difficulty; 5.2 percent indicated having self-care difficulty; and 8.2 percent indicated having difficulty with independent living. By cross-tabulating these four conditions, we identified 4.1 million (18.3 percent) service members and veterans experiencing one or more difficulties and that may need paid or unpaid caregiving. Of these, 5.3 percent of the 4.1 million potential care recipients indicate being on active duty in the post-9/11 era.

To estimate how this translates to the number of caregivers, we use data from our own survey and assume that 47 percent of post-9/11 care recipients and 71 percent of pre-9/11 care recipients have a caregiver with a caregiving network (see Table C.1). For post-9/11 care recipients, those with a caregiving network have 1 additional caregiver; for pre-9/11 care recipients, those with a caregiving network have an additional 1.5 caregivers. Using these data and under these assumptions, we estimate a total of 8.3 million military caregivers. This is larger than the estimate that we produce, and may be because we are overestimating the proportion of veterans (18.3 percent) in need of caregiving.

**Table C.1**
**Estimating the Number of Military Caregivers Using the ACS**

| Cohort | Need Caregiving Support | Caregivers Without a Network | Caregivers in a Network | Total |
|---|---|---|---|---|
| Post-9/11 | 225,500 | 119,515 | 211,970 | 331,485 |
| Pre-9/11 | 3,874,500 | 1,123,605 | 6,877,238 | 8,000,842 |
| Total | 4,100,000 | | | 8,332,327 |

# Environmental Scan Methods

This appendix describes the methods used to identify and categorize organizational entities that provide services to military caregivers, and the methods used to collect and analyze data pertaining to these services.

## Identifying Organizational Entities

We used a multipronged approach to identify organizational entities that provide services to military caregivers. Our general method was to identify a broad range of U.S.-owned or -operated organizational entities providing services that may be relevant to military caregivers. This included entities serving one or more of the following populations, either explicitly or as determined by RAND staff: caregivers, military families, or aging or disabled populations.

We identified the broad landscape of potentially relevant organizational entities through several mechanisms:

- web searches using key terms such as "caregiving," "caregiver," and "military family"
- the National Resource Directory's Family and Caregiver Support section
- resource directories of organizations included in our study
- consultations with nonprofit staff and subject-matter experts
- attendance at meetings and events relevant to caregiving or military families
- snowball sampling among interviewees (i.e., organizations were asked about, and referred us to, other organizations they knew of that offered programs and services to military caregivers).

Our search for organizational entities continued until we reached saturation, the point at which additional searches revealed no new entities.

Our analytical focus differed based on the type of "organizational entity" we encountered. We sometimes focused on organizations themselves, and at other times concentrated on departments or programs within those organizations, choosing the level that best allowed us to narrow in on caregiving services while not overlooking pertinent services in other areas of the organization. For example, the VA provides multiple services for caregivers, through several different programs within the Veterans Health Administration and Veterans Benefits Administration (VBA). However, given that the breadth of the VA's services for caregivers are administered through the VA Caregiver Support program, we focused specifically on this program rather than the VA as a whole.

## Categorizing Organizational Entities

As we identified the range of potential organizational entities providing services to military caregivers, we developed a framework for determining which were most pertinent to this population, and thus appropriate for inclusion in our analysis. Table D.1 outlines this framework. Our model was informed by the military family–specific approach developed by Miller et al. (2011). Their approach enables researchers to link service members' and spouses' most pressing problems to their self-defined needs. We tailored this approach specifically to military caregivers based on the needs of caregivers that we identified during the first phase of this work (Tanielian et al., 2013). We refined these categories as we identified organizational entities and learned the nuances of the available military caregiving services.

Our framework delineates several "common caregiving services" that involve direct or intensive interaction with caregivers. Specifically, these include respite care, patient advocacy or case management, a helping hand, financial stipend, structured social support, religious support, structured wellness activities, or structured education or training. If an organizational entity offered at least one of these services to caregivers currently caring for a care recipient (i.e., post-injury and still living), then we included it in our analysis. In some instances, as delineated in Table D.1, we required that the service be offered by a "caregiver specific" entity, or a "caregiver incidental" entity that targeted certain populations, such as military families.

We also included organizations that offered health care or mental health care outside of routine channels, such as common government or private-sector payment and delivery systems, or offered health care or mental health care explicitly to caregivers. Our distinction of "nonstandard" clinical care enabled us to focus on lesser-known avenues for caregiver health care and mental health care, as well as sources that may have been tailored specifically to caregivers' needs. Our definitions of "common caregiving services" and "nonstandard" health care and mental health care are further articulated in Table D.2.

In some instances, interviews revealed activities or services relevant to military caregiving that did not fit the categories in Table D.2 but still appeared to involve direct or intensive interaction with caregivers and help caregivers to address their most pressing

**Table D.1**
**Framework of Services Included in RAND's Analysis**

| Population of Focus for Organization or Program | Services Provided by Organizations or Programs | | | |
| --- | --- | --- | --- | --- |
| | Common Caregiving Services | Nonstandard Clinical Care | Information and Resources | Services Deemed Out-of-Scope[b] |
| | Respite care<br>Patient advocate<br>A helping hand<br>Financial stipend<br>Structured social support<br>Religious support<br>Structured wellness activities<br>Structured education/training<br>Other caregiving service[a] | Health care<br>Mental health care | Informal information source<br>Referral Service (veteran)<br>Referral Service (caregiver) | |
| Caregiver-specific | Included | Included | Excluded[c] | Excluded |
| Caregiver-incidental | Included if targets military families, aging populations, or disabled populations | Included if targets military families | Excluded[c] | Excluded |

[a] Services in this category are those that involve direct or intensive interaction with caregivers, but do not fit into a "common caregiving service" category, nor qualify as out-of-scope.

[b] Categories of out-of-scope services are listed in Appendix G.

[c] We collected information about these services when the organizational entity also offered a common caregiving service.

Table D.2
Definitions of Services Included

| Common Caregiving Service | Definition |
|---|---|
| Respite care | Care provided to the service member or veteran by someone other than the caregiver to give the caregiver a short-term, temporary "break." |
| Patient advocate or case manager | An individual acting as a liaison between the service member or veteran and his or her care providers, or coordinating care for the service member or veteran. |
| A helping hand | Direct support such as loans, donations, legal guidance, housing support, or transportation assistance. |
| Financial stipend | Compensation for a caregiver's time devoted to caregiving activities and/or for loss of wages due to one's caregiving commitment. |
| Structured social support | Online or in-person support groups for caregivers or military family members (which may incidentally include caregivers) that is likely to assist with caregiving-specific stresses or challenges. |
| Religious support | Religious- or spiritual-based guidance or counseling. |
| Structured wellness activities | Organized activities such as fitness classes or stress relief lessons that focus on improving mental or physical well-being. |
| Structured education or training | In-person or online classes, modules, or webinars, or manuals or workbooks that involve a formalized curriculum (rather than ad hoc information) related to caregiving activities. |

| Nonstandard Clinical Care | Definition |
|---|---|
| Nonstandard mental health care | Mental health care that is (1) offered outside of routine or traditional channels such as common government or private sector payment and delivery systems, or (2) offered specially to caregivers. |
| Nonstandard physical health care | Health care that is (1) offered outside of routine or traditional channel such as common government or private sector payment and delivery systems, or (2) offered specially to caregivers. |

problems. We collected this information for possible inclusion in an "other" category. However, this category was not designed to capture the full range of services that an organization may offer, and thus we excluded several types of entities or services they offered, as outlined in Appendix G. For organizational entities included in our environmental scan based on the criteria defined in Table D.2, we also noted whether they provided services fitting into one of the following three categories: informal information source, referral service for caregiver, and referral service for veteran.

## Collecting Data

RAND staff collected qualitative data about organizational entities from three sources: websites, publicly available documents, and semistructured interviews with organization staff. We developed and utilized a standardized data collection form that enabled us to systematically gather data pertaining to the following categories of information:

- history and origination date
- geographic reach, target population(s), and number of individuals served
- mission and goals
- services offered, including the mode of delivery, duration, and frequency of services
- outreach activities
- challenges encountered in providing services to caregivers
- evaluation activities
- funding sources, tax determination status, and staffing resources
- formal partnerships with other organizations.

The data collection period began on July 1, 2013, and ended on October 15, 2013.

We first perused websites to gather basic information about organizational entities such as their mission, goals, and services offered. Similarly, we perused relevant documents that RAND staff had obtained through web searches, consultations with nonprofit staff and subject-matter experts, or attendance at meetings and events. If our review of websites and documents revealed that the organizational entity did not meet the inclusion criteria listed in Table D.1, then we excluded it from our analysis. If the organizational entity met our criteria, or if we were unsure whether it met our criteria, then we conducted an interview with organization staff to gather additional information.

To arrange an interview, RAND staff contacted managers or directors of organizations, making at least three attempts to contact these individuals. Interviews were designed to confirm (or, in a limited number of instances, disconfirm) whether an organizational entity met our inclusion criteria, and to obtain more information about the organization utilizing our standardized data collection form as already described. For a small number of organizational entities that did not respond (n = 19) or declined to participate (n = 8), we relied on descriptions of these entities based on publicly available information and were able to include them in this report. We also created descriptions using publicly available information for a limited number of entities that we discovered after the data collection period had ended (n = 12). Often, we were unable to locate information on the following fields for organizational entities that we did not interview: outreach activities, challenges encountered in providing services to caregivers, evaluation activities, staffing resources, and formal partnerships with other organizations.

We included a total of 120 organizational entities, and interviewed staff from 81 of them. Table D.3 shows the number of organizational entities identified and then included or excluded.

Interviews with organizational staff lasted between 30 and 45 minutes. RAND staff took typewritten notes during each interview and shared these notes with the interviewee via email to ensure their accuracy. Notes were sent to all 81 programs that were interviewed and returned by 77 programs (a 95-percent return rate). Summaries drawn from our finalized notes describing each organizational entity are displayed in Appendix H.

## Analyzing Data

We analyzed the information collected during our review of websites and documents, and during our interviews with organizational staff, and coded this information in Microsoft Excel. Our coding categorized the breadth of organizational characteristics and services offered. A majority of our codes were defined by RAND staff prior to data collection, but a limited number of these codes (for example, the challenges reported by organizations) were determined inductively, subsequent to data collection. In these instances, we utilized constant comparative analysis (Glaser and Strauss, 1967; Strauss and Corbin, 1998) to move back and forth among the data and to identify similarities and differences among the data. Together, this range of categories represents the various dimensions of the organizational entities in our analysis, and the challenges faced or witnessed by these entities. These categories are represented in Table D.4; for the majority of these categories, the cells were populated with either text entries or with a binary indicator of whether a particular service was available.

We then tabulated selected information to illustrate the frequency with which these various dimensions existed across the organizational entities included in our analysis. Tables containing this information are shown in Appendix E and in chap-

**Table D.3**
**Number of Organizational Entities Identified and Included/Excluded**

| Organizational Entities Identified and Included/Excluded | Number |
| --- | --- |
| Number of potentially relevant unique entities | 502 |
| Excluded (ineligible) | 382 |
| No interview: identified as an ineligible | 375 |
| Interview: identified as ineligible | 7 |
| Included (eligible) and interviewed | 81 |
| Included (eligible) but not interviewed | 39 |
| (Included but not interviewed) No response | 19 |
| (Included but not interviewed) Declined to participate | 8 |
| (Included but not interviewed) Discovered after the data collection period ended | 12 |

**Table D.4**
**Dimensions of Organizational Entities Included in RAND's Analysis**

| Data Field |
| --- |
| Origination date |
| History |
| Target population(s) |
| Specific injury/illness |
| Geographic reach |
| Number of individuals served |
| Mission |
| Goals |
| Services for caregivers |
|     Respite care |
|     Patient advocacy |
|     Helping hand |
|     Financial stipend |
|     Structured social support |
|     Religious support |
|     Structured wellness activities |
|     Structured education/training |
|     Nonstandard physical health care |
|     Nonstandard mental health care |
|     Other |
| Mode of delivery |
| Duration and frequency |
| Information, resources, and guidance |
|     Informal informational source |
|     Referral service for veteran |
|     Referral service for caregiver |
| Outreach activities |
| Challenges faced by programs |
| Challenges faced by caregivers (as witnessed by programs) |
| Program evaluation |
| Key staff who provide services |
| Type of organization/tax determination status |
| Relationships the program has with other caregiving programs |

ters throughout this report. Appendix H contains descriptions of each organizational entity included in this analysis.

# Environmental Scan Organizational Characteristics

In this section, we describe the organizations identified in the environmental scan across a number of datapoints that we collected. First, we describe the services offered across these organizations, and then highlight the organizational landscape by tax determination status (i.e., nonprofit, government, or for-profit). Next we provide a breakdown of organizations by "service category," which is our classification for how these services are likely to assist caregivers. Since many organizations offer multiple services, several tables in this section have rows and columns that are not mutually exclusive. Therefore, these rows and columns do not equal the total number of organizations included in the environmental scan.

## Services Offered

Organizations included in our environmental scan offer varied arrays of services for caregivers. Some provide one service, while others offer multiple different services. As described in Appendix D, we included organizations in our environmental scan if they offered one or more "common caregiving service" or "nonstandard" clinical care. These categories are respite care, patient advocacy, helping hand, financial stipend, structured social support, religious support, structured wellness activities, structured education or training, health care, and mental health care. In Table E.1, we illustrate the number of programs that offer multiple services, by the services offered. This overlap, or lack thereof, provides insight into the number of organizations a caregiver must engage to fulfill a range of needs.

Several organizations offer more than one service. The greatest overlap exists at the intersection of structured social support and helping hand, with 18 organizations providing both. Thus, caregivers can often seek out assistance, such as miscellaneous financial support, and also access social support from the same organization, or vice versa. Substantial overlap also exists at the intersection of structured social support and structured wellness activities, as well as structured social support and structured education and training. We find this to be indicative of the fact that social support is offered quite commonly (although it varies in its frequency and intensity) and overlaps with

**Table E.1**
**Number of Organizations Providing Multiple Caregiving Services (n = 120)**

| Caregiving Services | Total | Respite Care | Patient Advocacy | Helping Hand | Financial Stipend | Social Support | Religious Support | Wellness Activities | Education/Training | Health Care | Mental Health Care |
|---|---|---|---|---|---|---|---|---|---|---|---|
| Respite Care | 9 | | 3 | 5 | 2 | 7 | 1 | 3 | 6 | 1 | 3 |
| Patient Advocacy | 21 | | | 10 | 5 | 5 | 0 | 1 | 5 | 1 | 2 |
| Helping Hand | 52 | | | | 6 | 18 | 1 | 9 | 5 | 3 | 6 |
| Financial Stipend* | 7 | | | | | 3 | 0 | 1 | 2 | 1 | 1 |
| Social Support | 53 | | | | | | 3 | 17 | 16 | 1 | 6 |
| Religious Support | 4 | | | | | | | 2 | 1 | 0 | 1 |
| Wellness Activities | 21 | | | | | | | | 5 | 0 | 4 |
| Education/Training | 37 | | | | | | | | | 2 | 2 |
| Health Care | 4 | | | | | | | | | | 2 |
| Mental Health Care | 13 | | | | | | | | | | |

\* Five programs offering financial stipend services to caregivers facilitate receipt of DoD's SCAADL stipend, which is offered via different programs across the branches of service. Here, we account for these programs separately; elsewhere in this report we considered them to be one "financial stipend" program.

numerous other services. We also note that structured social support and structured wellness activities often overlap because they are offered in conjunction at retreats, conferences, or other events.

Table E.2 displays the various modes of delivery of the services offered by organizations interviewed in the environmental scan. Here, we focus only on interviewed organizations because we were not able to ascertain reliable data on mode of delivery for programs that we did not interview. It is not surprising those services such as respite, religious support, and wellness activities are offered solely or largely in person. Patient advocacy, structured social support, and structured education and training are offered through a variety of modes. We have categorized helping-hand assistance and financial stipends as "other," which typically indicates support such as direct financial assistance or housing assistance.

Also of interest here is the fact that a substantial number of services, particularly structured social support and structured education and training, are offered via the

Table E.2
Percent of Organizations Offering Common Caregiving Services by Mode of Delivery
(n = 81)

| Common Caregiving Services | Mode of Delivery (%) | | | | | |
| --- | --- | --- | --- | --- | --- | --- |
| | Face to Face, Group | Face to Face, Individual | Internet | Phone | Printed | Other (e.g., Financial Assistance) |
| Respite Care | 71 | 100 | — | 14 | — | — |
| Patient Advocacy | 20 | 53 | 47 | 100 | 20 | — |
| Helping Hand | — | — | — | — | — | 100 |
| Financial Stipend | — | — | — | — | — | 100 |
| Social Support | 82 | 18 | 44 | 15 | — | — |
| Religious Support | 100 | 100 | — | — | — | — |
| Wellness Activities | 94 | 19 | 6 | 6 | 6 | — |
| Education/Training | 66 | 17 | 76 | 14 | 31 | 7 |

Internet. As previous research has noted, the Internet may be an important aspect of service delivery because caregivers can often go online from their homes at their own convenience amid their demanding schedules (Tanielian et al., 2013).

## Organizational Designation and Scope

In conducting our environmental scan, we also gathered information on organizations' tax determination. By this, we refer to their classification as a nonprofit, for-profit, or government entity. Table E.3 exhibits the number of organizations in the environmental scan, by tax determination status (as a proxy for sector) and "organizational scope." By organizational scope, we refer to a range of variables that, together, provide insight into how widespread these organizations are (over geographic space and time).

Notable is the fact that over half of the organizations serving caregivers (69) have been created in the last ten years. This likely reflects the fact that the organizational landscape expanded specifically to care for the wounded, ill, or injured service members returning from Iraq or Afghanistan. The government entities serving this popula-

Table E.3
Number of Organizations by Organizational Scope and Tax Determination Status (n = 119)

| Tax Status | Total | Organizational Scope | | | | | | | | | | | |
|---|---|---|---|---|---|---|---|---|---|---|---|---|---|
| | | Time in Operation (n = 114) | | | Geographic Reach | | | Target Population | | | | Specific Injury or Illness? | |
| | | 1–5 years | 5–10 years | >10 years | National/International | Local | National w/ local branches, locations, events | Caregiver Incidental | Caregiver Specific | Military Incidental | Military Specific | No | Yes |
| Nonprofit | 95 | 21 | 32 | 38 | 64 | 8 | 23 | 67 | 28 | 21 | 74 | 91 | 4 |
| For-Profit | 10 | 2 | 2 | 5 | 9 | 0 | 1 | 0 | 10 | 10 | 0 | 10 | 0 |
| Government | 14 | 4 | 8 | 2 | 10 | 1 | 3 | 11 | 3 | 1 | 13 | 12 | 2 |

tion are particularly recent, with only two having been in existence for more than ten years at the time of this study.

Most organizations included in the environmental scan (83 of the 120) are national or international in scope. Many organizations with international reach are focused military populations within the continental United States *and* at overseas military installations or treatment facilities. Twenty-seven organizations are national in scope, but tend to emphasize services for caregivers in certain geographic locations. For example, some organizations have regional branch offices where caregivers can receive in-person services, while others host conferences or events that are held in specific regions. Only nine organizations we identified are purely local in scope—for example, specific to a certain county or state. Nearly all of these are nonprofit organizations, with the exception of one government entity, the Virginia WWP.

A majority of the organizations in the environmental scan (78 of 120) are caregiver-incidental, meaning that caregivers are not a specific target population but are nonetheless served. Likewise, a majority of organizations (87) are military-specific, signifying that military service members, veterans, and/or family members are one of their target populations or their sole target population. Most organizations are not focused on caregivers of individuals with *specific* injuries or illnesses, although seven focus on certain conditions such as TBI or mental health issues.

Table E.4 shows the number of organizations by tax determination status and services provided. Nonprofit organizations offering helping-hand services are the most common (46). Nonprofits providing structured social support and structured educa-

**Table E.4**
**Number of Organizations by Services for Caregivers and Tax Determination Status (n = 119)**

| | Services for Caregivers | | | | | | | | | | | | |
| | Common Caregiving Services | | | | | | | | Nonstandard Clinical Care | | Information, Resources, and Guidance | | |
| Tax Status | Respite Care | Patient Advocacy | Helping Hand | Financial Stipend* | Structured Social Support | Religious Support | Structured Wellness Activities | Structured Education/Training | Physical Healthcare | Mental Healthcare | Informal Informational Source | Referral Service for Veteran | Referral Service for Caregiver |
|---|---|---|---|---|---|---|---|---|---|---|---|---|---|
| Nonprofit | 7 | 9 | 46 | 1 | 40 | 4 | 21 | 28 | 3 | 12 | 37 | 29 | 36 |
| For-Profit | 1 | 1 | 0 | 0 | 7 | 0 | 0 | 5 | 0 | 0 | 7 | 5 | 6 |
| Government | 1 | 11 | 6 | 2 | 5 | 0 | 0 | 4 | 1 | 1 | 4 | 8 | 10 |

tion or training are also quite common (40 and 28, respectively). Government and for-profit organizations are fewer than nonprofits and for-profits in all categories except financial stipend. This represents the fact that the VA and DoD are principal sources of financial stipends to offset the expenses that caregivers incur while providing care. We also included in this count the military services' "wounded warrior" programs, which facilitate access to DoD's SCAADL stipend.

We note, however, that the number of programs providing a service is not an indicator of the scope or reach of the total services provided or received. For example, in some categories (such as structured education or training), there exist numerous nonprofit organizations; yet government organizations—notably, the VA—appear to occupy a principal role in caregiver education, since the VA is a broad-reaching national organization, and since the VA caregiver training is a prerequisite to participate in the VA's Program of Comprehensive Assistance to Family Caregivers. Thus, Table E.4 should be interpreted with this caveat in mind.

## Service Category

We also clustered different types of services offered based on the goals of these services, as shown in Table E.5. Specifically, we created four categories: services aiding caregivers to provide better care (patient advocacy or case management and structured education or training), services addressing caregiver health and well-being (respite care, health and mental health care, structured social support, and structured wellness activities targeting caregivers solely), services addressing caregiver family well-being (structured wellness activities targeting care recipients and their family caregivers or family members of caregivers, a religious support network, and a helping hand), and services addressing income loss (financial stipend). Two of these categories—caregiver well-being and caregiver family well-being—are discussed in detail in Chapter Three of this report.

Notable here is that a high number of organizations aid caregivers in caring for their care recipient, and a low number of organizations address income loss.

## List of Organizations

This section displays two tables (E.6 and E.7), each listing all the organizations included in the environmental scan. The first displays programs by the caregiving services they provide. The second shows programs by a range of characteristics: origination date, tax status, caregiver specific or incidental, military specific or incidental, specific injury or illness, and geographic reach. Full descriptions of these organizations are included in Appendix H.

**Table E.5**
**Summary of Service Programs (n = 120)**

| Service Category | Total |
|---|---|
| Aiding Caregivers to Provide Better Care | 53 |
| Addressing Caregiver Health and Well-Being | 68 |
| Addressing Caregiver Family Well-Being | 66 |
| Addressing Income Loss | 3 |

**Table E.6**
**Organizations by Services Offered (n = 120)**

| Organization Name | Respite Care | Patient Advocacy | A Helping Hand | Financial Stipend | Structured Social Support | Religious Support Network | Structured Wellness Activities | Structured Education or Training | Health Care | Mental Health Care | Informal Informational Source | Referral Service for Veteran | Referral Service for Caregiver |
|---|---|---|---|---|---|---|---|---|---|---|---|---|---|
| AARP | 0 | 0 | 0 | 0 | 1 | 0 | 0 | 1 | 0 | 0 | 1 | 1 | 1 |
| AgingCare.com | 0 | 0 | 0 | 0 | 1 | 0 | 0 | 0 | 0 | 0 | 1 | 1 | 1 |
| AGIS | 0 | 0 | 0 | 0 | 1 | 0 | 0 | 0 | 0 | 0 | 1 | 1 | 1 |
| Air Force Aid Society | 0 | 0 | 1 | 0 | 0 | 0 | 0 | 0 | 0 | 0 | 0 | 0 | 0 |
| Air Force Wounded Warrior Program | 0 | 1 | 1 | 1 | 0 | 0 | 0 | 0 | 0 | 0 | 0 | 1 | 1 |
| Air Warrior Courage Foundation | 0 | 0 | 1 | 0 | 0 | 0 | 0 | 0 | 1 | 0 | 0 | 0 | 0 |
| American Bar Association Military Pro Bono Project and Veterans Claims and Assistance Network | 0 | 0 | 1 | 0 | 0 | 0 | 0 | 0 | 0 | 0 | 1 | 0 | 0 |
| American Legion Auxiliary | 0 | 0 | 0 | 0 | 1 | 0 | 0 | 0 | 0 | 0 | 0 | 0 | 0 |
| American Legion Family Support Network | 0 | 0 | 1 | 0 | 0 | 0 | 0 | 0 | 0 | 0 | 0 | 0 | 0 |
| American Red Cross | 0 | 0 | 0 | 0 | 0 | 0 | 0 | 1 | 0 | 0 | 0 | 1 | 1 |
| American Veterans with Brain Injuries | 0 | 0 | 0 | 0 | 1 | 0 | 0 | 0 | 0 | 0 | 1 | 1 | 1 |
| Armed Forces Foundation | 0 | 0 | 1 | 0 | 0 | 0 | 0 | 0 | 0 | 0 | 1 | 1 | 1 |
| Armed Forces Reserve Family Assistance Fund | 0 | 0 | 1 | 0 | 0 | 0 | 0 | 0 | 0 | 0 | 0 | 0 | 0 |
| Armed Services YMCA | 0 | 0 | 1 | 0 | 1 | 0 | 1 | 0 | 0 | 1 | 0 | 0 | 0 |
| Army Emergency Relief | 0 | 0 | 1 | 0 | 0 | 0 | 0 | 0 | 0 | 0 | 0 | 0 | 0 |
| Army Wounded Warrior Program | 0 | 1 | 1 | 1 | 0 | 0 | 0 | 0 | 0 | 0 | 0 | 1 | 1 |
| Association of the United States Army Family Readiness Directorate | 0 | 0 | 0 | 0 | 0 | 0 | 0 | 1 | 0 | 0 | 1 | 0 | 1 |
| Blue Star Families | 0 | 0 | 0 | 0 | 0 | 0 | 0 | 1 | 0 | 0 | 1 | 0 | 1 |
| Boulder Crest Retreat | 0 | 0 | 0 | 0 | 1 | 0 | 1 | 0 | 0 | 0 | 0 | 0 | 0 |
| Brain Injury Alliance and Brain Injury Alliance of Colorado | 0 | 0 | 0 | 0 | 1 | 0 | 0 | 1 | 0 | 0 | 1 | 1 | 1 |
| Brain Injury Association of America | 0 | 0 | 0 | 0 | 1 | 0 | 0 | 1 | 0 | 0 | 1 | 0 | 0 |
| Camaraderie Foundation | 0 | 0 | 0 | 0 | 1 | 0 | 1 | 0 | 0 | 1 | 0 | 0 | 0 |
| Care.com | 0 | 0 | 0 | 0 | 1 | 0 | 0 | 0 | 0 | 0 | 0 | 1 | 0 |
| Caregiver Action Network | 0 | 0 | 0 | 0 | 1 | 0 | 0 | 1 | 0 | 0 | 1 | 0 | 1 |

**Table E.6—Continued**

| Organization Name | Respite Care | Patient Advocacy | A Helping Hand | Financial Stipend | Structured Social Support | Religious Support Network | Structured Wellness Activities | Structured Education or Training | Health Care | Mental Health Care | Informal Informational Source | Referral Service for Veteran | Referral Service for Caregiver |
|---|---|---|---|---|---|---|---|---|---|---|---|---|---|
| CaregiverHelp.com | 0 | 0 | 0 | 0 | 0 | 0 | 0 | 1 | 0 | 0 | 0 | 0 | 0 |
| Caregivers Video Series: Walking on Eggshells | 0 | 0 | 0 | 0 | 0 | 0 | 0 | 1 | 0 | 0 | 0 | 0 | 0 |
| CaregivingHelp.org | 1 | 0 | 0 | 0 | 0 | 0 | 0 | 0 | 0 | 0 | 1 | 0 | 0 |
| CarePages | 0 | 0 | 0 | 0 | 1 | 0 | 0 | 0 | 0 | 0 | 0 | 0 | 0 |
| Caring From a Distance | 0 | 0 | 0 | 0 | 0 | 0 | 0 | 0 | 0 | 0 | 1 | 0 | 1 |
| Cause (Comfort for America's Uniformed Services) | 0 | 0 | 0 | 0 | 1 | 0 | 1 | 0 | 0 | 0 | 0 | 0 | 0 |
| Coaching Into Care | 0 | 1 | 0 | 0 | 0 | 0 | 0 | 0 | 0 | 0 | 0 | 0 | 1 |
| Coalition to Salute America's Heroes | 0 | 0 | 1 | 0 | 1 | 0 | 0 | 0 | 0 | 0 | 0 | 1 | 0 |
| Coast Guard Mutual Assistance | 0 | 0 | 1 | 0 | 0 | 0 | 0 | 0 | 1 | 1 | 0 | 1 | 1 |
| Code of Support Foundation | 0 | 1 | 0 | 0 | 0 | 0 | 0 | 0 | 0 | 0 | 0 | 0 | 0 |
| Coming Home Project | 0 | 0 | 0 | 0 | 0 | 0 | 1 | 1 | 0 | 0 | 1 | 1 | 1 |
| Compass Retreat Center | 0 | 0 | 0 | 0 | 1 | 0 | 1 | 1 | 0 | 0 | 0 | 0 | 0 |
| Courage Beyond | 0 | 0 | 0 | 0 | 1 | 0 | 1 | 0 | 0 | 1 | 1 | 1 | 1 |
| Defenders of Freedom | 0 | 0 | 1 | 0 | 0 | 0 | 0 | 0 | 0 | 0 | 0 | 0 | 0 |
| Defense and Veterans Brain Injury Center | 0 | 1 | 0 | 0 | 0 | 0 | 0 | 1 | 0 | 0 | 1 | 0 | 0 |
| Disabled American Veterans | 0 | 1 | 1 | 0 | 0 | 0 | 0 | 0 | 0 | 0 | 0 | 1 | 1 |
| DoD Office of Warrior Care Policy | 0 | 1 | 0 | 1 | 0 | 0 | 0 | 1 | 0 | 0 | 1 | 1 | 1 |
| Easter Seals Military and Veterans Services | 1 | 0 | 0 | 0 | 0 | 0 | 0 | 1 | 0 | 0 | 1 | 0 | 0 |
| Easter Seals New Hampshire Military and Veterans Services | 0 | 0 | 1 | 0 | 1 | 0 | 0 | 0 | 0 | 0 | 0 | 1 | 1 |
| EOD Warrior Foundation | 0 | 0 | 1 | 0 | 1 | 0 | 0 | 0 | 0 | 0 | 0 | 0 | 0 |
| Family & Friends for Freedom Fund | 0 | 0 | 1 | 0 | 0 | 0 | 0 | 0 | 0 | 0 | 0 | 0 | 0 |
| Family Caregiver Alliance | 1 | 0 | 1 | 0 | 1 | 0 | 0 | 1 | 0 | 1 | 1 | 0 | 0 |
| Federal Recovery Care Coordinator Program | 0 | 1 | 0 | 0 | 0 | 0 | 0 | 0 | 0 | 0 | 0 | 0 | 0 |
| Fisher House | 0 | 0 | 1 | 0 | 0 | 0 | 0 | 0 | 0 | 0 | 0 | 0 | 0 |
| Gary Sinise Foundation | 0 | 0 | 1 | 0 | 1 | 0 | 0 | 0 | 0 | 0 | 0 | 1 | 1 |

**Table E.6—Continued**

| Organization Name | Respite Care | Patient Advocacy | A Helping Hand | Financial Stipend | Structured Social Support | Religious Support Network | Structured Wellness Activities | Structured Education or Training | Health Care | Mental Health Care | Informal Informational Source | Referral Service for Veteran | Referral Service for Caregiver |
|---|---|---|---|---|---|---|---|---|---|---|---|---|---|
| Give an Hour | 0 | 0 | 0 | 0 | 0 | 0 | 0 | 0 | 0 | 1 | 0 | 0 | 0 |
| Her War, Her Voice | 0 | 0 | 0 | 0 | 1 | 0 | 0 | 0 | 0 | 0 | 0 | 0 | 0 |
| Home Front Hearts | 0 | 1 | 1 | 0 | 0 | 0 | 0 | 0 | 0 | 0 | 1 | 1 | 1 |
| Home Instead Senior Care | 1 | 1 | 0 | 0 | 1 | 0 | 0 | 1 | 0 | 0 | 1 | 0 | 1 |
| Hope for the Warriors | 1 | 1 | 1 | 0 | 1 | 0 | 1 | 0 | 0 | 1 | 1 | 1 | 1 |
| Hospice Foundation America | 0 | 0 | 0 | 0 | 0 | 0 | 0 | 1 | 0 | 0 | 1 | 1 | 0 |
| Impact a Hero | 0 | 0 | 1 | 0 | 1 | 0 | 0 | 0 | 0 | 0 | 0 | 0 | 0 |
| Iraq and Afghanistan Veterans of America | 0 | 1 | 0 | 0 | 0 | 0 | 0 | 0 | 0 | 0 | 1 | 1 | 1 |
| Jordan's Initiative | 0 | 0 | 1 | 0 | 0 | 0 | 0 | 0 | 0 | 0 | 0 | 0 | 0 |
| Lotsa Helping Hands | 0 | 0 | 0 | 0 | 1 | 0 | 0 | 0 | 0 | 0 | 1 | 1 | 1 |
| Marine Corps Wounded Warrior Regiment | 0 | 1 | 1 | 1 | 1 | 0 | 0 | 0 | 0 | 0 | 0 | 1 | 1 |
| Marine Parents | 0 | 0 | 0 | 0 | 1 | 1 | 0 | 0 | 0 | 0 | 1 | 0 | 1 |
| MBP Consulting | 0 | 0 | 0 | 0 | 0 | 0 | 0 | 1 | 0 | 0 | 1 | 0 | 0 |
| Mercy Medical Airlift and the Air Compassion for Veterans program | 0 | 0 | 1 | 0 | 0 | 0 | 0 | 0 | 0 | 0 | 0 | 0 | 0 |
| MHN Government Services' Military and Family Life Consultant and Joint Family Support Assistance Program | 0 | 0 | 0 | 0 | 0 | 0 | 0 | 0 | 0 | 1 | 0 | 0 | 0 |
| Military Child Education Coalition | 0 | 0 | 0 | 0 | 0 | 0 | 0 | 1 | 0 | 0 | 1 | 0 | 0 |
| Military Officer's Association of America | 0 | 0 | 0 | 0 | 0 | 0 | 0 | 1 | 0 | 0 | 0 | 1 | 1 |
| Military Order of the Purple Heart | 0 | 0 | 0 | 0 | 1 | 0 | 0 | 0 | 0 | 0 | 0 | 1 | 1 |
| Military Warriors Support Foundation | 0 | 0 | 1 | 0 | 0 | 0 | 1 | 0 | 0 | 0 | 1 | 0 | 0 |
| National Alliance on Mental Illness | 0 | 0 | 0 | 0 | 1 | 0 | 0 | 1 | 0 | 0 | 0 | 0 | 0 |
| National Association of American Veterans—Services | 0 | 0 | 0 | 0 | 1 | 0 | 0 | 0 | 0 | 0 | 0 | 1 | 1 |
| National Council on Aging—Building Better Caregivers | 0 | 0 | 0 | 0 | 0 | 0 | 0 | 1 | 0 | 0 | 0 | 1 | 1 |

**Table E.6—Continued**

| Organization Name | Respite Care | Patient Advocacy | A Helping Hand | Financial Stipend | Structured Social Support | Religious Support Network | Structured Wellness Activities | Structured Education or Training | Health Care | Mental Health Care | Informal Informational Source | Referral Service for Veteran | Referral Service for Caregiver |
|---|---|---|---|---|---|---|---|---|---|---|---|---|---|
| National Hospice and Palliative Care Organization's Caring Connections | 0 | 0 | 0 | 0 | 0 | 0 | 0 | 1 | 0 | 0 | 1 | 0 | 0 |
| National Military Family Association | 0 | 0 | 0 | 0 | 1 | 0 | 1 | 0 | 0 | 0 | 1 | 0 | 0 |
| Navy Safe Harbor Foundation | 0 | 0 | 1 | 0 | 0 | 0 | 0 | 0 | 0 | 0 | 0 | 0 | 0 |
| Navy Seal Foundation | 0 | 0 | 1 | 0 | 1 | 0 | 0 | 0 | 0 | 0 | 0 | 0 | 0 |
| Navy Wounded Warrior—Safe Harbor | 0 | 1 | 1 | 1 | 0 | 0 | 0 | 0 | 0 | 0 | 0 | 1 | 1 |
| Navy–Marine Corps Relief Society | 0 | 0 | 1 | 0 | 0 | 0 | 0 | 1 | 0 | 0 | 0 | 0 | 0 |
| Operation Family Fund | 0 | 0 | 1 | 0 | 0 | 0 | 0 | 0 | 0 | 0 | 0 | 0 | 0 |
| Operation First Response | 0 | 0 | 1 | 0 | 1 | 0 | 0 | 0 | 0 | 0 | 0 | 1 | 1 |
| Operation Heal Our Patriots | 0 | 0 | 0 | 0 | 1 | 1 | 1 | 0 | 0 | 0 | 0 | 0 | 0 |
| Operation Homefront | 0 | 0 | 1 | 0 | 1 | 0 | 0 | 1 | 0 | 0 | 1 | 0 | 1 |
| Patient Advocate Foundation | 0 | 1 | 0 | 0 | 0 | 0 | 0 | 1 | 1 | 0 | 1 | 1 | 1 |
| Pentagon Federal Credit Union Foundation | 0 | 0 | 1 | 0 | 0 | 0 | 0 | 0 | 0 | 0 | 0 | 0 | 0 |
| Project Sanctuary | 0 | 0 | 0 | 0 | 1 | 0 | 1 | 0 | 0 | 0 | 0 | 0 | 0 |
| Public Counsel Center for Veterans Advancement | 0 | 0 | 1 | 0 | 0 | 0 | 0 | 0 | 0 | 0 | 0 | 0 | 0 |
| Purple Heart Homes | 0 | 0 | 1 | 0 | 0 | 0 | 0 | 0 | 0 | 0 | 0 | 0 | 0 |
| Quality of Life Foundation | 0 | 1 | 1 | 0 | 0 | 0 | 0 | 0 | 0 | 0 | 1 | 0 | 1 |
| Rebuild Hope | 0 | 0 | 1 | 0 | 0 | 0 | 0 | 0 | 0 | 0 | 1 | 0 | 0 |
| Reserve Aid | 0 | 0 | 1 | 0 | 0 | 0 | 0 | 0 | 0 | 0 | 0 | 0 | 0 |
| Returning Heroes Home | 0 | 0 | 1 | 0 | 1 | 0 | 1 | 0 | 0 | 0 | 0 | 0 | 0 |
| Rosalynn Carter Institute for Caregiving | 0 | 0 | 0 | 0 | 0 | 0 | 0 | 1 | 0 | 0 | 1 | 1 | 1 |
| Salute, Inc. | 0 | 0 | 1 | 0 | 0 | 0 | 0 | 0 | 0 | 0 | 0 | 1 | 1 |
| Semper Fi Fund | 0 | 0 | 1 | 0 | 0 | 0 | 1 | 0 | 0 | 0 | 0 | 1 | 1 |
| Semper Max | 0 | 0 | 0 | 0 | 1 | 0 | 0 | 0 | 0 | 0 | 0 | 0 | 0 |
| Share the Care | 0 | 0 | 0 | 0 | 0 | 0 | 0 | 1 | 0 | 0 | 1 | 0 | 0 |
| Shepherds Centers of America | 1 | 0 | 1 | 0 | 1 | 1 | 1 | 1 | 0 | 0 | 1 | 1 | 1 |

## Table E.6—Continued

| Organization Name | Respite Care | Patient Advocacy | A Helping Hand | Financial Stipend | Structured Social Support | Religious Support Network | Structured Wellness Activities | Structured Education or Training | Health Care | Mental Health Care | Informal Informational Source | Referral Service for Veteran | Referral Service for Caregiver |
|---|---|---|---|---|---|---|---|---|---|---|---|---|---|
| Special Operations Command Care Coalition | 0 | 1 | 0 | 0 | 0 | 0 | 0 | 0 | 0 | 0 | 0 | 1 | 1 |
| Special Operations Warrior Foundation | 0 | 1 | 1 | 0 | 0 | 0 | 0 | 0 | 0 | 1 | 0 | 0 | 0 |
| Sportsmen's Foundation for Military Families | 0 | 0 | 0 | 0 | 1 | 0 | 1 | 0 | 0 | 0 | 0 | 0 | 0 |
| Strategic Outreach to Families of All Reservists | 0 | 0 | 0 | 0 | 0 | 0 | 0 | 0 | 0 | 1 | 0 | 0 | 0 |
| Strength for Caring | 0 | 0 | 0 | 0 | 1 | 0 | 0 | 1 | 0 | 0 | 1 | 0 | 1 |
| Support & Family Education (SAFE)—Mental Health Facts for Families | 0 | 0 | 0 | 0 | 1 | 0 | 0 | 1 | 0 | 0 | 0 | 0 | 0 |
| Terra Nova Films and Video Caregiving | 0 | 0 | 0 | 0 | 0 | 0 | 0 | 1 | 0 | 0 | 0 | 0 | 0 |
| The Soldier's Project | 0 | 0 | 0 | 0 | 0 | 0 | 0 | 0 | 0 | 1 | 1 | 0 | 0 |
| Them Bones Veteran Community | 0 | 0 | 0 | 0 | 0 | 1 | 0 | 0 | 0 | 1 | 0 | 0 | 0 |
| Today's Caregiver | 0 | 0 | 0 | 0 | 0 | 0 | 0 | 1 | 0 | 0 | 1 | 1 | 1 |
| USA Cares | 0 | 0 | 1 | 0 | 0 | 0 | 0 | 0 | 0 | 0 | 0 | 0 | 1 |
| USO Warrior and Family Care | 0 | 0 | 0 | 0 | 1 | 0 | 1 | 1 | 0 | 0 | 1 | 0 | 0 |
| VA Caregiver Support Program | 1 | 0 | 1 | 1 | 1 | 0 | 0 | 1 | 1 | 1 | 0 | 0 | 1 |
| VA OEF/OIF/OND Care Management Program | 0 | 1 | 0 | 0 | 0 | 0 | 0 | 0 | 0 | 0 | 0 | 0 | 0 |
| VeteranCaregiver.com | 0 | 0 | 0 | 0 | 1 | 0 | 0 | 0 | 0 | 0 | 1 | 0 | 0 |
| Virginia Navigator | 0 | 0 | 0 | 0 | 1 | 0 | 0 | 0 | 0 | 0 | 1 | 1 | 1 |
| Virginia Wounded Warrior Program | 0 | 1 | 1 | 0 | 1 | 0 | 0 | 0 | 0 | 0 | 1 | 1 | 1 |
| Well Spouse Association | 0 | 0 | 0 | 0 | 1 | 0 | 1 | 1 | 0 | 0 | 0 | 0 | 1 |
| Wounded Heroes Foundation | 0 | 0 | 1 | 0 | 0 | 0 | 1 | 0 | 0 | 0 | 1 | 0 | 0 |
| Wounded Heroes Fund | 0 | 0 | 1 | 0 | 0 | 0 | 0 | 0 | 0 | 0 | 0 | 0 | 0 |
| Wounded Warrior Project | 1 | 1 | 0 | 0 | 1 | 0 | 0 | 1 | 0 | 0 | 1 | 1 | 1 |
| Wounded Warriors Family Support | 1 | 0 | 1 | 1 | 1 | 0 | 1 | 0 | 0 | 0 | 1 | 1 | 1 |
| Yellow Ribbon Fund | 0 | 0 | 1 | 0 | 1 | 0 | 1 | 0 | 0 | 0 | 0 | 0 | 0 |
| Yellow Ribbon Reintegration Program | 0 | 0 | 0 | 0 | 1 | 0 | 0 | 0 | 0 | 0 | 1 | 1 | 1 |

**Table E.7**
**Organizations by Miscellaneous Characteristics (n = 120)**

| Organization Name | Origination Date | Tax Status | Caregiver Specific or Incidental | Military Specific or Incidental | Specific Injury or Illness | Geographic Reach |
|---|---|---|---|---|---|---|
| AARP | 1958 | Nonprofit | Incidental | Incidental | No | National or international |
| AgingCare.com | 2007 | For-profit | Specific | Specific | No | National or international |
| AGIS | 1998 | For-profit | Specific | Specific | No | National or international |
| Air Force Aid Society | 1942 | Nonprofit | Incidental | Incidental | No | National or international |
| Air Force Wounded Warrior Program | 2005 | Government | Incidental | Incidental | No | National or international |
| Air Warrior Courage Foundation | 1998 | Nonprofit | Incidental | Incidental | No | National or international |
| American Bar Association Military Pro Bono Project and Veterans Claims and Assistance Network | 2008; 2013 | Nonprofit | Incidental | Incidental | No | National or international |
| American Legion Auxiliary | 1919 | Nonprofit | Incidental | Incidental | No | National w/local activities |
| American Legion Family Support Network | 1990 | Nonprofit | Incidental | Incidental | No | National w/local activities |
| American Red Cross | 1881 | Nonprofit | Incidental | Incidental | No | National or international |
| American Veterans with Brain Injuries | 2004 | Nonprofit | Incidental | Incidental | Yes | National or international |
| Armed Forces Foundation | 2001 | Nonprofit | Incidental | Incidental | No | National or international |
| Armed Forces Reserve Family Assistance Fund (AFRFAF) | 2003 | Nonprofit | Incidental | Incidental | No | National or international |
| Armed Services YMCA | 1861 | Nonprofit | Incidental | Incidental | No | National w/local activities |
| Army Emergency Relief | 1942 | Nonprofit | Incidental | Incidental | No | National or international |
| Army Wounded Warrior Program | 2004 | Government | Incidental | Incidental | No | National or international |

## Table E.7—Continued

| Organization Name | Origination Date | Tax Status | Caregiver Specific or Incidental | Military Specific or Incidental | Specific Injury or Illness | Geographic Reach |
|---|---|---|---|---|---|---|
| Association of the United States Army Family Readiness Directorate | 1999 | Nonprofit | Incidental | Incidental | No | National or international |
| Blue Star Families | 2008 | Nonprofit | Specific | Specific | No | National or international |
| Boulder Crest Retreat | 2012 | Nonprofit | Specific | Specific | No | National or international |
| Brain Injury Alliance and Brain Injury Alliance of Colorado | 1980s | Nonprofit | Incidental | Incidental | Yes | National w/local activities |
| Brain Injury Association of America | 1980 | Nonprofit | Incidental | Incidental | Yes | National w/local activities |
| Camaraderie Foundation | N/A | Nonprofit | Incidental | Incidental | No | Local |
| Care.com | 2006 | For-profit | Specific | Specific | No | National or international |
| Caregiver Action Network | 1993 | Nonprofit | Specific | Specific | No | National or international |
| CaregiverHelp.com | N/A | For-profit | Specific | Specific | No | National or international |
| Caregivers Video Series: Walking on Eggshells | N/A | Nonprofit | Specific | Specific | No | National or international |
| CaregivingHelp.org | 1995 | Nonprofit | Specific | Specific | No | National w/local activities |
| CarePages | 2000 | For-profit | Specific | Specific | No | National or international |
| Caring From a Distance | 2002 | Nonprofit | Specific | Specific | No | National or international |
| Cause (Comfort for America's Uniformed Services) | 2003 | Nonprofit | Incidental | Incidental | No | National w/local activities |
| Coaching Into Care | 2010 | Government | Specific | Specific | No | National or international |
| Coalition to Salute America's Heroes | 2004 | Nonprofit | Incidental | Incidental | No | National or international |

**Table E.7—Continued**

| Organization Name | Origination Date | Tax Status | Caregiver Specific or Incidental | Military Specific or Incidental | Specific Injury or Illness | Geographic Reach |
|---|---|---|---|---|---|---|
| Coast Guard Mutual Assistance | 1924 | Nonprofit | Incidental | Incidental | No | National or international |
| Code of Support Foundation | 2010 | Nonprofit | Specific | Specific | No | National or international |
| Coming Home Project | 2007 | Nonprofit | Incidental | Incidental | No | National or international |
| Compass Retreat Center | 2009 | Nonprofit | Incidental | Incidental | No | Local |
| Courage Beyond | 2010 | Nonprofit | Incidental | Incidental | No | National or international |
| Defenders of Freedom | 2004 | Nonprofit | Incidental | Incidental | No | National w/local activities |
| Defense and Veterans Brain Injury Center | 1992 | Government | Incidental | Incidental | Yes | National or international |
| Disabled American Veterans | 1921 | Nonprofit | Incidental | Incidental | No | National w/local activities |
| DoD Office of Warrior Care Policy | 2008 | Government | Specific | Specific | No | National or international |
| Easter Seals Military and Veterans Services | 1919 | Nonprofit | Specific | Specific | No | National or international |
| Easter Seals New Hampshire Military and Veterans Services | 2005 | Nonprofit | Incidental | Incidental | No | Local |
| EOD Warrior Foundation | 2013 | Nonprofit | Incidental | Incidental | No | National or international |
| Family & Friends for Freedom Fund | 2004 | Nonprofit | Specific | Specific | No | National or international |
| Family Caregiver Alliance | 1977 | Nonprofit | Specific | Specific | No | National w/local activities |
| Federal Recovery Care Coordinator Program | 2007 | Government | Incidental | Incidental | No | National or international |
| Fisher House | 1990 | Nonprofit | Specific | Specific | No | National or international |
| Gary Sinise Foundation | 2011 | Nonprofit | Incidental | Incidental | No | National or international |

**Table E.7—Continued**

| Organization Name | Origination Date | Tax Status | Caregiver Specific or Incidental | Military Specific or Incidental | Specific Injury or Illness | Geographic Reach |
|---|---|---|---|---|---|---|
| Give an Hour | 2005 | Nonprofit | Incidental | Incidental | No | National or international |
| Her War, Her Voice | N/A | Nonprofit | Incidental | Incidental | No | National or international |
| Home Front Hearts | 2008 | Nonprofit | Incidental | Incidental | No | Local |
| Home Instead Senior Care | 1994 | For-profit | Specific | Specific | No | National w/local activities |
| Hope for the Warriors | 2006 | Nonprofit | Incidental | Incidental | No | National w/local activities |
| Hospice Foundation America | 1982 | Nonprofit | Specific | Specific | No | National or international |
| Impact a Hero | 2004 | Nonprofit | Incidental | Incidental | No | National or international |
| Iraq and Afghanistan Veterans of America | 2004 | Nonprofit | Incidental | Incidental | No | National w/local activities |
| Jordan's Initiative | 2008 | Nonprofit | Incidental | Incidental | No | National or international |
| Lotsa Helping Hands | 2008 | For-profit | Specific | Specific | No | National or international |
| Marine Corps Wounded Warrior Regiment | 2007 | Government | Incidental | Incidental | No | National or international |
| Marine Parents | 2003 | Nonprofit | Incidental | Incidental | No | National or international |
| MBP Consulting | 2009 | For-profit | Specific | Specific | No | National or international |
| Mercy Medical Airlift and the Air Compassion for Veterans program | 1972 | Nonprofit | Incidental | Incidental | No | National or international |
| MHN Government Services' Military & Family Life Consultant and Joint Family Support Assistance Program | 2004 | Nonprofit | Incidental | Incidental | No | National or international |
| Military Child Education Coalition | 1998 | Nonprofit | Incidental | Incidental | No | National or international |
| Military Officer's Association of America | 1929 | Nonprofit | Specific | Specific | No | National or international |

**Table E.7—Continued**

| Organization Name | Origination Date | Tax Status | Caregiver Specific or Incidental | Military Specific or Incidental | Specific Injury or Illness | Geographic Reach |
|---|---|---|---|---|---|---|
| Military Order of the Purple Heart | 1932 | Nonprofit | Incidental | Incidental | No | National w/local activities |
| Military Warriors Support Foundation | 2007 | Nonprofit | Incidental | Incidental | No | National or international |
| National Alliance on Mental Illness | 1979 | Nonprofit | Incidental | Incidental | Yes | National w/local activities |
| National Association of American Veterans—Services | 2005 | Nonprofit | Incidental | Incidental | No | National or international |
| National Council on Aging—Building Better Caregivers | 2012 | Nonprofit | Specific | Specific | No | National or international |
| National Hospice and Palliative Care Organization's Caring Connections | 2004 | Nonprofit | Specific | Specific | No | National or international |
| National Military Family Association | 1969 | Nonprofit | Incidental | Incidental | No | National or international |
| Navy Safe Harbor Foundation | 2009 | Nonprofit | Specific | Specific | No | National or international |
| Navy Seal Foundation | 2000 | Nonprofit | Incidental | Incidental | No | National or international |
| Navy Wounded Warrior—Safe Harbor | 2008 | Government | Incidental | Incidental | No | National or international |
| Navy–Marine Corps Relief Society | 2006 | Nonprofit | Incidental | Incidental | No | National or international |
| Operation Family Fund | 2003 | Nonprofit | Incidental | Incidental | No | National or international |
| Operation First Response | 2004 | Nonprofit | Incidental | Incidental | No | National or international |
| Operation Heal Our Patriots | 2012 | Nonprofit | Incidental | Incidental | No | National or international |
| Operation Homefront | 2002 | Nonprofit | Specific | Specific | No | National w/local activities |
| Patient Advocate Foundation | 1996 | Nonprofit | Incidental | Incidental | No | National or international |

**Table E.7—Continued**

| Organization Name | Origination Date | Tax Status | Caregiver Specific or Incidental | Military Specific or Incidental | Specific Injury or Illness | Geographic Reach |
|---|---|---|---|---|---|---|
| Pentagon Federal Credit Union Foundation | 2001 | Nonprofit | Incidental | Incidental | No | National or international |
| Project Sanctuary | 2007 | Nonprofit | Incidental | Incidental | No | National w/local activities |
| Public Counsel Center for Veterans Advancement | 2009 | Nonprofit | Specific | Specific | No | National w/local activities |
| Purple Heart Homes | 2008 | Nonprofit | Incidental | Incidental | No | National or international |
| Quality of Life Foundation | 2008 | Nonprofit | Specific | Specific | No | National or international |
| Rebuild Hope | 2007 | Nonprofit | Incidental | Incidental | No | National or international |
| Reserve Aid | 2006 | Nonprofit | Incidental | Incidental | No | National or international |
| Returning Heroes Home | 2006 | Nonprofit | Incidental | Incidental | No | National or international |
| Rosalynn Carter Institute for Caregiving | 1987 | Nonprofit | Specific | Specific | No | National or international |
| Salute, Inc. | 2003 | Nonprofit | Incidental | Incidental | No | National or international |
| Semper Fi Fund | 2003 | Nonprofit | Incidental | Incidental | No | National or international |
| Semper Max | 2009 | Nonprofit | Incidental | Incidental | No | National or international |
| Share the Care | 1988 | Nonprofit | Specific | Specific | No | National w/local activities |
| Shepherd's Centers of America | 1975 | Nonprofit | Specific | Specific | No | National w/local activities |
| Special Operations Command Care Coalition | 2005 | Government | Incidental | Incidental | No | National or international |
| Special Operations Warrior Foundation | 1980 | Nonprofit | Incidental | Incidental | No | National or international |

**Table E.7—Continued**

| Organization Name | Origination Date | Tax Status | Caregiver Specific or Incidental | Military Specific or Incidental | Specific Injury or Illness | Geographic Reach |
|---|---|---|---|---|---|---|
| Sportsmen's Foundation for Military Families | 2008 | Nonprofit | Incidental | Incidental | No | National w/local activities |
| Strategic Outreach to Families of All Reservists | 2004 | Nonprofit | Incidental | Incidental | No | National w/local activities |
| Strength for Caring | 1993 | For-profit | Specific | Specific | No | National or international |
| Support & Family Education (SAFE)—Mental Health Facts for Families | 1999 | Government | Incidental | Incidental | Yes | National or international |
| Terra Nova Films and Video Caregiving | 1981 | Nonprofit | Specific | Specific | No | National or international |
| The Soldier's Project | 2004 | Nonprofit | Incidental | Incidental | No | National w/local activities |
| Them Bones Veteran Community | 2001 | Nonprofit | Incidental | Incidental | No | Local |
| Today's Caregiver | 1995 | For-profit | Specific | Specific | No | National or international |
| USA Cares | 2003 | Nonprofit | Incidental | Incidental | No | National or international |
| USO Warrior and Family Care | 2009 | Nonprofit | Specific | Specific | No | National or international |
| VA Caregiver Support Program | 2007 | Government | Specific | Specific | No | National w/local activities |
| VA OEF/OIF/OND Care Management Program | 2007 | Government | Incidental | Incidental | No | National w/local activities |
| VeteranCaregiver.com | 2010 | Unknown | Specific | Specific | No | National or international |
| Virginia Navigator | N/A | Nonprofit | Specific | Specific | No | Local |
| Virginia Wounded Warrior Program | 2008 | Government | Incidental | Incidental | No | Local |
| Well Spouse Association | 1988 | Nonprofit | Specific | Specific | No | National or international |
| Wounded Heroes Foundation | 2007 | Nonprofit | Incidental | Incidental | No | National or international |

**Table E.7—Continued**

| Organization Name | Origination Date | Tax Status | Caregiver Specific or Incidental | Military Specific or Incidental | Specific Injury or Illness | Geographic Reach |
|---|---|---|---|---|---|---|
| Wounded Heroes Fund | 2008 | Nonprofit | Incidental | Incidental | No | Local |
| Wounded Warrior Project | 2003 | Nonprofit | Incidental | Incidental | No | National w/local activities |
| Wounded Warriors Family Support | 2003 | Nonprofit | Specific | Specific | No | National or international |
| Yellow Ribbon Fund | 2008 | Nonprofit | Specific | Specific | No | Local |
| Yellow Ribbon Reintegration Program | 2007 | Government | Incidental | Incidental | No | National w/local activities |

# Federal and State Policies and Programs to Support Military Caregivers

In this appendix, we provide a summary of several federal policies and programs that support caregivers broadly, and military caregivers specifically. We also describe the availability of state-based programs to support military caregivers and include maps to indicate which states offer caregiver support programs that would apply to post-9/11 caregivers across different categories.

## Federal Policies to Support Caregiving

We identified several federal policies that support caregiving. These policies serve as the foundation for multiple caregiver support programs throughout the United States. Here, we summarize some of the key federal policies and programs as context for the landscape of military caregiver policies and programs. These policies are listed in alphabetical order.

### Affordable Care Act

In March 2010, Congress enacted the Affordable Care Act, a health care law that brings a number of benefits to all Americans. Many provisions are now in place. Others are being phased in over several years. There are provisions of this law that directly affect family caregivers (FCA, 2013c). For example, it:

- expands home- and community-based services through Medicaid, allowing more people to receive care at home rather than going into a nursing home
- provides training for family caregivers and home care workers
- expands coverage for care coordination and transitional care services
- establishes a new, voluntary, long-term services and support insurance program.

### Americans with Disabilities Act

The ADA of 1990 prohibits discrimination and ensures equal opportunity for persons with disabilities in employment, state and local government services, public accommodations, commercial facilities, and transportation. It also mandates the establishment of TDD/telephone relay services. The ADA was originally enacted in public law format and later rearranged and published in the U.S. Code.[1] In addition to ensuring equal opportunity for persons with a disability, the ADA also protects those related to an individual with a disability. For example, the ADA prohibits "excluding or otherwise denying equal jobs or benefits to a qualified individual because of the known disability of an individual with whom the qualified individual is known to have a relationship or association" (FCA, 2013f). This can include a caregiver, depending on the relationship with the care recipient.

The ADA does not require an employer to reasonably accommodate an employee's wish to attend to caregiving obligations (FCA, 2013f). However, in 2007, the EEOC issued guidance to clarify the circumstances under which discrimination against workers with caregiving responsibilities might violate federal employment discrimination laws. The EEOC provided several examples of best practices for employers that go beyond federal discrimination requirements and that would remove barriers for caregivers in the workplace (this information is presented in Table 5.1; EEOC, 2007).

### The Family and Medical Leave Act

The FMLA provides certain employees with up to 12 weeks of unpaid, job-protected leave per year. It also requires that their group health benefits be maintained during the leave (DoL, 2013). FMLA is designed to help employees balance their work and family responsibilities by allowing them to take reasonable unpaid leave for certain family and medical reasons. It also seeks to accommodate the legitimate interests of employers and promote equal employment opportunity for men and women (DoL, 2013). FMLA applies to all public agencies, all public and private elementary and secondary schools, and companies with 50 or more employees. These employers must provide an eligible employee with up to 12 weeks of unpaid leave each year for any of the following reasons (2012a):

- birth and care of a newborn child of an employee
- placement with the employee of a child for adoption or foster care
- care for an immediate family member (spouse, child, or parent) with a serious health condition
- medical leave when the employee is unable to work because of a serious health condition.

Employees are eligible for leave if they have worked for their employer at least 12 months, at least 1,250 hours over the past 12 months, and work at a location where the company employs 50 or more employees within 75 miles (DoL, 2013).

---

[1]  The current text of the ADA includes changes made by the ADA Amendments Act of 2008 (P.L. 110-325), which became effective on January 1, 2009.

Following expansions of FMLA as a result of the NDAAs for fiscal years 2008 and 2010, the law now also provides certain military family leave entitlements. Military family members may take FMLA leave for special reasons related to certain military deployments. Additionally, a family of a military member may take up to 26 weeks of FMLA leave in a single 12-month period to care for a covered service member with a serious injury or illness (as compared with other, nonmilitary related employees who may only be eligible for up to 12 weeks leave in a year). We discuss details about these expansions in greater detail later.

### Lifespan Respite Care Act

The Lifespan Respite Care Act, signed into law in December 2006, established a program to assist family caregivers in accessing affordable and high-quality respite care. Specifically, this new law authorizes:

- lifespan respite programs at the state and local levels
- planned and emergency respite for family caregivers
- training/recruitment of respite workers and volunteers
- provision of information to caregivers about respite/support services
- assistance for caregivers in gaining access to such services
- establishment of a National Resource Center on Lifespan Respite Care.

Although the law authorizes Congress to spend approximately $50 million annually on these activities, annual allocations have been in the amount of $2.5 million per year since 2009. The funds are used to award grants to individual states as they implement specific Lifespan Respite programs. Figure F.1 displays the states that have received funding through the Lifespan Respite programs. In these maps, we color the states to demonstrate the density of the veteran population as defined by data from the VA. For the states that have received funding under this program, we also show the years in which they have been funded.

### Older Americans Act

Signed into law in 1965, the OAA set out specific objectives for maintaining the dignity and welfare of older individuals and created the primary vehicle for organizing, coordinating, and providing community-based services and opportunities for older Americans and their families. The original legislation established authority for grants to states for community planning and social services, research and development projects, and personnel training in the field of aging. The law also established the Administration on Aging to administer the grant programs and to serve as the federal focal point on matters concerning older persons. Although older individuals may receive services under many other federal programs, the OAA is considered to be the major vehicle for the organization and delivery of social and nutrition services to this group

**Figure F.1**
**States Receiving Funding Under the Lifespan Respite Care Program**

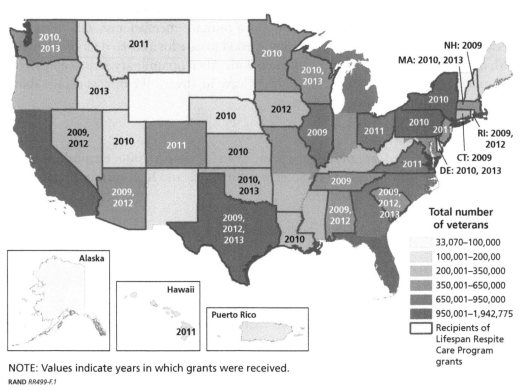

NOTE: Values indicate years in which grants were received.
RAND RR499-F.1

and their caregivers. It authorizes a wide array of service programs through a national network of 56 state agencies on aging, 629 area agencies on aging, nearly 20,000 service providers, 244 tribal organizations, and two Native Hawaiian organizations representing 400 tribes. The OAA also includes community service employment for low-income older Americans; training, research, and demonstration activities in the field of aging; and vulnerable elder rights protection activities.

## Federal Policies to Support Military Caregivers Specifically

Several pieces of federal legislation have been written in recent years to establish or improve the benefits of caregivers of veterans. The defense authorization bills that Congress cleared in 2008 and 2010 made amendments to FMLA and established new benefits within DoD. Additionally, the Caregivers and Veterans Omnibus Health Benefits Act of 2010 (CVOHSA) established the Caregiver Support Program within the VA.

## National Defense Authorization Acts for Fiscal Years 2008 and 2010

In fiscal years 2008 and 2010, Congress introduced changes to FMLA for military caregivers. Section 585 of the 2008 NDAA amended FMLA to include caregivers of injured military members and veterans as eligible for receiving job-protected leave. It also entitled eligible caregivers to 26 work weeks of leave in a 12-month period and outlined the eligibility requirements.[2] Section 1616 required the Secretary of Defense to establish a Wounded Warrior Resource Center to provide services and support to injured service members, their families, and their caregivers.[3] Lastly, Section 1633 also amended Section 1074(c) of Title 10 of the U.S. Code to include respite care for caregivers of service members who were injured or became ill in the line of duty.[4]

Congress amended FMLA again through the fiscal year 2010 NDAA by expanding definitions and eligibility requirements to give greater benefits to injured or ill service members and their caregivers. Specifically, Section 565 made amendments to allow family members of recent veterans with serious injuries or illnesses to take job-protected leave, and expanded the definition of serious injuries and illnesses to include those resulting from preexisting conditions. It also establishes the term "covered active duty" in its eligibility requirements, stating that regular service members and activated reserve service members deployed to a foreign country are eligible for family and medical leave under FMLA (P.L. 111-84, 2009).

## Veterans' Caregiver and Omnibus Health Benefits Act

This 2010 law combined the key provisions of the Veterans Health Care Authorization Act (S. 252) and the Veterans Insurance and Benefits Enhancement Act (S. 728) to provide family caregivers of veterans with information and training, respite, counseling, and other supportive services. In addition, family caregivers of veterans who were injured in the line of duty after September 11, 2001, are also eligible for training and certification, health care, and a caregivers' stipend. The law also sought to improve health care for veterans in rural areas, help the VA adapt to the needs of women veterans, and expand supportive services for homeless veterans (FCA, 2013g).

The caregiver provision duplicated a program that already exists, but was deemed to be underutilized. The VA's Aid and Attendance program provides up to $2,900

---

[2]  A "Covered Servicemember" is defined as "a member of the Armed Forces, including a member of the National Guard or Reserves, who is undergoing medical treatment, recuperation, or therapy, is otherwise in outpatient status, or is otherwise on the temporary disability retired list, for a serious injury or illness."

[3]  The document specifically calls for "a wounded warrior resource center to provide wounded warriors, their families, and their primary caregivers with a single point of contact for assistance with reporting deficiencies in covered military facilities, obtaining health care services, receiving benefits information, and any other difficulties encountered while supporting wounded warriors."

[4]  The amount of coverage to be provided is comparable to that outlined in subsections (d) and (e) of Section 1079 of Title 10, U.S. Code.

additionally a month for veterans who need caregiver assistance for daily living. This program is currently authorized by law and available to all veterans who served during wartime and were injured. The CVOHSA of 2010 is also directly responsible for the forming of VA's Program of Comprehensive Assistance for Family Caregivers.

This act amended Title 38 of the U.S. Code and called on the VA Secretary to set up a program to provide benefits and services to caregivers of veterans who were injured while in the line of duty on or after September 11, 2001. It outlines the eligibility and requirements of caregivers to receive benefits, as well as the services to be provided to eligible caregivers.[5]

It should be noted that the Caregivers Expansion and Improvement Act of 2013 (S. 851) was introduced in April 2013. This would allow all veterans with a serious service-connected injury the eligibility to participate in the VA's Program of Comprehensive Assistance for Family Caregivers of such veterans. Under current law, such eligibility is limited to those veterans who incurred such an injury on or after September 11, 2001 (S. 851, 2013; H.R. 3383, 2013).

## Federal Caregiver Support Programs

As a result of these federal policies, there are several programs across HHS, DoL, and VA that directly support caregivers. We provide some description and highlights of some of the programs most relevant to military caregivers.

---

[5]  An eligible veteran is defined as "any individual who: is a veteran or member of the Armed Forces undergoing medical discharge from the Armed Forces; has a serious injury (including traumatic brain injury, psychological trauma, or other mental disorder) incurred or aggravated in the line of duty in the active military, naval, or air service on or after September 11, 2001; and is in need of personal care services because of an inability to perform one or more activities of daily living, a need for supervision or protection based on symptoms or residuals of neurological or other impairment or injury, or such other matters as the Secretary considers appropriate." The following services are to be provided to family caregivers of eligible veterans: "(I) such instruction, preparation, and training as the Secretary considers appropriate for the family caregiver to provide personal care services to the eligible veteran; (II) ongoing technical support consisting of information and assistance to address, in a timely manner, the routine, emergency, and specialized caregiving needs of the family caregiver in providing personal care services to the eligible veteran; (III) counseling; and (IV) lodging and subsistence under section 111(e) of this title." Additionally, the following services are to be provided to primary providers of personal care services: "(I) the assistance described in clause (i); (II) such mental health services as the Secretary determines appropriate; (III) respite care of not less than 30 days annually, including 24-hour-per-day care of the veteran commensurate with the care provided by the family caregiver to permit extended respite; (IV) medical care under section 1781 of this title; and (V) a monthly personal caregiver stipend."

### National Family Caregiver Support Program

The Administration on Community Living,[6] a component of HHS, runs the National Family Caregiver Support Program. Since its establishment in 2000 with the enactment of the OAA, the National Family Caregiver Support Program has provided support and program funds to all U.S. states and territories. The amount of funding that each state or territory receives depends on the share of the population aged 70 and over that is represented (AARP, 2013). The program offers a range of services to support family caregivers, and states are expected to provide five types of services (National Family Caregiver Support Program, 2013):

- information to caregivers about available services
- assistance to caregivers in gaining access to the services
- individual counseling, organization of support groups, and caregiver training
- respite care
- supplemental services, on a limited basis.

By creating the National Family Caregiver Support Program, Congress explicitly recognized the role that family caregivers occupy in our nation's long-term services and supports system. As of the 2006 Reauthorization of the Older Americans Act, the following specific populations of family caregivers are eligible to receive services (AARP, 2013):

- adult family members or other informal caregivers ages 18 and older providing care to individuals ages 60 and older
- adult family members or other informal caregivers ages 18 and older providing care to individuals of any age with Alzheimer's disease and related disorders
- grandparents and other relatives (not parents) ages 55 and older providing care to children under the age of 18
- grandparents and other relatives (not parents) ages 55 and older providing care to adults ages 18–59 with disabilities.

In fiscal 2013, the most recent year for which service data is available, over 750,000 caregivers received services through the National Family Caregiver Support Program. Military caregivers providing assistance for veterans over the age of 60 or with Alzheimer's disease may be eligible for services through the National Family Caregiver Support Program.

---

[6] ACL brings together the Administration on Aging, the Administration on Intellectual and Developmental Disabilities, and the HHS Office on Disability to serve as the federal agency responsible for increasing access to community supports, while focusing attention and resources on the unique needs of older Americans and people with disabilities across the lifespan.

**Medicaid Home- and Community-Based Service Program**

Within CMS, the Medicaid HCBS waiver program is the largest single payer of long-term care caregiving services in the country (HHS, 2013a). The legislative language authorizing the program is broad and inclusive, defining a family caregiver as "an adult family member, or another individual, who is an informal provider of in-home and community care to an older individual" (HHS, 2013b). The wide-ranging definition allows states to tailor unique requirements for residents receiving and providing care (FCA, 2013b). Programs can provide a combination of standard medical services and nonmedical services. Standard services include but are not limited to: case management (i.e., supports and service coordination), homemaker, home health aide, personal care, adult day health services, habilitation (both day and residential), and respite care. States can also propose "other" types of services that may assist in diverting and/or transitioning individuals from institutional settings into their homes and community (HHS, 2013b). To be eligible for the HCBS waiver program, caregivers must be rendering care for an individual eligible for and covered by Medicaid. In order to participate in Medicaid, federal law requires states to cover certain population groups (mandatory eligibility groups) and gives them the flexibility to cover other population groups (optional eligibility groups). States set individual eligibility criteria within federal minimum standards and states can apply to CMS for a waiver of federal law to expand health coverage beyond these groups.

Individuals with disabilities are eligible to receive both mandatory and optional coverage under Medicaid. Once a disability determination is made, the individual must then undergo an asset test and meet specific income requirements to be considered for Medicaid eligibility. In the next section, we provide more detail about the Medicaid HCBS Waiver-Funded programs at the state level, where eligibility requirements are defined more specifically based upon the characteristics of the care recipient and the caregiver in some cases.

**Special Compensation for Assistance with Activities of Daily Living**

SCAADL was authorized by the fiscal 2010 NDAA and provides for special monthly compensation for service members who incur a permanent catastrophic injury or illness and require caregiving assistance. SCAADL helps offset the loss of income by a primary caregiver who provides nonmedical care, support, and assistance for the service member (VA, 2011b). DoD Instruction 1341.12 (published in August 2011 and updated in May 2012) established SCAADL. The Under Secretary of Defense for Personnel and Readiness is responsible for managing and administering the program in coordination with the VA Under Secretary for Benefits.

To be eligible for SCAADL benefits, a service member must be suffering from a catastrophic injury or illness incurred in the line of duty,[7] in need of assistance to perform tasks of everyday living, or otherwise require residential institutional care if not for the assistance of a caregiver. SCAADL eligibility stops when a service member recovers from his or her injuries (or is no longer eligible for SCAADL benefits as determined by a primary care provider), begins to receive VA caregiver benefits (this prevents dual compensation for caregiving assistance), reaches 90 days after separation from the military, or dies.

Monetary stipends and compensations from SCAADL are paid directly to the service member. It is expected that the service member then transfer this money to their caregiver as appropriate. Therefore, the caregiver does not have to be related to the service member in any way to receive benefits from SCAADL, as long as they provide care to the service member. However, other military members are not eligible to be considered caregivers by SCAADL standards. As such, any dual military couples would not be eligible to receive SCAADL payments. It should also be noted that the money paid by SCAADL to service members is subject to taxation.

The SCAADL stipend is intended to cover the cost of additional expenses accrued by caregivers as well as lost wages. The amount is dependent on the geographic location of the service members and the amount of care required (and are determined based upon DoL wage rates for home health aids, as well as the amount of caregiving assistance required as determined by the certifying physician). SCAADL requires reauthorization every 180 days. Travel expenses, such as hotel rooms and transportation, are eligible for compensation when the travel is necessary to receive care.

It should be noted that caregivers for wounded, ill, or injured service members are also eligible for patient advocacy and helping-hand services through WWPs in each of the service branches.[8] The duration of these services is unspecified but may be limited to the period of time while a service member is on active duty or reserve status. We note these programs here, as the SCAADL financial stipends are accessed through the service-specific wounded warrior programs (these programs were described in Appendix F).

---

[7]  A catastrophic injury or illness is defined as "a permanent severely disabling injury, disorder, or illness incurred or aggravated in the line of duty that the Secretary of the Military Department concerned determines compromises the ability of the afflicted person to carry out ADL [activities of daily living] to such a degree that the person requires personal or mechanical assistance to leave home or bed, or constant supervision to avoid physical harm to self or others."

[8]  DoD Wounded Warrior programs include Air Force Wounded Warrior Program, Army Wounded Warrior Program, Care Coalition—United States Special Operations Command, Marine Corps Wounded Warrior Regiment, and Navy Wounded Warrior Safe Harbor. DoD's Office of Warrior Care Policy oversees these programs.

### VA Caregiver Support Program

The VA Caregiver Support Program was originally launched in 2007 to support the funding of a series of pilot programs to provide assistance and support of family caregivers of veterans. However, the program was significantly expanded after 2010, with the signing of the CVOHSA, which directed the Secretary of the VA to establish two programs to assist family caregivers of veterans. First, the Program of Comprehensive Assistance for Family Caregivers supports family caregivers of veterans who were seriously injured in the line of duty on or after September 11, 2001, and who are in need of personal care services. Second, the Program of General Caregiver Support Services provides support and assistance to family caregivers of veterans of all eras. Together, these programs make up the VA's Caregiver Support Program.

It should be noted that the Program of General Caregiver Support Services was an existing, albeit underutilized, program within the VA, through which the department provided a monthly stipend and respite services to caregivers of veterans. Through the Aid and Attendance program, the VA provides additional funding of up to $2,900 a month for veterans who need caregiver assistance for daily living. Several opportunities for respite care were and are also available through this general caregiver support program (for example, caregivers of veterans in this program can receive up to 30 days of respite in a given year, either at home or by placing the veteran in a VA facility temporarily). This program is currently available to all veterans who served during wartime and were injured. VA officials have reported, however, that this benefit is underutilized. Only 27 percent of veterans and 14 percent of veterans' widows who qualify for aid and attendance benefits receive them. The others are either unaware of this benefit or do not choose to apply for it (FCA, 2013g).

The second caregiver program authorized by the CVOHSA, the VA's Comprehensive Assistance for Caregivers Program, provides additional benefits and services to caregivers of veterans who were injured while in the line of duty on or after September 11, 2001. This program provides training and certification, ongoing education, and access to mental health services and counseling, as well as a monthly financial stipend and health insurance to those who qualify.

To provide assistance to caregivers and help facilitate the Caregiver Support Programs, starting in February 2011, the VA placed Caregiver Support Coordinators in each VA medical center. These individuals serve as a local resource for caregivers, and facilitate caregivers' access to training and educational opportunities, as well as provide feedback to the Central Office with respect to evolving needs and issues facing the caregivers. The VA Caregiver Support Program also hosts a Caregiver Support Line (toll-free line/call center), which provides caregivers with information about their eligibility for the VA, connects caregivers to services and local Caregiver Support Coordinators, and listens to caregivers' issues and concerns. In January 2012, the VA initiated caregiver peer support mentoring to link new caregivers with peer mentors who have more experience. More information about the additional services available through the VA Caregiver Support Program can be found in Appendix H.

### Veteran-Directed, Home- and Community-Based Services Program

In 2008, the Administration on Aging, now part of ACL, formally announced its collaboration with the Veterans Health Administration to provide an opportunity for states and local aging and disability network agencies to serve veterans of all ages at risk of nursing home placement through the Veteran Directed Home and Community Based Service Program, which involves providing one-on-one counseling to veterans and their families and helps the veteran determine how to use a flexible HCBS service budget to meet long-term service and support needs, goals, and preferences. The ACL website reports that more than 1,400 veterans had been served through this program in 23 states and the District of Columbia as of April 2012. These programs are operated with VA Medical Centers. In addition, in 2012, HHS announced that the Veterans Health Administration would purchase the support of Aging and Disability Resource Centers to assist veterans and their families as they determine how to use their flexible HCBS service budgets.

## State Programs to Support Caregiving

Many of the federal policies and programs that support caregivers are administered and managed through the individual states. For example, the National Family Caregiver Program, Medicaid-HCBS program, and the Lifespan Respite Care Program are administered at the state level. Often, states will authorize their own expansions of these programs either by changing the eligibility criteria or changing the caps on benefits (for example, in respite care). Through cross-cutting state-based initiatives, these programs and services seek to maximize the quality of life, functional independence, health, and well-being of individuals served by the programs.

Many states also have task forces, coalitions, or other state-level organizations that focus on caregiving. These may be grassroots membership organizations, either run by volunteers or paid staff. These organizations may work either formally (through grant or contract mechanisms) or informally with the state agencies to implement state programs to support caregiving. For example, states agencies may work with state respite coalitions to implement the Lifespan Respite Programs.

We next describe our process and findings with respect to the states in which military caregivers may be eligible for the state-based programs. Readers interested in detailed information about state-based resources should review the FCA report, *The State of the States in Family Caregiving: A 50 State Study.*

## State Availability of Caregiver Resources

To identify state-funded programs that might support military caregivers, we conducted Internet searches during October and November 2013. Using common search engines, we searched for information on state programs by using various keywords (state, caregiver, caregiver support, etc.) and—when available—names of specific programs. We also explored available informational resources through clearinghouses like the ones compiled and maintained by the FCA and through state and federal government websites.[9] Discovery of programs was aided by publicly available resource directories.

We extracted names and basic information about the state-funded programs and created an Excel spreadsheet. For each program, we extracted details about:

- type of program: options included Aged/Disabled Medicaid HCBS wavier program, state-funded program, or National Family Caregiver Support program
- the program's intended client: options included care recipient, family caregiver, or both
- the geographic region served by the program
- the minimum age requirement to receive benefits (for both the caregiver and care recipient)
- the state's administering agency
- several variables regarding the services provided to support family caregivers and the regulations of the services; e.g., whether family members are paid to provide care.

During the abstraction process, we received guidance from FCA staff members. Along with their online directory resource, the organization confirmed the structural makeup of specific programs we found and provided us with recently updated program information that was not publicly available.

We abstracted information about all the programs we found that provide services to caregivers, recipients of informal caregiving, or both. Most commonly, a state's Department of Human Services or its Department of Aging is the administering agency for the service programs.

Of the 147 state-based programs we abstracted, 62 provide services to individuals at a minimum age of 18 or 21. We focused on these programs because the minimum age allows for the inclusion of post-9/11 veterans. Using this additional criterion, all the National Family Caregiver Support Programs were excluded because of the senior age requirement for recipients of caregiving.

Figure F.2 displays how the states with caregiver support programs using a minimum care recipient age of 18 or 21 years distribute geographically across the United

---

[9]  See their Family Care Navigator website.

**Figure F.2**
**States with a Program with Minimum Care Recipient Age ≤ 21**

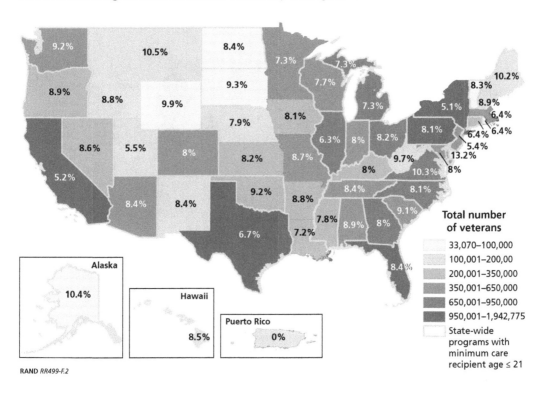

RAND *RR499-F.2*

States. The 40 states (out of 51 options[10]) that offer such program are highlighted by a yellow boundary. These maps also show the density of the veteran population by state (using the shading scheme defined in the color key at the bottom of each figure) and display the proportion of the state population that is a veteran (displayed as the percentage for each state). We used these as context to assess whether states might have a higher number of military caregivers (as a result of having higher density and proportions of veteran residents).

States can offer a variety of unlimited services under an HCBS waiver program. Programs can provide a combination of standard medical services and nonmedical services (AARP, 2013). Standard services include but are not limited to: case management (i.e., service coordination), homemaker, home health aide, personal care, adult day health services, habilitation (both day and residential), and respite care. States can also propose "other" types of services that may assist in diverting and/or transitioning individuals from institutional settings into their homes and community (HHS, 2013a).

---

[10] The maps we used include all 50 U.S states and Puerto Rico. Washington, D.C., was not included. The results for Washington, D.C., are included in the results' footnotes.

**Figure F.3**
**States with Programs That Are Family Caregiver Specific**

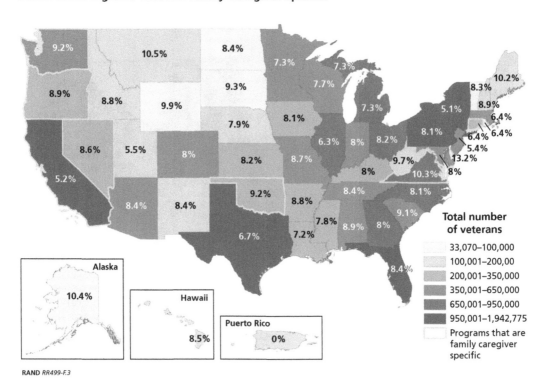

RAND *RR499-F.3*

For the states highlighted in Figure F.2, these benefits are available to care recipients as young as 21 (some states have a minimum age as young as 18).

Within the 40 states that serve care recipients as young as 21 years, seven (13.7 percent) have programs that are specific to caregivers who are family members. These are highlighted in Figure F.3. The most common services provided by these programs are caregiver support programs, education and training programs, and respite programs.

We also identified 19 states (37.3 percent) that have programs that pay family members to provide caregiving services (displayed in Figure F.4). The waiver and state programs are called "consumer-directed," "participant-directed," "cash and counseling," or other titles. Income amounts differ enormously by program. California, Ohio, and Pennsylvania have higher-than-average monthly income maximums at $2,130 (FCA, 2013b).

Many state programs also offer respite services; however, more than half of these programs have a maximum cap on the amount of respite benefit to be provided per care recipient. Programs with respite care caps confine the service by expense or time depending on the type of program. A typical cap is between $1,000 and $2,500 in expense or 720 hours of care per year (FCA, 2013a). In Figure F.5, we highlight the 23

**Figure F.4**
**States Where Family Members Can Be Paid to Provide Care**

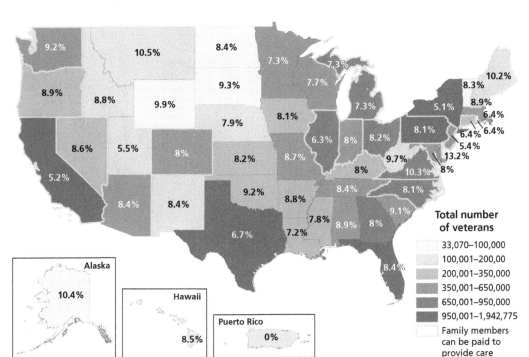

RAND RR499-F.4

states (45.1 percent) that have programs with no cap in respite care.[11] As such, military caregivers living in these states may have greater access to respite care services than those living in other areas.

---

[11] The maps we used include all 50 U.S states and Puerto Rico. Washington, D.C., does have a program that provides services for those 18 and older but does not have a program we would include in our other three variables.

**Figure F.5**
**States That Have a Program with No Maximum on Respite Care**

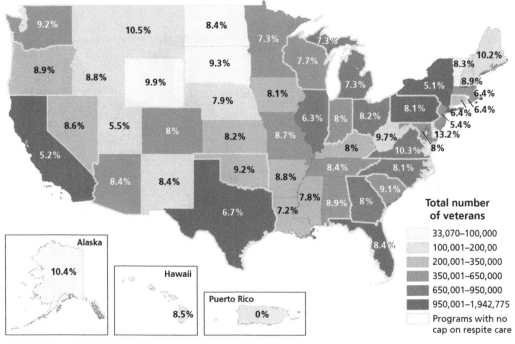

RAND *RR499-F.5*

# Programs and Organizations Excluded from the Environmental Scan

In this appendix, we describe the organizational entities that we considered for inclusion in the environmental scan but ultimately excluded (n = 382) because, after closer review, they did not meet our inclusion criteria. As noted in Appendix D, we *included* organizational entities if they offered certain types of common caregiving services or "nonstandard" health or mental health care (n = 120); thus, we *excluded* organizational entities that did not offer these services. It should be noted that while many of these resources may be informative or useful for caregivers, we excluded these services to maintain our core focus on *services that involve direct or intensive interaction with caregivers and help caregivers to address their most pressing problems (e.g., performing caregiving activities or maintaining their own health or well-being)*. Table G.1 illustrates the various types excluded organizations that we identified. In the following paragraphs, we describe the types of services that did not prompt inclusion of organizational entities, highlighting specific examples of excluded organizations.

## Informal Informational Sources

This category includes a range of information on a variety of topics. Some informational sources are directly related to caregiving (e.g., caregiving tips or navigating systems of care), while others are not. By "informal," we refer to sources that do not qualify as formal education or training, as described in Appendix D. The information is delivered through various modes, including the Internet, printed materials, and events such as conferences or seminars. Following is an example of an excluded organization that provided informal information:

- **HealthCentral.com (also CareConnection.com)** provides a range of information and resources for caregivers via its website and Web-based newsletter. The website includes a "Health A–Z" section that provides information on a number of common health and mental health conditions. It also provides detailed information on several prescription medications, and offers screening tools such as a "Symptom Checker" and "Stress Test."

**Table G.1**
**Types of Excluded Organizations**

| Service | Excluded | Included If Organization Also Had a Caregiving Service |
|---|---|---|
| Informal Informational Sources | | X[a] |
| Referral Services (for caregivers or service members/veterans) | | X[b] |
| Adapted Housing | X | |
| "Umbrella" Organizations or Websites | X | |
| Claims and Benefits Assistance | X | |
| Educational Assistance | X | |
| Employment Services | X | |
| Family Readiness, Resilience, or Transition Programs | X | |
| Financial Services | X | |
| General Relocation Assistance | X | |
| Homelessness Programs | X | |
| Parenting Resources, Child Care, or Activities for Children | X | |
| Professional Caregiver Resources | X | |
| Scheduling and Communication Tools | X | |
| Screening Tools for Caregivers | X | |
| Survivor Services | X | |

[a] Although this service category did not prompt inclusion in our environmental scan, we collected data on informal informational sources for organizations that were included in our scan for other reasons, but only if the information offered was directly related to caregiving or health or mental health conditions.

[b] Although this service category did not prompt inclusion in our environmental scan, we collected data on referral services for organizations that were included in our scan for other reasons.

## Referral Services

This category includes activities and efforts that connect caregivers (or other individuals) with health or social services. Referral services range from web-based or printed materials involving a passive, one-way transmittal of information to interactive mechanisms such as telephone hotlines or "warm hand-offs" to service providers. Referral services differ from "patient advocacy or case management" (an included category in our environmental scan), which involves a process of ongoing, active, care coordination or liaison activities, versus the one-time hand-off that many of these other organizations provide. Following is an example of an excluded organization that provided referral services:

- **Military OneSource** is a government-sponsored program that offers confidential services, including nonmedical counseling, specialty consultations, and resource and referral services to active-duty, National Guard and reserve members and their families located in the continental United States. Services are available online, in person, and via the Internet. Although Military OneSource offers nonmedical counseling, it does not meet our criteria for clinical (mental health) counseling. Nor does it meet our criteria for patient advocacy or case management, since a primary aim of the program is referral services rather than ongoing case management.

## Adapted Housing

This category includes services that help care recipients to purchase or construct a modified home, or alter an existing home to accommodate a care recipient's disability. Although this category borders upon services that may be considered helping-hand assistance (an included category in our environmental scan), we distinguish the former by the fact that it typically involves a one-time substantial home modification or the purchase of a new home, rather than routine maintenance support. Following is an example of an excluded organization that provided adapted housing:

- **VA Specially Adapted Housing and Special Housing Adaptation** assist veterans with certain service-connected disabilities and their families in adapting their homes or buying homes to accommodate their disabilities. Although these programs may be of use to caregivers indirectly, we considered these programs out of scope because they do not involve a direct service to caregivers.

## "Umbrella" Organizations

These are formal administrative structures that "house" organizational entities offering services to caregivers. Often, the distinction between "umbrella" organizations and the entities providing services was not immediately clear. We researched interrelated organizations until we determined the appropriate entity for inclusion and exclusion. Typically, we chose to include the organizational entity that best allowed us to narrow in on caregiving services while not overlooking pertinent services in other areas of the organization. Often, this resulted in the exclusion of "umbrella" organizations. Following is an example of an excluded organization that provided employment services:

- The **Defense Centers of Excellence for Psychological Health and Traumatic Brain Injury (DCoE)** is composed of three centers that, together, seek to improve the lives of service members, families, and veterans by advancing excellence in psychological health and TBI prevention and care. The centers include the Defense and Veterans Brain Injury Center, the National Center for Telehealth and Technology, and the Deployment Health Clinical Center. Instead of focusing on DCoE as an entity for inclusion in our environmental scan, we searched the programs and initiatives within DCoE, and included the Defense and Veterans Brain Injury Center, which offers an educational and training through its "Family Caregiver Curriculum."

## Claims and Benefits Assistance

This includes assistance provided by a range of organizations—most notably veterans service organizations. These groups assist service members or veterans, and sometimes their caregivers or family members, with obtaining benefits. They may provide general information about benefits, assistance preparing benefits paperwork, or guidance if and when claims are denied. Although this category borders upon "patient advocacy or case management" (an included category in our environmental scan), the latter typically links individuals with a broader range of health and social services. Further, patient advocacy or case management is also ongoing, whereas claims and benefits assistance tends to be one time only. Following is an example of an excluded organization that provided claims and benefits assistance:

- **Paralyzed Veterans of America Veterans Benefits Department** offers free, comprehensive benefits assistance and advocacy to veterans with spinal cord injury and disease, as well as other veterans needing assistance or their family members. Staff work through a national network of National Service Offices to provide services. These services vary from bedside visits, to guidance in the VA claims process, to legal representation for appealing denied claims.

## Educational Assistance

This category is largely composed of scholarship or grant assistance programs and organizations, but also includes student loan assistance and other services that promote the attainment of higher education among service members, veterans, or their family members or caregivers. Following is an example of an excluded organization that provided educational assistance:

- The **Air Force Association (Spouse Scholarship)** is designed to encourage Air Force spouses to pursue associate's, bachelor's, graduate, or postgraduate degrees. Scholarships are awarded annually and are nonrenewable. Funds can be used to pay for any reasonable cost related to pursuing a degree. This includes tuition, books, transportation, or child care costs.

## Employment Services

Employment services assist individuals by offering job training or resumé assistance, or by connecting job seekers with employers. We encountered a range of such services targeting caregivers as well as service members or veterans. Following is an example of an excluded organization that provided employment services:

- **DoD Education and Employment Initiative** is a DoD-sponsored program that assists recovering service members early in their recovery process, by identifying their skills and matching them with education and career opportunities that will help them successfully transition to civilian life. Services are offered through the program's regional coordinators, who work with the military departments, federal agencies, and private-sector organizations to locate training, employment, and education opportunities.

## Family Readiness, Resilience, or Transition Services

This includes services that seek to improve the overall "readiness" or "resilience" of military families, or services that facilitate the transition of service members back into family or civilian life after deployment. Such offerings tend to focus on broader issues of family functioning or military mission readiness rather than on the needs of caregivers, per se. Specifically, readiness and resilience programs tend to focus on coping during the deployment period or on preparing for upcoming deployments, and as a result are typically only available for those still in the military. Transition programs emphasize the "reintegration" of service members into their families or communities, and often facilitate access to needed services or benefits. These programs tend to be general in nature and not focused on specific issues related to caregiving. Following is an example of an excluded organization that provided family readiness and resilience services:

- **Family Readiness Groups** are military command–sponsored organizations that operate on military installations with the goal of increasing soldier and family readiness and resilience. Among the aims of these groups is to build family cohesion and morale, and to prepare families for the stresses of deployment. These groups offer social activities and provide a range of information and referral services. Group members typically include spouses, but may also include a range of other family members. Family Readiness Groups do not meet our inclusion criteria since they do not formally offer caregiving services.

## Financial Services

This category includes a range of services, such as financial advice or planning, or insurance services. Following is an example of an excluded organization that provided financial services:

- **Military HUB Financial Management Center** is a private organization that provides information and advice to assist military service members and families in making good money management choices. For example, it assists these individuals with budgeting, choosing from available military and VA benefits, and financial and retirement planning.

## General Relocation Assistance

This includes financial assistance with relocations that are not a direct result of a service member or veteran's injury or illness. Relocation assistance that is directly related to the injury or illness of a service member or veteran—for example, reimbursement for a caregiver's move to a VA medical center location—would fall under a helping hand (an included category in our environmental scan). Following is an example of an excluded organization that provided general relocation assistance:

- The **Navy Family Support Relocation Assistance Program** offers a range of relocation services to help ease the stress of transition for Navy families. Assistance includes links to relocation information and resources, relocation workshops, and individual or family consultations. The relocation assistance provided is not directly related to the injury or illness of a service member or veteran; thus, we excluded it from our environmental scan.

## Homelessness Services

Homelessness services are designed to assist individuals or families who are, or are at risk of becoming, homeless. They focus largely on providing or maintaining shelter or housing for these populations. Although some caregiving families may be homeless or at risk for homelessness, the specific needs of caregivers are not likely to be addressed by homelessness services. Following is an example of an excluded organization that provided such services:

- The **Supportive Services for Veteran Families** program assists low-income veterans and family members who are at risk of homelessness. With grants provided by the VA, various nonprofit organizations (e.g., the Salvation Army) assist eligible recipients with obtaining and maintaining housing. This assistance may take the form of direct housing assistance, temporary financial assistance, help obtaining other VA or public benefits, or referrals to other resources.

## Parenting Resources, Child Care, or Activities for Children

This category includes a diverse range of services such as child care, activities for children (e.g., summer camps or after school programs), and services for children with special needs. The focus of these services is the parent and/or child, generally, rather than the caregiver in their caregiver role. Following is an example of an excluded organization that provided parenting resources, child care, or activities for children:

- The **General's Kids** provides assistance for military children facing the life-changing injury or illness of a parent. The program grew from the founder's experiences as a caregiver at Walter Reed National Military Medical Center, but is now national in scope. It helps connect military children and teenagers with others across the country who are going through similar struggles; provides sponsors who will send encouraging cards or care packages to children; and offers financial assistance for things like special interests or school funding. Although the program may indirectly assist caregivers by improving their children's experiences, its primary focus is children rather than caregivers.

## Planning and Scheduling Tools

This category includes programs that engage caregivers with other individuals in their preexisting social networks, such as connecting with friends or family. These programs often take the form of online platforms that communicate to friends and family members what the caregiver needs, and when. Programs that link caregivers with new peers are not included in this category. Following is an example of an excluded organization that provided planning and scheduling tools:

- **Care Central** connects family and friends by providing an online platform that allows users to keep others updated, for example, on a loved one's medical condition or on the ongoing needs expressed by a caregiver. The program's primary intent is to connect those who are already socially connected through a private, centralized hub.

## Professional Caregiver Resources

This category includes programs that serve those in the caregiving industry. Services for professional caregivers can be wide-ranging and are exclusive. A program under this category provides resources that can be unavailable or impractical for many nonprofessional family caregivers. Following is an example of an excluded organization that provided professional caregiver resources:

- The **National Association for Home Care and Hospice** professionally represents and legislatively advocates for its members, which are primarily nurses, therapists, or other caregiving professionals. In addition to legislative and professional advocacy, the organization provides private educational workshops and webinars for its members. The organization's emphasis on serving the professional caregiving population was the reason for exclusion.

## Screening Tools for Caregivers

Caregiver screening tools help individuals determine whether they are, indeed, caregivers, or to analyze their own health risks and behaviors. Assessment tools that we reviewed for inclusion were typically online questionnaires. Following is an example of an excluded organization that provided caregiver screening tools:

- The **American Medical Association Caregiver Self-Assessment** helps caregivers analyze their own health risks and behaviors and, with their physician's help, make decisions that will benefit them as well as the care recipient. The assessment enables physicians to identify and provide preventive services and improve communication and enhance the physician-family caregiver health partnership. The assessment can be downloaded from the Internet and disseminated by physicians caring for caregivers.

## Survivor Services

Survivor services target caregivers whose care recipient has passed away. Although these services are critical to caregivers' health and well-being, they generally do not offer services while the care recipient is living. The array of survivor services is broad, ranging from social support and mental health services to instrumental assistance with things such as funeral arrangements. Following is an example of an excluded organization that provided survivor services:

• **Tragedy Assistance Program for Survivors (TAPS)** offers support to families and friends who are grieving the loss of a military service member. The program provides care through a range of services and programs, including peer-based emotional support, benefits assistance, connections to community-based care, and grief and trauma resources. Although TAPS is an important service for former caregivers, it does not provide direct services during the caregiving period; thus, we excluded it from our environmental scan.

In addition to these categories of excluded services (and organizational entities offering these services), we also excluded entities that were not U.S. owned or operated; not in operation any longer; or duplicates of other entities (e.g., organizations listed under a slightly different name).

## Excluded Entities

We now list the entities that we considered but excluded in our environmental scan. These entities fell into one or more of the categories previously described.

Achilles International
Advancing the Health of the Family Left Behind
Afterdeployment.org
Aging with Dignity
Air Force Assistance Fund (AFAF)
Air Force Association (AFA) Spouse Scholarship
Air Force Community
Air Force Enlisted Village
Air Force Personnel Center
Air Force Villages Charitable Foundation
AirCraft Casualty Emotional Support Services (ACCESS)
Alaska's Healing Hearts
American Cancer Society
American Combat Veterans of War (ACVOW)
American Gold Star Mothers, Inc.
American Medical Association (Caregiver Health Self-Assessment)
American Psychological Association
American Widow Project
AMVETS
ARCH National Respite Network and Resource Center
Armed Forces Communications & Electronics Association (AFCEA) Educational Foundation
Armed Forces Crossroads—Deployment & Reintegration
Armed Forces Services Corporation

Army Aviation Association of America Scholarships (AAAA)
Army Behavioral Health
Army Career Alumni Program (ACAP XXI)
Army Casualty Web Site
Army Combat-Related Special Compensation (CRSC)
Army Community Covenant
Army Family Action Plan
Army Homefront Fund
Army Long Term Family Case Management
Army National Guard (ARNG) GI—Deployment Support for Families
Army Non-Service-Connected Death Compensation
Army OneSource
Army Reserve Recovery Care Coordination Program[1]
Army Reserve Warrior and Family Assistance Center
Army Survivor Benefits Calculator
Army Well Being
Battered Women's Justice Project—Military Advocacy Resource Network
Benefits Check-Up and Benefits Check-Up RX
The Blue Box—Resources for Soldiers, Civilians and Family Members
Blue Button
Blue Star Mothers of America, Inc.
Bob Woodruff Foundation
The Boot Campaign
Brain Injury Association of America
Brainline.org
Camp Hometown Heroes
Camp Lejeune Deployment & Reunion Programs
CAN Center for Health Research And Policy
CareCentral
CareConnection.com
Career One Stop
Caregivingcafe.com
The Caregiving Connection
Caring Connection
CaringBridge
Challenged Athlete's Foundation
Charlotte Bridge Home
Chief Petty Officer Scholarship Fund
Child Care Subsidy for Dependents of Severely Injured Military Members

---

[1]   We were unable to gather sufficient information about this program to determine its suitability for inclusion.

ChildCare Aware
Children of Aging Parents
Children of Fallen Soldiers Relief Fund
Children of Military Service Members Resource Guide
Chippewa County Veterans Services
Christopher & Dana Reeve Foundation
Coalition for Iraq & Afghanistan Veterans
Coast Guard Child Care Subsidy Rates
Coast Guard Exchange System Scholarship Program
Coast Guard Family Child Care Program & Resources
Coming Home—A Guide for Spouses
Compensation for Abused Family Members
Consumer Consortium of Assisted Living
Consumer Financial Protection Bureau (CFPB)—Servicemembers Civil Relief Act Information
Courage to Care
Courage to Talk—Communicating with Your Children about Parental Injury
Defense Centers of Excellence (DCoE)
Defense Finance & Accounting Service (DFAS)
Deployment Guide for Families
Deployment Health & Family Readiness Library
Desert Veterans Program
Disability.gov
Disabled Sports USA
DoD Compensation and Benefits Handbook for Wounded, Ill, and Injured Service Members
DoD Military Community and Family Policy
DoD Military Family Support
DoD Military Pay & Benefits
DoD Recovering Warrior Task Force
DoD Safe Helpline Sexual Assault Support
DoD Sexual Assault Prevention and Response Programs (within each service branch)
DoD Strengthening Our Military Families Homepage and Strengthening Our Military Families Initiative 2011
Dolphin Scholarship Foundation
Donald Rumsfeld Foundation
Eagles Watch Foundation
eArmy Family Messaging System
Education and Employment Initiative (E2I)
Effects of PTSD on the Family
Eldercare.gov

The Entrepreneurship Bootcamp for Veterans' Families
Exceptional Family Member Programs (within each service branch)
eXtension Military Families Learning Network—Military Caregiving educational
    initiative
Faith in Action
Fallen Patriot Fund
Family & Friends: Deployment & DoD Health Care Services
Family Advocacy Program (in each service branch)
Family Caregiver Toolbox
Family Counselor Fellowship for Military Spouses
Family Delta Force Program
Family Friends
Family of a Vet
Family Readiness Groups (FRGs) (in each service branch and Reserve Affairs)
Family Reading Program—United Through Reading
Federal Benefits for Veterans, Dependents and Survivors, 2011 Edition
Federal Trade Commission
Feds Hire Vets
Focus on Family—Know Before You Go
Folds of Honor Foundation
Force Health Protection & Readiness—Deployment Tips
Fort Campbell Survivor Outreach Services (SOS)
Fort Family Outreach and Support
Fort Meade Child Care Programs
Fort Stewart Survivor Outreach Services (SOS)
Free Respite Child Care for Soldiers
Free Tax Help for Military Personnel & Their Families
Frequently Asked Questions about Traumatic Servicemember's Group Life Insurance
    (TSGLI)
Friends' Health Connection
Friendship Place (Washington, D.C., Maryland, Virginia)
Game on Nation
The General's Kids
GenWorth
Gift from Within
Gold Star Dads of America
Gold Star Mothers
Gold Star Wives of America
The Greatest Generation Foundation
Grief Comfort Kit for Kids
Grief Guidelines for Parents

Grieving as a Family—Finding Comfort Together
Growth House
Guide to Reserve Family Member Benefits
Handbook for Injured Service Members and Their Families
Health Wise
Health.net
Healthinsurance.com
Helmets to Hardhats
Helpguide.org
Hero 2 Hired
Higher Ground
Hire Heroes USA
Hiring Heroes Program
Hiring Our Heroes
Homefront America, Inc.
Homes for our Troops
HomeWatch Caregiver Franchise
Hope 4 Heroes
Hope for the Homefront
HospiceDirectory.org
ICF International
International Franchise Association's VetFran Toolkit
InTransition Mental Health Coaching and Support
ITN Men's Caregiver Support Group Program
Jeffrey Bean Foundation
Job Explorer
Job Opportunities for Disabled American Veterans
John A. Keller Scholarship
Johnson and Johnson
Joining Forces
Joint Family Support Assistance Program
Joint Services Support
Ladies Auxiliary of the Fleet Reserve Association
Leaders Guide for Managing Marines in Distress
Lemay Foundation
Leukemia Lymphoma Society
Lewy Body Dementia Association
Liberty University's Heroes Fund Scholarship
Lifestyle Insights, Networking, Knowledge & Skills (LINKS)
Magellan Health
Marine Corps—Law Enforcement Foundation, Inc.

Marine Corps—Resources for Parents
Marine Corps Casualty Assistance
Marine Corps Community Services Quantico
Marine Corps Family Team Building
Marine Corps Gold Star Family Support
Marine Corps League—Scholarship Program
Marine Corps Marine and Family Programs Division
Marine Corps Scholarship Foundation
Marine Corps Transition Assistance Management Program
Medicare
Medicare Rights Center
Medicare RX Matters (My Medicare Matters)
The Medicine Program
Medline Plus—Hospice
Mental Health America
MetLife Foundation
Military Child Education Coalition
Military Crisis Line
Military Families—Learning Communities
Military Families Learning Network
Military Families United
Military Family Link
Military Family Network
Military Family Program
Military Family Support
Military Homefront
Military HUB Financial Management Center
Military Kids Connect
The Military Ministry
Military Money
Military One Source-Tax Filing Service
Military OneSource
Military Saves
Military Significant Other Support
Military Spouse Corporate Career Network
Military Spouse Employment Partnerships
Military Spouse Fellowship Program for Financial Counseling
Military Spouse Program at Excelsior College
Military.com (Veterans Disability Compensation Information)
MilitaryFamily.com Deployment Readiness
MilSpouse eMentoring Program

Mission Continues
Morale, Welfare, and Recreation (MWR)
My HealtheVet
MyArmyBenefits
National Adult Day Services Association
National Alliance for Caregiving
National Association for Home Care and Hospice
National Association of Hospital Hospitality Houses
National Association of Professional Geriatric Care Managers
National Citizens' Coalition for Nursing Reform
National Clearing House for Long-term Care Information
National Fatherhood Initiative
National Guard Child and Youth Program
National Guard Family Program
National Guard Local Resource Finder
National Labor Exchange
National Resource Directory
National Veterans Foundation
National Veterans Transition Services
Naval Services FamilyLine
Navy Casualty Assistance
Navy Child and Youth Programs
Navy Family Preparedness
Navy Family Support and Relocation Assistance
Navy Fleet and Family Support Program
Navy League of the United States Scholarship Program
Navy Life Pacific Northwest
Navy Marine Corps Relief Society
Navy Mutual
Navy Ombudsman Program
Navy Returning Warrior Workshop (RWW)
Navy Supply Corps Foundation Scholarship Program
Navy Transition GPS/TAP
Navy Wives Clubs of America
Navy/Marine Corps Housing
Network of Care
New Health Partnerships
Next Step in Care
NFCA Senior Housing Locator
Nursing Home Compare
Office of the Assistant Secretary of Defense for Health Affairs

One Freedom
Operation Forever Free
Operation Healthy Reunion
Operation Military Kids
Operation Mom
Operation RE/MAX
Operation Shower
Our Military Kids
Paralyzed Veterans of America
Patriot Foundation
Pfizer
Pfizer Helpful Answers
PTSD Treatment Help
Ranger Memorial Foundation Scholarship Fund
Rape, Abuse, Incest National Network
Real Warriors Campaign
REALifelines
Recruit Military
Reserve Component Resource Center
Respect A Caregiver's Time (ReACT)
Retirement Pay Calculator
Return and Reunion Guide for Marines and Families
Returning from the War Zone—A Guide for Families of Military Members
Reuniting with Your Loved One—Helpful Advice for Families
Rewarding Work Resources
Rural Caregivers
RxCompare
SBA loans for individuals, families and caregivers in cases of disasters and emergencies
Scan Foundation
Scholarship for Graphic and Web Design Careers
Scholarship for Military Aviators
Scholarships for Military Children
Sea Legs
Sesame Workshop
Shepherds for Lost Sheep
Sittercity Childcare Program for All Service Members
Social Security Disability Benefits for Wounded Warriors
Society of Military Widows
Society of the First Infantry Division—Scholarships and Grants
Soldier for Life
Soul Repair Center

Specialized Training of Military Parents (STOMP)
State respite coalitions
Still Serving Veterans
Strategic Resources Incorporated (SRI)
STRIDE
Stronger Families
Student Veterans of America
Supportive Services for Veteran Families (SSVF) Program
Substance Abuse and Mental Health Services Administration
Tailhook Education Foundation
Taking Care of America's Armed Force Families
ThanksUSA Scholarship Program
That Others May Live Scholarships
Tillman Military Scholarships
Tips for Caring for Your Newborn and Yourself
Tragedy Assistance Program for Survivors
Transition Assistance Advisors
Troops First Foundation
Tug McGraw Foundation
Turbo Transition Assistance Program
Tutor.com
Tyze
U.S. Administration on Aging
U.S. Army Warrior Care and Transition Program (WCTP)
U.S. Army Warrior Transition Command (WTC)
U.S. Coast Guard Chief Petty Officers Association
U.S. Coast Guard Office of Work-Life Programs—Ombudsman Program
U.S. Coast Guard Special Needs Program
U.S. Coast Guard Spouses Information
U.S. Department of Agriculture Extension/4-H Support for Military Youth and
    Family Programs
U.S. Military Handbook
United Hospital Fund
United States Army Survivor Outreach Services
USA4Military Families
VA Adaptive Housing
VA Benefits Page
VA Caregiver Coalition
VA Civilian Health and Medical Program of the Department of Veterans Affairs
VA Family Support
VA for Vets

VA Home Health and Hospice Care
VA Life Insurance Policies
VA Mental Health Services
VA Specially Adapted Housing and Special Housing Adaptation
VA Suicide Prevention Program
VA Survivors' and Dependents' Educational Assistance (SDEA)
VA VBA Disability Compensation
VA VBA Vocational Rehabilitation and Employment
VA Vet Centers
VA Veteran Crisis Hotline
VA Women Veterans Call Center
Vet Center Combat Call Center
Vet Power
Vet Success
VeteranAid.org
Veterans and Families Foundation
Veterans Across America
Veterans Enterprise
Veterans of Foreign Wars (VFW) National Home for Children
Veterans Retraining Assistance Program
Veterans' Widows/ers International Network, Inc.
Veterans' Families United Foundation
VeteransPlus
VetNet
Vets 4 Warriors
Vets-help.org
Vet-Trans
VFW
Visiting Nurse Associations of America
Warrior Gateway (WarriorGateway.org)
We Honor Veterans
Wings Over America Scholarship Foundation
Women's Army Corps Veterans Association Scholarship
Wounded Soldier and Family Hotline
Wounded Warrior Entitlements Handbook
Wounded Warrior Resource Center
Wounded Warriors in Action
Yoga for Caregivers: Relax Your Stressed Body and Restore Yourself
Zero to Three

# Military Support Programs and Organizations Included in the Environmental Scan

Readers are encouraged to go to RAND's website to access Appendix H,[1] which contains summary information for each of the 120 programs identified in our scan as meeting our eligibility criteria. This information is available to readers interested in learning more about the details for each program, and is summarized using the format from our semistructured data abstraction form. These entries appear in alphabetical order and correspond to the summary information contained in Appendix D.

---

[1]  http://www.rand.org/pubs/research_reports/RR499.html

# References

AARP, Inc., *Access to Long-Term Services and Supports: A 50-State Survey of Medicaid Financial Eligibility Standards*, web page, 2013. As of January 5, 2014:
http://assets.aarp.org/rgcenter/ppi/ltc/i44-access-ltss_revised.pdf

AARP Public Policy Institute, *Valuing the Invaluable: 2011 Update: The Economic Value of Family Caregiving*, Washington, D.C., 2011.

ACL—*See* Administration for Community Living.

Administration for Community Living, *Lifespan Respite Care Program*, web page, undated. As of November 30, 2013:
http://acl.gov/Programs/CDAP/OIP/LifespanRespite/index.aspx

Alzheimer's Association and the National Alliance for Caregiving, *Caring for Persons with Alzheimer's: 2004 National Survey*, September 2004. As of January 5, 2014:
http://www.alz.org/national/documents/report_familiescare.pdf

Amato, P. R., "Research on Divorce: Continuing Trends and New Developments," *Journal of Marriage and Family*, Vol. 72, No. 3, 2010, pp. 650–666.

Archbold, P. G., B. J. Stewart, M. R. Greenlick, and T. Harvath, "Mutuality and Preparedness as Predictors of Caregiver Role Strain," *Research in Nursing and Health*, Vol. 13, No. 6, December 1990, pp. 375–384.

Arno, P. S., C. Levine, and M. M. Memmott, "The Economic Value of Informal Caregiving," *Health Affairs*, Vol. 18, No. 2, March–April 1999, pp. 182–188.

Attridge, M., *Personal and Work Outcomes of Employee Assistance Services*, paper presented at American Psychological Association Annual Conference, San Francisco, CA, 2001.

Attridge, M., *Employee Assistance Program Outcomes Similar for Counselor (Phone and In-Person) and Legal/Finance Consultation Clients*, paper presented at American Psychological Society Annual Conference, New Orleans, LA, June 2002.

Bass, D. M., K. S. Judge, A. L. Snow, N. L. Wilson, W. J. Looman, C. McCarthy, R. Morgan, C. Ablorh-Odjidja, and M. E. Kunik, "Negative Caregiving Effects Among Caregivers of Veterans with Dementia," *American Journal of Geriatric Psychiatry*, Vol. 20, No. 3, March 2012, pp. 239–247.

Beach, S. R., R. Schulz, J. L. Yee, and S. Jackson, "Negative and Positive Health Effects of Caring for a Disabled Spouse: Longitudinal Findings from the Caregiver Health Effects Study," *Psychology and Aging*, Vol. 15, No. 2, 2000, pp. 259–271.

Berglass, N., *America's Duty: The Imperative of a New Approach to Warrior and Veteran Care*, Washington, D.C.: Center for a New American Security, 2010.

Bigby, C., and E. Ozanne, "Comparison of Specialist and Mainstream Programs for Older Carers of Adults with Intellectual Disability: Considerations for Service Development," *Australian Social Work*, Vol. 57, No. 273–287, 2004.

Bilmes, L. J. "The Financial Legacy of Iraq and Afghanistan: How Wartime Spending Decisions Will Constrain Future National Security Budgets," HKS Faculty Research Working Paper Series RWP13-006, March 2013. As of January 5, 2014:
https://research.hks.harvard.edu/publications/workingpapers/citation.aspx?PubId=8956&type=WPN

Booth, A., and D. R. Johnson, "Declining Health and Marital Quality," *Journal of Marriage and the Family*, 1994, pp. 218–223.

Bowey, L., and A. McGlaughlin, "Older Carers of Adults with a Learning Disability Confront the Future: Issues and Preferences in Planning," *British Journal of Social Work*, Vol. 37, No. 1, 2007, pp. 39–54.

Bray, R. M., L. L. Hourani, K. L. Rae Olmsted, M. Witt, J. M. Brown, M. R. Pemberton, M. E. Marsden, B. Marriott, S. Scheffler, and R. Vandermaas-Peeler, *2005 Department of Defense Survey of Health-Related Behaviors Among Active-Duty Military Personnel*, Raleigh, NC: RTI International, 2006.

Bray, R. M., M. R. Pemberton, L. L. Hourani, M. Witt, K. L. Rae Olmsted, J. M. Brown, B. J. Weimer, M. Lane, M. E. Marsden, S. A. Scheffler, R. Vandermaas-Peeler, K. R. Aspinwall, E. M. Anderson, K. Spagnola, K. Close, J. L. Gratton, S. L. Calvin, and M. R. Bradshaw, *2008 Department of Defense Survey of Health-Related Behaviors Among Active-Duty Military Personnel*, Raleigh, NC: RTI International, 2009.

Brodaty, H., A. Green, and A. Koschera, "Meta-Analysis of Psychosocial Interventions for Caregivers of People with Dementia," *Journal of the American Geriatrics Society*, Vol. 51, No. 5, May 2003, pp. 657–664.

Brown, S. L., I.-Fen Lin, and K. K. Payne, *Age Variation in the Divorce Rate, 1990–2010 (FP-12-05)*, web page, 2012. As of November 30, 2013:
http://ncfmr.bgsu.edu/pdf/family_profiles/file108695.pdf

Calhoun, P. S., J. C. Beckham, and H. B. Bosworth, "Caregiver Burden and Psychological Distress in Partners of Veterans with Chronic Posttraumatic Stress Disorder," *Journal of Traumatic Stress*, Vol. 15, No. 3, June 2002, pp. 205–212.

Carr, J., "Families of 30–35-Year-Olds with Down's Syndrome," *Journal of Applied Research in Intellectual Disabilities*, Vol. 18, No. 1, 2005, pp. 75–84.

Carter, P., *Expanding the Net: Building Mental Health Care Capacity for Veterans*, Washington, D.C.: Center for a New American Security, 2013.

Chien L., H. Chu, J. Guo, Y. Liao, L. Chang, C. Chen, K. Chou, "Caregiver Support Groups in Patients with Dementia: A Meta-Analysis," *International Journal of Geriatric Psychiatry*, Vol. 26, No. 10, 2011, pp. 1089–1098.

Chien, W.T., I. Norman, "The Effectiveness and Active Ingredients of Mutual Support Groups for Family Caregivers of People with Psychotic Disorders: A Literature Review," *International Journal of Nursing Studies*, Vol. 46, No. 12, December 2009, pp. 1604–1623.

Christensen, A., and C. L. Heavey, "Interventions for Couples," *Annual Review of Psychology*, Vol. 50, 1999, pp. 165–190.

Cohen, S., and T. A. Wills, "Stress, Social Support, and the Buffering Hypothesis," *Psychological Bulletin*, Vol. 98, No. 2, 1985, pp. 310–357.

Coppus, A. M., "People with Intellectual Disability: What Do We Know About Adulthood and Life Expectancy?" *Developmental Disabilities Research Reviews*, Vol. 18, No. 1, August 2013, pp. 6–16.

Cox, C., "Findings from a Statewide Program of Respite Care: A Comparison of Service Users, Stoppers, and Nonusers," *Gerontologist*, Vol. 37, 1997, pp. 511–517.

Cozza, S. J., A. K. Holmes, and S. L. Van Ost, "Family-Centered Care for Military and Veteran Families Affected by Combat Injury," *Clinical Child and Family Psychology Review*, Vol. 16, No. 3, September 2013, pp. 311–321.

Degeneffe, C. E., "Family Caregiving and Traumatic Brain Injury," *Health and Social Work*, Vol. 26, No. 4, November 2001, pp. 257–268.

DiSogra, C., C. Cobb, E. Chan, and J. M. Dennis, "Calibrating Non-Probability Internet Samples with Probability Samples Using Early Adopter Characteristics," *Joint Statistical Meetings Proceedings*, Section on Survey Research Methods, Alexandria, VA, 2011, pp. 4501–4515.

DoL—*See* U.S. Department of Labor.

Dunbrack, J., "Respite for Family Caregivers: An Environmental Scan of Publicly Funded Programs in Canada," *Health Canada*, 2003.

Eaton, W. W., H. Armenian, J. Gallo, L. Pratt, and D. E. Ford, "Depression and Risk for Onset of Type II Diabetes: A Prospective Population-Based Study," *Diabetes Care*, Vol. 19, No. 10, October 1996, pp. 1097–1102.

EEOC—*See* U.S. Equal Employment Opportunities Commission.

Erel, O., and B. Burman, "Interrelatedness of Marital Relations and Parent-Child Relations: A Meta-Analytic Review," *Psychological Bulletin*, Vol. 118, No. 1, July 1995, pp. 108–132.

Etters, L., D. Goodall, and B. E. Harrison, "Caregiver Burden Among Dementia Patient Caregivers: A Review of the Literature," *Journal of the American Academy of Nurse Practitioners*, Vol. 20, No. 8, August 2008, pp. 423–428.

Family Caregiver Alliance, caregiver.org website, undated a. As of January 2014: http://www.caregiver.org/caregiver/jsp/content/pdfs/fs_caregiver_stats_side_by_side.pdf

———, *Innovations Clearinghouse on Family Caregiving*, web page, undated b. As of January 5, 2014: http://caregiver.org/caregiver/jsp/content_node.jsp?nodeid=2319

———, *National Policy Statement*, web page, undated c. As of January 5, 2014: http://www.caregiver.org/caregiver/jsp/content_node.jsp?nodeid=2279

———, *State of the States in Family Caregiver Support: A 50-State Study*, web page, 2013a. As of January 5, 2014: http://www.caregiver.org/caregiver/jsp/content_node.jsp?nodeid=1276

———, *State Profiles*, web page, 2013b. As of January 5, 2014: http://www.caregiver.org/caregiver/jsp/content_node.jsp?nodeid=1271

———, *Health Care Reform and Family Caregivers*, web page, 2013c. As January 5, 2014: http://www.caregiver.org/jsp/content_node.jsp?nodeid=2397

———, *Proceedings from the National Conference: Family Caregiving: State of the Art, Future Trends*, web page, 2013d. As of January 5, 2014: http://www.caregiver.org/caregiver/jsp/content_node.jsp?nodeid=2043

———, *Selected Caregiver Assessment Measures: A Resource Inventory for Practitioners*, web page 2013e. As of January 5, 2014: http://www.caregiver.org/caregiver/jsp/content_node.jsp?nodeid=2604

————, *Laws Protect Employees Who Serve as Caregivers*, 2013f.

———— —, *Family Caregiving and Transitional Care: A Critical Review*, web page, 2013g. As of January 5, 2014:
http://www.caregiver.org/caregiver/jsp/content_node.jsp?nodeid=2603

FCA—*See* Family Caregiver Alliance.

Feinberg, L., S. C. Reinhard, A. Houser, and R. Choula, "Valuing the Invaluable: 2011 Update—The Growing Contributions and Costs of Family Caregiving," *Insight on the Issues*, Vol. 51, 2011.

Fox, S., and J. Brenner, *Family Caregivers Online*, Washington, D.C.: Pew Research Center, 2012.

Garin, O., J. L. Ayuso-Mateos, J. Almansa, M. Nieto, S. Chatterji, G. Vilagut, J. Alonso, A. Cieza, O. Svetskova, H. Burger, V. Racca, C. Francescutti, E. Vieta, N. Kostanjsek, A. Raggi, M. Leonardi, M. Ferrer, and Mhadie consortium, "Validation of the 'World Health Organization Disability Assessment Schedule, WHODAS-2' in Patients with Chronic Diseases," *Health and Quality of Life Outcomes*, Vol. 8, 2010, p. 51.

GfK, *KnowledgePanel Design Summary*, 2013. As of October 11, 2013:
http://www.knowledgenetworks.com/knpanel/docs/knowledgePanel%28R%29-design-summary-description.pdf

Glaser, B. G., and A. L. Strauss, *Discovery of Grounded Theory: Strategies for Qualitative Research*, Chicago: Aldine, 1967.

Goetzel, R. Z., K. Hawkins, R. J. Ozminkowski, and S. Wang, "The Health and Productivity Cost Burden of the 'Top 10' Physical and Mental Health Conditions Affecting Six Large U.S. Employers in 1999," *Journal of Occupational and Environmental Medicine*, Vol. 45, No. 1, January 2003, pp. 5–14.

Goodman, S. H., M. H. Rouse, A. M. Connell, M. R. Broth, C. M. Hall, and D. Heyward, "Maternal Depression and Child Psychopathology: A Meta-Analytic Review," *Clinical Child and Family Psychology Review*, Vol. 14, No. 1, March 2011, pp. 1–27.

Gottlieb, B. H., and J. Johnson, "Respite Programs for Caregivers of Persons with Dementia: A Review with Practice Implications," *Aging and Mental Health*, Vol. 4, 2000, pp. 119–129.

Griffin, J. M., G. Friedemann-Sánchez, A. C. Jensen, B. C. Taylor, A. Gravely, B. Clothier, A. B. Simon, A. Bangerter, T. Pickett, and C. Thors, "The Invisible Side of War: Families Caring for U.S. Service Members with Traumatic Brain Injuries and Polytrauma," *Journal of Head Trauma Rehabilitation*, Vol. 27, No. 1, 2012, pp. 3–13.

Grych, J. H., and F. D. Fincham, "Marital Conflict and Children's Adjustment: A Cognitive-Contextual Framework," *Psychological Bulletin*, Vol. 108, No. 2, September 1990, pp. 267–290.

Hanks, R. A., L. J. Rapport, J. Wertheimer, and C. Koviak, "Randomized Controlled Trial of Peer Mentoring for Individuals with Traumatic Brain Injury and Their Significant Others," *Archives of Physical Medicine and Rehabilitation*, Vol. 93, No. 8, August 2012, pp. 1297–1304.

Harrell, M. C., and N. Berglass, *Well After Service: Veteran Reintegration and American Communities*, Washington, D.C.: Center for a New American Security, 2012.

Harris, E. C., and B. Barraclough, "Suicide as an Outcome for Mental Disorders: A Meta-Aanalysis," *British Journal of Psychiatry*, Vol. 170, March 1997, pp. 205–228.

Hartwell, T., P. Steele, M. T. French, F. J. Potter, N. F. Rodman, and G.A. Zarkin, "Aiding Troubled Employees: The Prevalence, Cost and Characteristics of Employee Assistance Programs in the United States," *American Journal of Public Health*, Vol. 86, 1996, pp. 804–808.

Hays, R. D., C. D. Sherbourne, and R. M. Mazel, "The RAND 36-Item Health Survey 1.0," *Health Economics*, Vol. 2, No. 3, 1993, pp. 217–227.

Heller, T., and J. Caldwell, "Supporting Aging Caregivers and Adults with Developmental Disabilities in Future Planning," *Mental Retardation*, Vol. 44, No. 3, June 2006, pp. 189–202.

Heller, T., J. Caldwell, and A. Factor, *Supporting Aging Caregivers and Adults with Developmental Disabilities in Future Planning*, Chicago, IL: University of Illinois, 2005.

Hendrick, S. S., "A Generic Measure of Relationship Satisfaction," *Journal of Marriage and the Family*, Vol. 50, 1988, pp. 93–98.

Hendrick, S. S., A. Dicke, and Clyde Hendrick, "The Relationship Assessment Scale," *Journal of Social and Personal Relationships*, Vol. 15, No. 1, February 1, 1998, pp. 137–142.

Henry J. Kaiser Family Foundation, "Uninsured Estimates of Adults 18–64, American Community Survey," 2013. As of December 2, 2013:
http://kff.org/uninsured/state-indicator/adults-18-64/

Hickey, A., "Focusing on People: A Review of VA's Plans for Employee Training, Accountability, and Workload Management to Improve Disability Claims Processing," testimony before the House Committee on Veterans Affairs hearing for the U.S. Department of Veterans Affairs, March 20, 2013. As of January 5, 2014:
http://veterans.house.gov/witness-testimony/the-honorable-allison-hickey-0

Holmes, W. C., E. B. Foa, and M. D. Sammel, "Men's Pathways to Risky Sexual Behavior: Role of Co-Occurring Childhood Sexual Abuse, Posttraumatic Stress Disorder, and Depression Histories," *Journal of Urban Health*, Vol. 82, No. 1, Supplement 1, March 2005, pp. 89–99.

H. R. 3383, *Caregiver Expansion and Improvement Act of 2013*, introduced in the House, 113th Congress, first session.

Hudson, P., T. Trauer, B. Kelly, M. O'Connor, K. Thomas, M. Summers, R. Zordan, and V. White, "Reducing the Psychological Distress of Family Caregivers of Home-Based Palliative Care Patients: Short-Term Effects from a Randomised Controlled Trial," *Psychooncology*, Vol. 22, No. 9, September 2013, pp. 1987–1993.

———, *Returning Home from Iraq and Afghanistan: Readjustment Needs of Veterans, Service Members, and Their Families*, Washington, D.C.: National Academy Press, 2013.

Institute of Medicine, *Returning Home from Iraq and Afghanistan: Readjustment Needs of Veterans, Service Members, and Their Families*, Washington, D.C., March 26, 2013.

Jeon, Y-H., H. Brodaty, and J. Chesterson, "Respite Care for Caregivers and People with Severe Mental Illness: Literature Review," *Journal of Advanced Nursing*, Vol. 49, 2005, pp. 297–306.

Joiner, T. E., and J. Katz, "Contagion of Depressive Symptoms and Mood: Meta-Analytic Review and Explanations from Cognitive, Behavioral, and Interpersonal Viewpoints," *Clinical Psychology Science and Practice*, No. 6, 1999, pp. 149–164.

Karney, B. R., and T. N. Bradbury, "The Longitudinal Course of Marital Quality and Stability: A Review of Theory, Method, and Research," *Psychological Bulletin*, Vol. 118, No. 1, July 1995, pp. 3–34.

Kessler, R. C., M. Ames, P. A. Hymel, R. Loeppke, D. K. McKenas, D. E. Richling, P. E. Stang, and T. B. Ustun, "Using the World Health Organization Health and Work Performance Questionnaire (HPQ) to Evaluate the Indirect Workplace Costs of Illness," *Journal of Occupational and Environmental Medicine*, Vol. 46, No. 6, Supplement, June 2004, pp. S23–S37.

Kessler, R., C. Barber, A. Beck, P. Berglund, P. Cleary, and D. Mckenas, "The World Health Organization Health and Work Performance Questionnaire (HPQ)," *Journal of Occupational and Environmental Medicine*, Vol. 45, 2003, pp. 156–174.

Kessler, R. C., C. B. Nelson, K. A. McGonagle, M. J. Edlund, R. G. Frank, and P. J. Leaf, "The Epidemiology of Co-Occurring Addictive and Mental Disorders: Implications for Prevention and Service Utilization," *American Journal of Orthopsychiatry*, Vol. 66, No. 1, January 1996, pp. 17–31.

Kiecolt-Glaser, J. K., L. D. Fisher, P. Ogrocki, J. C. Stout, C. E. Speicher, and R. Glaser, "Marital Quality, Marital Disruption, and Immune Function," *Psychosomatic Medicine*, Vol. 49, No. 1, January–February 1987, pp. 13–34.

Knol, M. J., J. W. Twisk, A. T. Beekman, R. J. Heine, F. J. Snoek, and F. Pouwer, "Depression as a Risk Factor for the Onset of Type II Diabetes Mellitus: A Meta-Analysis," *Diabetologia*, Vol. 49, No. 5, May, 2006, pp. 837–845.

Kosloski, K., and R. J. V. Montgomery, "The Effects of Respite Care on Caregivers of Alzheimer's Patients: One-Year Evaluation of the Michigan Model Respite Program," *Journal of Applied Gerontology*, Vol. 12, 1993, pp. 4–17.

Kramer, B. J., "Gain in the Caregiving Experience: Where Are We? What Next?" *The Gerontologist*, Vol. 37, No. 2, 1997, pp. 218–232.

Krauss, M. W., M. M. Seltzer, R. Gordon, and D. H. Friedman, "Binding Ties: The Roles of Adult Siblings of Persons with Mental Retardation," *Mental Retardation*, Vol. 34, No. 2, April 1996, pp. 83–93. As of January 5, 2014:
http://www.ncbi.nlm.nih.gov/pubmed/8935888

Kroenke, K., R. L. Spitzer, and J. B. W. Williams, "The PHQ-9," *Journal of General Internal Medicine*, Vol. 16, No. 9, 2001, pp. 606–613. As of January 5, 2014:
http://dx.doi.org/10.1046/j.1525-1497.2001.016009606.x

Kroenke, K., T. W. Strine, R. L. Spitzer, J. B. W. Williams, J. T. Berry, and A. H. Mokdad, "The PHQ-8 as a Measure of Current Depression in the General Population," *Journal of Affective Disorders*, Vol. 114, 2009, pp. 163–173.

Lasser, K., J. W. Boyd, S. Woolhandler, D. U. Himmelstein, D. McCormick, and D. H. Bor, "Smoking and Mental Illness: A Population-Based Prevalence Study," *Journal of the American Medical Association*, Vol. 284, No. 20, November 22–29, 2000, pp. 2606–2610. As of January 5, 2014:
http://www.ncbi.nlm.nih.gov/pubmed/11086367

Lawrence, R. H., S. L. Tennstedt, and S. F. Assmann, "Quality of the Caregiver–Care Recipient Relationship: Does It Offset Negative Consequences of Caregiving for Family Caregivers?" *Psychology and Aging*, Vol. 13, No. 1, 1998, p. 150.

Lawton, M. P., E. M. Brody, and A. R. Saperstein, "A Controlled Study of Respite Service for Caregivers of Alzheimer's Patients," *Gerontologist*, Vol. 29, 1989, pp. 8–16.

Lebow, J. L., A. L. Chambers, A. Christensen, and S. M. Johnson, "Research on the Treatment of Couple Distress," *Journal of Marital and Family Therapy*, Vol. 38, No. 1, January 2012, pp. 145–168.

Lee, H., and M. Cameron, "Respite Care for People with Dementia and Their Carers," *Cochrane Database and Systematic Reviews*, No. 1, 2004.

Lerner, D., D. Adler, H. Chang, L. Lapitsky, M. Hood, and C. Perissinotto, "Unemployment, Job Retention, and Productivity Loss Among Employees with Depression," *Psychiatric Services*, Vol. 55, 2004, pp. 1371–1378.

Lerner, D., and R. Henke, "What Does Research Tell Us About Depression, Job Performance and Work Productivity?" *Journal of Occupational and Environmental Medicine*, Vol. 50, 2008. pp. 401–410.

Lincoln, Abraham, *Second Inaugural Address*, Washington, D.C.: American Memory Project, 2000–2002, April 10, 1865. As of January 5, 2014: http://memory.loc.gov/ammem/alhtml/alhome.html

Lofvenmark, C., F. Saboonchi, M. Edner, E. Billing, and A. C. Mattiasson, "Evaluation of an Educational Programme for Family Members of Patients Living with Heart Failure: A Randomised Controlled Trial," *Journal of Clinical Nursing*, Vol. 22, No. 1–2, January 2013, pp. 115–126.

Mansell, I., and C. Wilson, "'It Terrifies Me, the Thought of the Future': Listening to the Current Concerns of Informal Carers of People with a Learning Disability," *Journal of Intellect Disabilities*, Vol. 14, No. 1, March 2010, pp. 21–31.

Mason, A., H. Weatherly, K. Spilsbury, S. Golder, H. Arksey, J. Adamson, and M. Drummond, "The Effectiveness and Cost-Effectiveness of Respite for Caregivers of Frail Elderly People," *Journal of the American Geriatric Society*, Vol. 55, 2007, pp. 290–299.

McDonough, J., "Strengthening and Transforming Local Partnerships to Serve Veteran Families," in *VAntage Point: Dispatches from the U.S. Department of Veterans Affairs*, 2013. As of January 5, 2014: http://www.blogs.va.gov/VAntage/11496/serve-veteran-families/

McNally, S., Y. Ben-Shlomo, and S. Newman, "The Effects of Respite Care on Informal Carers' Well-Being: A Systematic Review," *Disability and Rehabilitation*, Vol. 21, 1999, pp. 1–14.

MetLife, *The MetLife Study of Working Caregivers and Employer Health Care Costs: New Insights and Innovations for Reducing Health Care Costs for Employers*, February 2010.

Mezuk, B., W. W. Eaton, S. Albrecht, and S. H. Golden, "Depression and Type 2 Diabetes Over the Lifespan: A Meta-Analysis," *Diabetes Care*, Vol. 31, No. 12, December 2008, pp. 2383–2390.

Miller, L. M., B. Rostker, R. M. Burns, D. Barnes-Proby, S. Lara-Cinisomo, and T. R. West, *A New Approach for Assessing the Needs of Service Members and Their Families*, Santa Monica, CA: RAND Corporation, MG-1124-OSD, 2011. As of January 5, 2014: http://www.rand.org/pubs/monographs/MG1124.html

Mochari-Greenberger, H., and L. Mosca, "Caregiver Burden and Nonachievement of Healthy Lifestyle Behaviors Among Family Caregivers of Cardiovascular Disease Patients," *American Journal of Health Promotion*, Vol. 27, No. 2, November–December 2012, pp. 84–89.

Montgomery, R. J. V., and E. F. Borgatta, "The Effects of Alternative Support Strategies on Family Caregiving," *Gerontologist*, Vol. 29, 1989, pp. 457–464.

Moore, P. M., S. Rivera Mercado, M. Grez Artigues, and T. A. Lawrie, "Communication Skills Training for Healthcare Professionals Working with People Who Have Cancer," *Cochrane Database Systemaic Review*, Vol. 3, 2013, p. CD003751. As of January 5, 2014: http://www.ncbi.nlm.nih.gov/pubmed/23543521

NAC—*See* National Alliance for Caregiving.

National Alliance for Caregiving, *Evercare Study of Caregivers in Decline: A Close-Up Look at the Health Risks of Caring for a Loved One*, Washington, D.C., 2006.

———, *Caregivers of Veterans—Serving on the Homefront: Report of Study Findings*, Washington, D.C.: 2010.

National Alliance for Caregiving and AARP, *Family Caregiving in the U.S.: Findings from a National Survey*, 1997.

———, *Caregiving in the U.S., 2004*, 2004.

———, *Caregiving in the U.S.: A Focused Look at Those Caring for Someone Age 50 or Older*, 2009.

National Alliance for Caregiving and UHF, *Young Caregivers in the U.S.: Report of Findings*, 2005.

National Family Caregiver Support Program, "National Family Caregiver Support Program," fact sheet, 2013. As of January 5, 2014:
http://www.aoa.gov/aoaroot/Press_Room/Products_Materials/fact/pdf/Natl_Family_Caregiver_Support.pdf

National Research Council, *Crossing the Quality Chasm: A New Health System for the 21st Century*, Washington, D.C.: The National Academies Press, 2001.

National Resource Directory, home page, undated. As of January 5, 2014:
http://www.nrd.gov

Negrusa, B., and S. Negrusa, *Home Front: Post-Deployment Mental Health and Divorces*, Santa Monica, CA: RAND Corporation, WR-874-OSD, 2012. As of January 5, 2014:
http://www.rand.org/pubs/working_papers/WR874.html

Nerenberg, L., *Caregiver Stress and Elder Abuse*, Washington, D.C.: National Center for Elder Abuse, 2002.

Ohio Respite Coalition, *Ohio State Respite Coalition: Lifespan Strategic Plan 2013–2018*, Ohio Department of Aging, undated. As of November 30, 2013:
http://www.lifespanrespite.memberlodge.org/Resources/Documents/Strategic%20Plans/Lifespan%20Respite%20Strategic%20Plan%202013-2018%20Final.pdf

Osilla, K. C., and K. R. Van Busum, *Labor Force Reentry: Issues for Injured Service Members and Veterans*, Santa Monica, CA: RAND Corporation, 2012. As of January 5, 2014:
http://www.rand.org/pubs/occasional_papers/OP374.html

P.L. 109-442, *An Introduction to the Family and Medical Leave Act*, 109th Congress, second session, 2006. As of January 2013:
http://www.gpo.gov/fdsys/pkg/PLAW-109publ442/html/PLAW-109publ442.htm

P.L. 110-325, *ADA Amendments Act of 2008*, 110th Congress, second session, 2008.

P.L. 111-84, *National Defense Authorization Act of 2010*, 111th Congress, second session, 2010.

Pauly, M. V., S. Nicholson, J. Xu, D. Polsky, P. M. Danzon, J. F. Murray, and M. L. Berger, "A General Model of the Impact of Absenteeism on Employers and Employees," *Health Economics*, Vol. 11, No. 3, April 2002, pp. 221–231.

Paveza, G., D. Cohen, C. Eisdorfer, S. Freels, T. Semla, J. W. Ashford, P. Gorelick, R. Hirschman, D. Luchins, and P. Levy, "Severe Family Violence and Alzheimer's Disease: Prevalence and Risk Factors," *The Gerontologist*, Vol. 32, No. 4, 1992, pp. 493–497.

Pearlin, L. I., "Conceptual Strategies for the Study of Caregiver Stress," in *Stress Effects on Family Caregivers of Alzheimer's Patients: Research and Interventions*, eds. E. Light, G. Niederehe, & B.D. Lebowitz; New York: Springer, 1994, pp. 3–21.

Pearlin, L. I., E. G. Menaghan, M. A. Lieberman, and J. T. Mullan, "The Stress Process," *Journal of Health and Social Behavior*, 1981, pp. 337–356.

Pearlin, L. I., J. T. Mullan, S. J. Semple, and M. M. Skaff, "Caregiving and the Stress Process: An Overview of Concepts and Their Measures," *The Gerontologist*, Vol. 30, No. 5, 1990, pp. 583–594.

Pew Research Center, *War and Sacrifice in the Post-9/11 Era*, Washington, D.C.: Pew Research Center, 2011. As of November 30, 2013:
http://www.pewsocialtrends.org/2011/10/05/war-and-sacrifice-in-the-post-911-era/

Phelan, S. M., J. M. Griffin, W. L. Hellerstedt, N. A. Sayer, A. C. Jensen, D. J. Burgess, and M. van Ryn, "Perceived Stigma, Strain, and Mental Health Among Caregivers of Veterans with Traumatic Brain Injury," *Disability and Health Journal*, Vol. 4, No. 3, July 2011, pp. 177–184.

Pinquart, M., and S. Sörensen, "Associations of Stressors and Uplifts of Caregiving with Caregiver Burden and Depressive Mood: A Meta-Analysis," *The Journals of Gerontology Series B: Psychological Sciences and Social Sciences*, Vol. 58, No. 2, 2003a, pp. P112–P128.

———, "Differences Between Caregivers and Noncaregivers in Psychological Health and Physical Health: A Meta-Analysis," *Psychology and Aging*, Vol. 18, No. 2, 2003b, pp. 250–267.

Ramchandani, P., A. Stein, J. Evans, T. G. O'Connor, and Alspac study team, "Paternal Depression in the Postnatal Period and Child Development: A Prospective Population Study," *Lancet*, Vol. 365, No. 9478, June 25–July 1, 2005, pp. 2201–2205.

Redfoot, D., L. Feinberg, and A. Houser, "The Aging of the Baby Boom and the Growing Care Gap: A Look at Future Declines in the Availability of Family Caregivers," *Insight on the Issues,* AARP Public Policy Institute, Vol. 85, August 2013.

Robinson, B. C., "Validation of a Caregiver Strain Index," *Journal of Gerontology*, Vol. 38, No. 3, 1983, pp. 344–348.

Robinson-Whelen, S., and D. H. Rintala, "Informal Care Providers for Veterans with SCI: Who Are They and How Are They Doing?" *Journal of Rehabilitation Research and Development*, Vol. 40, No. 6, November–December, 2003, pp. 511–516.

Rone-Adams, S. A., D. F. Stern, and V. Walker, "Stress and Compliance with a Home Exercise Program Among Caregivers of Children with Disabilities," *Pediatric Physical Therapy*, Vol. 16, No. 3, Fall 2004, pp. 140–148.

Rostker, B. D., *Providing for the Casualties of War: The American Experience Through World War II*, Santa Monica, CA: RAND Corporation, MG-1164-OSD, 2013. As of January 5, 2014:
http://www.rand.org/pubs/monographs/MG1164.html

Rubin, D. B., *Multiple Imputation for Nonresponse in Surveys*, New York: John Wiley, 1987.

Rugulies, R., "Depression as a Predictor for Coronary Heart Disease: A Review and Meta-Analysis," *American Journal of Preventive Medicine*, Vol. 23, No. 1, 2002, pp. 51–61.

S. 252, *Veterans Health Care Authorization Act of 2009*, 111th Congress, first session.

S. 728, *Veterans Insurance and Benefits Enhancement Act of 2009*, 111th Congress, first session.

S. 851, *Caregiver Expansion and Improvement Act of 2013*, 113th Congress, first session.

S. 851, *Caregivers Expansion and Improvement Act of 2013*, 113th Congress, first session.

Särndal, C.-E., "The Calibration Approach in Survey Theory and Practice," *Survey Methodology*, Vol. 33, No. 2, 2007, pp. 99–119

Shaw, C., R. McNamara, K. Abrams, R. Cannings-John, K. Hood, M. Longo, S. Myles, S. O'Mahony, B. Roe, and K. Williams, "Systematic Review of Respite Care in the Frail Elderly," *Health Technology Assessment*, Vol. 13, 2009.

Shen, C. C., S. J. Tsai, C. L. Perng, B. I. Kuo, and A. C. Yang, "Risk of Parkinson Disease After Depression: A Nationwide Population-Based Study," *Neurology*, Vol. 81, No. 17, October 22, 2013, pp. 1538–1544.

Sherbourne, C. D., R. D. Hays, L. Ordway, M. R. DiMatteo, and R. L. Kravitz, "Antecedents of Adherence to Medical Recommendations: Results from the Medical Outcomes Study," *Journal of Behavioral Medicine*, Vol. 15, No. 5, October 1, 1992, pp. 447–468.

Simon, M. A., B. Gunia, E. J. Martin, C. E. Foucar, T. Kundu, D. M. Ragas, and L. L. Emanuel, "Path Toward Economic Resilience for Family Caregivers: Mitigating Household Deprivation and the Health Care Talent Shortage at the Same Time," *The Gerontologist*, Vol. 53, No. 5, October 2013, pp. 861–873

Skaff, M. M., and L. I. Pearlin, "Caregiving: Role Engulfment and the Loss of Self," *The Gerontologist*, Vol. 32, No. 5, 1992, pp. 656–664.

Smith, L. N., M. Lawrence, S. M. Kerr, P. Langhorne, and K. R. Lees, "Informal Carers' Experience of Caring for Stroke Survivors," *Journal of Advanced Nursing*, Vol. 46, No. 3, 2004, pp. 235–244.

Sörensen, S., M. Pinquart, and P. Duberstein, "How Effective Are Interventions with Caregivers? An Updated Meta-Analysis," *The Gerontologist*, Vol. 42, No. 3, June 2002, pp. 356–372.

Strauss, A., and J. Corbin, *Basics of Qualitative Research: Techniques and Procedures for Developing Grounded Theory*, 2nd ed., Thousand Oaks, CA: Sage, 1998.

Taggart, L., M. Truesdale-Kennedy, A. Ryan, and R. McConkey, "Examining the Support Needs of Aging Family Carers in Developing Future Plans for a Relative with an Intellectual Disability," *Journal of Intellectual Disability Research*, Vol. 16, No. 3, September 2012, pp. 217–234.

Tanielian, T., R. Ramchand, M. P. Fisher, C. S. Sims, R. Harris, and M. C. Harrell, *Military Caregivers: Cornerstones of Support for Our Nation's Wounded, Ill, and Injured Veterans*, Santa Monica, CA: RAND Corporation, RR-244-TEDF, 2013. As of January 5, 2014: http://www.rand.org/pubs/research_reports/RR244.html

Thompson, D., and S. Wright, *Misplaced and Forgotten: People with Learning Disabilities in Residential Services for Older People*, London: The Foundation for People with Learning Disabilities, 2001.

U.S. Census Bureau, *American Community Survey*, web page, December 2013. As of January 2014: https://www.census.gov/acs/www/

U.S. Census Bureau and Bureau of Labor Statistics, *Current Population Survey*, web page, undated. As of January 2014: http://www.census.gov/cps

U.S. Centers for Disease Control and Prevention, *National Health Interview Study*, web page, updated December 2013. As of January 2014: http://www.cdc.gov/nchs/nhis.htm

U.S. Department of Defense, "Final Rule to Implement Statutory Amendments to the Family And Medical Leave Act Military Family Leave Provisions," 2013. As of January 5, 2014: http://www.dol.gov/whd/fmla/2013rule/fs-military.htm

U.S. Department of Health and Human Services, "Section 1915(c) Home and Community-Based Services Waivers," 2013a. As of January 5, 2014: http://www.medicaid.gov/Medicaid-CHIP-Program-Information/By-Topics/Waivers/Waivers.html

———, "National Family Caregiver Support Program," 2013b. As of January 5, 2014: http://www.aoa.gov/aoa_programs/hcltc/caregiver/index.aspx

U.S. Department of Labor, "An Employee's Guide to the Family and Medical Leave Act," 2013. As of January 5, 2014: http://www.dol.gov/whd/fmla/employeeguide.pdf

U.S. Department of Veterans Affairs, *Web Automated Reference Material System: 38 CFR Book C, Schedule for Rating Disabilities*, web page, undated. As of January 2014:
http://www.benefits.va.gov/warms/bookc.asp

———, *Annual Benefits Report, Fiscal Year 2011*, Washington, D.C., 2011a.

———, "New and Enhanced VA Benefits Provided to Caregivers of Veterans: Unprecedented Law Augments Commitment to Nation's Most Vulnerable Veterans," 2011b. As of 2013:
http://www.va.gov/opa/pressrel/pressrelease.cfm?id=2048

———, *National Center for Veterans Analysis and Statistics*, 2012. As of November 30, 2013:
http://www.va.gov/vetdata/docs/quickfacts/Utilization-slideshow.pdf

———, "America's Wars Fact Sheet, 2013," 2013a. As of February 26, 2014:
http://www.va.gov/opa/publications/factsheets/fs_americas_wars.pdf

———, *Annual Benefits Reports, 2000–2012*, 2013b.

———, *Guide to Long Term Care: Explore Your Options*, web page updated October 2013c. As of January 5, 2014:
http://www.va.gov/GERIATRICS/Guide/LongTermCare/Respite_Care.asp#

———, *2013 Monday Morning Workload Reports: Compensation and Pension Rating Bundle as of November 23, 2013*, 2013d. As of December 11, 2013:
http://www.vba.va.gov/reports/mmwr/

U.S. Equal Employment Opportunity Commission, "Employer Best Practices for Workers with Caregiving Responsibilities," 2007 (updated 2011). As of November 30:
http://www.eeoc.gov/policy/docs/caregiver-best-practices.html

Uchino, B. N., "Social Support and Health: A Review of Physiological Processes Potentially Underlying Links to Disease Outcomes," *Journal of Behavioral Medicine*, Vol. 29, No. 4, 2006, pp. 377–387.

———, "Understanding the Links Between Social Support and Physical Health: A Life-span Perspective with Emphasis on the Separability of Perceived and Received Support," *Perspectives on Psychological Science*, Vol. 4, No. 3, 2009, pp. 236–255.

Ustün T. B., S. Chatterji, N. Kostanjsek, J. Rehm, C. Kennedy, J. Epping-Jordan, S. Saxena, M. von Korff, and C. Pull, WHO/NIH Joint Project, *Bulletin of the World Health Organization*, Vol. 88, No. 11, November 1, 2010, pp. 815–823.

VA—*See* U.S. Department of Veterans Affairs.

Van Houtven, C. H., E. Z. Oddone, and M. Weinberger, "Informal and Formal Care Infrastructure and Perceived Need for Caregiver Training for Frail U.S. Veterans Referred to Home and Community-Based Services," *Chronic Illness*, Vol. 6, No. 1, 2010, pp. 57–66.

Varni, J. W., M. Seid, and C. A. Rode, "The PedsQL (TM): Measurement Model for the Pediatric Quality of Life Inventory," *Medical Care*, Vol. 37, No. 2, 1999, pp. 126–139.

Wahlbeck, K., J. Westman, M. Nordentoft, M. Gissler, and T. M. Laursen, "Outcomes of Nordic Mental Health Systems: Life Expectancy of Patients with Mental Disorders," *British Journal of Psychiatry*, Vol. 199, No. 6, December 2011, pp. 453–458.

Waldron, E. A., E. A. Janke, C. F. Bechtel, M. Ramirez, and A. Cohen, "A Systematic Review of Psychosocial Interventions to Improve Cancer Caregiver Quality of Life," *Psychooncology*, Vol. 22, No. 6, June 2013, pp. 1200–1207.

Wang, P. S., G. E. Simon, J. Avorn, F. Azocar, E. J. Ludman, J. McCulloch, M. Z. Petukhova, and R. C. Kessler, "Telephone Screening, Outreach, and Care Management for Depressed Workers and Impact on Clinical and Work Productivity Outcomes: A Randomized Controlled Trial," *Journal of the American Medicine Association*, Vol. 298, 2007, pp. 1401–1411.

Weinick, R. M., E. B. Beckjord, C. M. Farmer, L. T. Martin, E. M. Gillen, J. Acosta, M. P. Fisher, J. Garnett, G. C. Gonzalez, T. C. Helmus, L. H. Jaycox, K. Reynolds, N. Salcedo, and D. M. Scharf, *Programs Addressing Psychological Health and Traumatic Brain Injury Among U.S. Military Servicemembers and Their Families*, Santa Monica, CA: RAND Corporation, TR-950-OSD, 2012. As of January 5, 2014:
http://www.rand.org/pubs/technical_reports/TR950.html

Weinraub, M., and B. M. Wolf, "Effects of Stress and Social Supports on Mother-Child Interactions in Single- and Two-Parent Families," *Child Development*, Vol. 54, No. 5, October 1983, pp. 1297–1311.

Whittier, S., A. E. Scharlach, and T. S. Dal Santo, "Availability of Caregiver Support Services: Implications for Implementation of the National Family Caregiver Support Program," *Journal of Aging and Social Policy*, Vol. 17, No. 1, 2005, pp. 45–62.

Wickrama, K.A.S., F. O. Lorenz, R. D. Conger, and G. H. Elder Jr., "Marital Quality and Physical Illness: A Latent Growth Curve Analysis," *Journal of Marriage and Family*, Vol. 59, No. 1, 1997, pp. 143–155.

Wilks, S. E., and B. Croom, "Perceived Stress and Resilience in Alzheimer's Disease Caregivers: Testing Moderation and Mediation Models of Social Support," *Aging and Mental Health*, Vol. 12, No. 3, May 2008, pp. 357–365.

Willliamson, V., *Supporting Our Troops, Veterans, and Their Families: Lessons Learned and Future Opportunities for Philanthropy*, Los Angeles, Calif.: California Community Foundation, 2009.

Wilsum, L. R., and B. M. Singal, "Do Depressive Symptoms Increase the Risk for the Onset of Coronary Disease? A Systematic Quantitative Review," *Psychosomatic Medicine*, Vol. 65, 2003, pp. 201–210.

Witters, D., "Caregiving Costs U.S. Economy $25.2 Billion in Lost Productivity," Gallup.com, 2011. As of November 30, 2013:
http://www.gallup.com/poll/148670/caregiving-costs-economy-billion-lost-productivity.aspx

World Health Organization, *WHO Disability Assessment Schedule 2.0 WHODAS 2.0*, 2011. As of January 5, 2014:
http://www.who.int/classifications/icf/whodasii/en/

Wulsin, L. R., G. E. Vaillant, and V. E. Wells, "A Systematic Review of the Mortality of Depression," *Psychosomatic Medicine*, Vol. 61, No. 1, January–February, 1999, pp. 6–17.

Zarit, S. H., M. A. Stephens, A. Townsend, and R. Greene, "Stress Reduction for Family Caregivers: Effects of Adult Day Care Use," *Journal of Gerontology*, Vol. 53B, 1998, pp. S267–S277.